COUNTERTERRORISM
STRATEGIES

More Advance Praise for *Counterterrorism Strategies*

The quality of the organization, research, and writing makes *Counterterrorism Strategies* invaluable for the critical and dynamic areas of criminal justice and international security policies. Editor Yonah Alexander has worked for many decades on international and comparative counterterrorism and is a giant without equal in the field of counterterrorism policy. As usual, he has compiled an excellent research product for policymakers, academics, journalists, and professionals.

—Bruce Zagaris, editor-in-chief of the
International Enforcement Law Reporter

Counterterrorism Strategies is a must-read for specialists in the growing field of counterterrorism and homeland security as well as the general public. The six countries it examines are good examples of how much work still needs to be done to fully comprehend the true dimensions of the new global threat of terrorism. The book also emphasizes the need for more and deeper international cooperation in order to meet this complex challenge.

—Dieter Dettke, Transatlantic Fellow of the
German Marshall Fund of the United States
and adjunct professor, Security Studies Program,
Georgetown University

COUNTERTERRORISM
STRATEGIES

*Successes and Failures
of Six Nations*

Edited by
YONAH ALEXANDER

Foreword by
JOSÉ MARÍA AZNAR

Potomac Books, Inc.
Washington, D.C.

Library of Congress Cataloging-in-Publication Data
Counterterrorism strategies : successes and failures of six nations / edited by Yonah Alexander.—1st ed.
    p. cm.
  Includes bibliographical references and index.
  ISBN 1-59797-018-2 (hc : alk. paper)—ISBN 1-59797-019-0 (pb : alk. paper)
  1. Terrorism—Prevention—Cross-cultural studies. 2. Terrorism—Government policy—Cross-cultural studies. I. Alexander, Yonah.
   HV6431.C6915 2006
   363.325'17—dc22
                                    2006015385

ISBN 1-59797-018-2

(alk. paper)

Potomac Books, Inc.
22841 Quicksilver Drive
Dulles, Virginia 20166

First Edition

10 9 8 7 6 5 4 3 2 1

CONTENTS

*This book is dedicated
to the victims of contemporary terrorism with the
hope that future generations will not know fear and
bloodshed anymore.*

ACKNOWLEDGMENTS

The academic research in contemporary terrorism studies, that was initiated some forty years ago, adapted almost immediately traditional interdisciplinary methodologies for the purpose of exploring the nature of the emerging phenomenon of ideological and political violence and how societies can and should confront the expanding challenge.

As founder and editor-in-chief of *Terrorism: An International Journal* (published first in 1977 by Crane Russak in New York and subsequently by Taylor and Francis Group in London), I have had the opportunity to collaborate with many contributors focusing on a new broad-range of issues, including political, social, economic, legal, intelligence, law enforcement, military, diplomatic, medical, and technological considerations. In an effort to broaden the research offerings, I developed and edited two additional academic publications, namely, *Political Communication and Persuasion: An International Journal* (published in 1980 also by Crane and Russak and then by the Taylor and Francis Group), and the *International Journal on Minority and Group Rights* (appeared in 1990 as the *International Journal on Group Rights* by Martinus Nijhoff and currently published by Brill in the Netherlands).

These two journals dealt, inter alia, with various contributing factors that encourage the proliferation of terrorist activities such as the role of propaganda and psychological warfare and ethnic, racial, and religious intolerance.

To the numerous individuals, representing different disciplines and nationalities, who participated in promoting these scientific undertakings, I owe my own intellectual development, particularly gaining a better understanding of the nature of the terrorist threat and the strategies that are needed to combat the growing challenge on national and international levels. In particular, I wish to recognize the unique inspiration and guidance provided to me by Professor Hans J. Morgenthau (the University of Chicago) and Professor Raymond Aron

(Centre Européan de Sociologie Historique, Paris), both of whom served at different times as Chairman, International Advisory Board, *Terrorism: An International Journal.*

Additionally, I wish to acknowledge the support of several universities and think tanks that have afforded me the opportunity to conduct relevant research since the late 1960s in this important area of public concern: the Institute for Studies in International Terrorism, State University of New York; the Graduate School of Journalism, Columbia University; the Center for Strategic and International Studies, Georgetown University; the Institute of Social and Behavioral Pathology, University of Chicago; and the Terrorism Studies Program, the George Washington University.

Special thanks are due to three institutions for assisting me in directing the interdisciplinary research project "Counter Terrorism Strategies in the Twenty-first Century: National, Regional, and Global Agenda," which resulted in the publication of *Combating Terrorism: Strategies of Ten Countries* (University of Michigan Press, 2002) and this volume, *Counterterrorism Strategies: Successes and Failures of Six Countries.* These academic bodies are the Inter-University Center for Terrorism Studies (a consortium of universities and think tanks in over thirty countries); the International Center for Terrorism Studies at the Potomac Institute for Policy Studies (Arlington, Virginia); and the Inter-University Center for Legal Studies at the International Law Institute (Washington, D.C.). The encouragement and support of Michael S. Swetnam, Chairman and CEO of the Potomac Institute of Policy Studies and Professor Edgar H. Brenner, Co-director, Inter-University Center for Legal Studies, are particularly appreciated.

In conducting the research for this book, initially developed in 1998 and completed in early 2006, I was assisted by two dozen project advisors in the United States and abroad and benefited from the important contributions of my five co-authors, who provided extraordinary insights from the academic and practitioners' perspectives. This volume could have not been realized without their professional cooperation over the years.

Thanks also goes to the research team in 2005–2006 that included Benjamin Feinberg (American University), Jeffrey Tang (Wheaton College), Karen Davis (Susquehanna University), Brian Terranova (University of Delaware), Daniel Kirch (University of Trier), Katrine Halskov (University of Copenhagen), Adriana Plata (Unversidad Externado de Colombia), Lea Pyne (Sweet Briar College), James Mersereau (Tulane University), Jack Baber (Rhodes College), Agnes Pernicaut (University of Nanterre), Laura Bondesen (Georgetown University), Elizabeth Constable (Lafayette College), Dave Madden (San Diego State University), Sarah Bar (American University), and Kara Hess (Western Illinois University).

The editorial guidance provided by Rajika Jayatilake and Professor Herbert Levine of the Inter-University Center for Terrorism Studies, and the Potomac Books staff, especially Donald Jacobs, Lisa Camner, and Laura Hymes is also appreciated.

Finally, the generous grants from several foundations in supporting the research for this publication is also acknowledged.

This book is published in cooperation with
the Inter-University Center for Terrorism Studies, administered
by the International Center for Terrorism Studies at the
Potomac Institute for Policy Studies
and the Inter-University Center for Legal Studies at the
International Law Institute.

FOREWORD

I have always believed that victory over terrorism is possible, that terrorism can be defeated. The only recourse is to set in motion and implement opportune policies. I know well what it is like to have to live with the fear that terrorism creates in the heart of our societies. Spain has unfortunately had to battle against the violence of the terrorist group Euskadi Ta Askatasuna (ETA) for more than thirty years. ETA's aim is to achieve the independence of the Basque Country by force and to set up a Marxist-style government. What is more, I myself have been a victim of a terrorist attack, a car bomb that ETA planted in an attempt to kill me, but which I survived, thank God. On that day in 1995, ETA blew up my car, but they did not change my convictions. We must and we can fight effectively against terrorism. And all those who believe that it is better to make concessions in order to achieve an unstable peace and those who fall prey to defeatism are quite frankly deluded.

Terrorists are people just like us, nothing more. They eat, they move around, they need money, they need the media to convey their messages of fanaticism. And they can be pursued, arrested, and jailed. Their plans can be foiled, and the credibility of their causes can be called into question. What is more, the law that governs the state requires that all this can and must be carried out, and our liberal democratic societies have the necessary instruments at their disposal to combat and defeat terrorism. This has always been my philosophy, and it formed the basis of the policies that I implemented for eight years as head of the Spanish government. And I have to say that the results were good. When I chose to step down from government in March 2004, ETA had not been entirely destroyed, but its operational capacity had been reduced to a minimum. It had failed to kill anyone for a year because it no longer had the means to do so. What is more, its arguments were less credible and convincing than ever.

In order to defeat terrorism, we must gain an intimate knowledge of the enemy we are facing. We must attempt to dismantle terrorist cells and imprison as many members of the organization as possible. This is the work of the intelligence services, the police, and the army, in their application of the laws of the land. However, terrorism goes well beyond the terrorists themselves. Terrorism is sustained through ongoing extortion, including organized crime; terrorism tends to use a political wing in order to legitimize its crimes; terrorism frequently uses the media to present its propaganda; and terrorism depends on its ability to continue recruiting new members. In order to defeat terrorism, therefore, we need a policy that touches upon all of these aspects as part of an integrated approach. Only then will terrorist organizations and their members be isolated and alienated from the societies that they claim to represent.

Terrorism is nothing new. However, since we became first-hand witnesses to the largest terrorist attack in history on that tragic day, September 11, 2001, we know that local terrorist threats have now been augmented by an additional threat, that of jihadist terrorism. Jihad, as a global vision and an entirely reactionary phenomenon—it seeks to bring about the total destruction of our way of life, which is to say, our free societies—is something that goes way beyond the scope of traditional counterterrorist policies. It goes beyond national borders, it surpasses the lethal actions we have become accustomed to and makes a mockery of the degree of criminal activity that democratic governments have had to face up until now. We must understand that a phenomenon that unites and informs a cause that can ram a barge full of explosives against a U.S. warship, the USS *Cole*, carry out the attacks of 9/11, blow up the underground in London, assassinate Theo Van Gogh, and attack a school in Russia, requires us to rethink the resources we need in order to combat it. It explains how armed intervention to bring down Saddam Hussein can be viewed as being part of this great war on terrorism.

Professor Yonah Alexander, a veritable institution in his own right with regard to studies on terrorism, is well aware of the ideas I have expressed here. He has not only been studying terrorism for decades, but has analyzed the most effective ways of combating it. By presenting an analysis of the successes and failures of six nations in their battle against terrorism, he is offering us a useful tool to help us learn from one another, so that we might develop a philosophy that inspires a shared strategy against terrorism, a phenomenon that threatens us all equally.

Al Qaeda has already revealed its extraordinary capacity to adapt to circumstances that have made it more difficult for terrorists to operate. This is because it has learned its lessons. Now is the time for us to carry out our duty and to learn the important lessons of our past actions. This is the best way of ensuring that what we do in the future will serve to bring about the final defeat of terrorism.

−**José María Aznar**
former president of the government of Spain (1996–2004)

INTRODUCTION

Yonah Alexander

From time immemorial, terrorism, one of the most common expressions of man's inhumanity to man, has taken on the form of random, selected, and systematic intimidation, coercion, repression, or destruction of human lives and property. Used intentionally by individuals, groups, and state actors to create a climate of intense fear in order to obtain avowed realistic or imaginary political, social, economic, and strategic goals, terrorism has been a strategy utilized by both the strong and the weak in the struggle for power within and among communities and nations.

Numerous historical examples underscore the fact that the employment of violence in the name of "higher" principles or specifically desired objectives has always been common place. Aggravated by nationalistic fanaticism, ideological extremism, religious animosities, ethnic hatred, and racial prejudices, this form of psychological and physical force has consistently been justified and rationalized by terms such as "rights," "justice," and even "peace."

The Oxford English Dictionary specifies, for instance, two primary meanings of "terrorism":

> First, it is government by intimidation as directed and carried out by the party in power in France during the revolution of 1789–1794: the system of terror (1793–4).
>
> Second, it connotes a policy intended to strike with terror those against whom it is adopted; the employment of methods of intimidation; the fact of terrorizing.

What is obviously a missing element in the standard dictionary is a more comprehensive list of different types of "terrorism" as it is activated from both "above" and "below." Suffice, therefore, to recall some of these notable precedents:

1

- Roman emperors during the first century A.D. against their own populations to maintain domestic oppression;
- Zealot Jewish group the Sicarii ("dagger men"), targeting the Roman occupiers of Judea and their collaborators during the first century A.D.;
- assassinations by the Hashasheen of Christian and Muslim adversaries between the eleventh and thirteenth centuries to advance religious-political goals;
- ritual killing and cannibalism by the religious group Binderwurs, worshipping the god Kali in India;
- domestic oppression and violence utilized by Dracula against the Ottoman armies in the fifteenth century in Wallachia (present-day Romania);
- religious atrocity by the Aztecs of their own people in Mexico in the sixteenth and seventeenth centuries;
- Spanish Inquisition from the fifteenth to the nineteenth centuries in an effort to "cleanse" Catholicism and convert Jews to Christianity;
- Thuggee cult carrying out ritual murders for Kali in India between the thirteenth and nineteenth centuries;
- pirates, or privateers, employed by several European countries between the sixteenth and eighteenth centuries;
- enslavement and killing of millions of Congo's black population by Belgium rulers in the nineteenth century;
- the revolutionary activities of the Narodnaya Volya (People's Will) in Czarist Russia in the nineteenth century;
- Bolshevik-Soviet, Maoist, and Nazi terror in the twentieth century.

The tyranny and fear instituted throughout recorded history have been duplicated often in contemporary times. In the post–World War II period, psychological and physical terrorism employed by nonstate and state actors became a permanent feature of international life. Advances in modern technology, developments in communications, rapid travel opportunities, and availability of funds and weapons have partly, at least, contributed to the proliferation of terrorist acts both domestically and internationally. Moreover, unique political circumstances led to this development, including the emergence of national liberation movements in Asia, Africa, and Latin America; the Six-Day War of 1967 and rise of Palestinian terrorism worldwide; the adversarial relationship and physical proximity of the United States to Cuba, leading to numerous aircraft hijackings; the Vietnam War and the universal reaction against it; the Paris students' revolt in 1968; the existence of the Cold War; and the religionization of politics, particularly the proliferation of radical Islamic groups and networks regionally and globally.

To be sure, in the broad non-state category of contemporary terrorist perpetrators, included are, on the one hand, marginal antisocial elements, conspiratorial adventurers, pseudo-ideological extremists, religious fanatics, and racial bigots, and, on the other hand, more institutionalized opposition movements such as banned political parties and "military wings" or paramilitary underground resistance movements. To put it differently, the terrorist framework consists of individual "free-lancers" (e.g. mentally deranged, "crusaders," or "martyrs"); single-issue political desperates; ultra "diehard" ethnic, tribal, and religious bodies; uncompromising nationalist and separatist groups; and criminal and political mercenaries.

Although these actors are nourished by various political and social roots sustained by wide-ranging ideologies and theologies, terrorists have, nevertheless, a common disposition. More specifically, they have contempt and hostility toward the moral and legal norms of the domestic and international order. Also, terrorists glorify their violent deeds for the sake of the cause they seek to advance, regarding themselves beyond the limits of any society and system of government. They do not feel bound by any obligations or constraints, except those they have imposed on themselves to succeed.

Among the hundreds of nationally and internationally designated terrorist groups, mention should be made, for instance, of past and current better-known perpetrators, including the Puerto Rican Armed Forces of National Liberation; the Palestinian Abu Nidal Organization, Hamas, and the al-Jihad; the Lebanese Hizbollah; the Egyptian Islamic Group; the Jewish Kach and Kahane Chai; the Kurdish Workers Party; the Irish Republican Army; the Basque Fatherland and Liberty; the Japanese Red Army; the Liberation Tigers of Tamil Ealam of Sri Lanka; Peru's Shining Path and Tupac Amaru Revolutionary Movement; the Revolutionary Armed Forces of Colombia; the Moroccan Islamic Combatant Group; Abu Sayyaf Group in the Philippines; and al Qaeda in Iraq.

What makes the challenge of substate terrorism particularly dangerous is the existence of an international network of groups that cooperate informally and formally with each other. This collaborative relationship operates in many ways, such as ideological and theological alliances; organizational assistance; propaganda and psychological warfare; financial help; recruitment support; intelligence sharing; supply of weapons; operational activities; and availability of sanctuaries.

Indeed, experience since the 1970s shows that shared ideologies, theologies, and commitments to radical causes and strategies such as professed struggles against capitalism, imperialism, racism, Zionism, and Western-oriented cultures and policies, motivated a wide range of terrorist movements to collaborate across national boundaries. A case in point is a former regional framework, the European anti-imperialist network consisting of several Marxist-Leninist groups, such as France's *Action Directe,* Germany's Red Army Faction, and Italy's Red Brigades.

Since the 1990s, however, al Qaeda (also known as the International Islamic Front for Jihad Against Jews and Crusaders, Islamic Salvation Foundation, and the Islamic Army for the Liberation of the Holy Shrines), serves as an international terrorist network operating in some ninety countries around the world. Headed by Osama bin Laden, this loosely knit framework of radical co-religionists are spreading their jihad (holy war) around the world with the stated objective of uniting all Moslems under one flag and establishing a unified government under the rule of the Caliphs.

It is not surprising, therefore, that the sanctification and justification of violence, coupled with global networks and modern technological advantages, have raised the magnitude and intensification of modern terrorism to a level unknown in previous centuries. In the past, terrorists have utilized both primitive and technologically advanced tactics in their operations, including arson, bombings, kidnappings, assassinations, hijacking, and facility attacks. Their arsenal consisted not only of explosives and arms, such as guns, but also of more sophisticated weapons, such as anti-tank rockets and ground-to-air missiles. It is highly likely, however, that in the future, these forms of conventional threats will expand even further and terrorists will also resort to unconventional or "super" terrorism—chemical, biological, radiological, and nuclear attacks. The prospect of the use of mass destruction weapons could inflict unprecedented devastation and affect thousands and perhaps millions of innocent victims.

Thus far, at least, the record of worldwide brutalization written by perpetrators during the past four decades consists of tens of thousands of terrorist acts. The number of fatalities and persons injured have increased steadily over the years as the value of resulting property damage and economic costs reached billions of dollars. Some of the more spectacular attacks include the following:

- 1970 hijacking and destruction of four western airliners by the Popular Front for the Liberation of Palestine, a Marxist-Leninist group;
- killing of eleven Israeli athletes at the Munich Olympic games in Munich in 1972, carried out by the Black September Organization headed by Yasser Arafat;
- takeover of the Grand Mosque of Mecca in 1979 by a coalition of international Islamic extremists opposing the Saudi monarchy;
- 1981 assassination of President Anwar el-Sadat of Egypt by Gama'at Islamia members as revenge for his 1978 peace treaty with Israel;
- Hizbollah bombing in 1983 of the marine base in Beirut, killing 241 Americans;

● 1985 hijacking of the Italian cruise ship *Achille Lauro* by operatives of the Palestine Liberation Front, killing a crippled U.S. passenger;

● Hizbollah bombing in 1992 of the Israeli Embassy in Argentina;

● 1993 truck bombing of the World Trade Center in New York by Islamic operatives organized by the newly formed al Qaeda;

● bombing of the Federal Building in Oklahoma City in 1995 by an American right-wing radical;

● 1995 sarin gas attack on Tokyo's subway system by Japan's Aum Shinrikyo group;

● assassination of Israel's Prime Minister Itzhak Rabin in 1995 by a Jewish fanatic opposing the 1993 Oslo Agreement with the Palestinian Authority;

● 1996 seizure of the Japanese Embassy in Lima by Tupac Amaru Revolutionary Movement, a Maoist group;

● destruction in 1996 of the U.S. military base at Khobar Towers in Dhahran, Saudi Arabia by Islamic terrorists, killing nineteen soldiers and wounding hundreds more;

● 1998 car bombings of U.S. embassies in Kenya and Tanzania by al Qaeda members, killing 234 people and wounding more than five thousand;

● suicide bombing of the USS *Cole* in Aden, Yemen, perpetrated by al Qaeda, killing seventeen and wounding thirty-nine American sailors;

● 9/11 multiple attacks directed by the al Qaeda hijackers against the World Trade Center in New York, the Pentagon in Washington, DC, and United Flight 93;

● al Qaeda bombing of international tourist facilities in Bali, Indonesia, and Mombassa, Kenya, in 2002;

● 2003 al Qaeda suicide bombings of civilian targets in Casablanca, Morocco, and Riyadh, Saudi Arabia;

● bombings of trains in Madrid in 2004 by al Qaeda operatives, killing some two hundred people and wounding one thousand more;

● killing of some three hundred civilian hostages, mostly children, in a school in Beslan, Russia, by Chechen terrorists;

● 2005 attacks on London transport system by British national members of al Qaeda;

● 2005 suicide bombings of hotels in Egypt's Sharem el-Sheik and Amman, Jordan, by al Qaeda terrorists;

● 2006 al Qaeda suicide attack against a Shiite mosque in Karbala, Iraq.

The foregoing disturbing record is due, in part at least, to the direct or indirect involvement of certain states in encouraging and directing terrorism. More specifically, a number of nations such as the former Soviet Union, Cuba, and North Korea, as well as Iran, Iraq, Libya, and the Sudan, have sponsored terrorist operations as a form of secret or undeclared warfare in situations where overt or declared warfare could be inconvenient and riskier. Because modern weapons and all-out wars are so expensive and destructive, these states, ideologically inclined to fight nations they perceive as enemies, may wish to restrict themselves to low-intensity conflict. In this mode, they attack their adversaries but confine their violence to the lower end of the spectrum of conflict, well away from the high-intensity of open, organized military hostilities.

The modus operandi of totalitarian and radical state sponsors of terrorism illustrate the complexity of the challenge and the difficulties in combating this form of violence. Traditionally, these governments have indoctrinated, funded, trained, armed, shared intelligence, and provided sanctuary to groups of diverse ideological, religious, and national dispositions. Many of the terrorist groups were directly supported or indirectly guided and encouraged, thereby becoming tools of the sponsoring states. The contemporary historical record indicates that many terrorist movements operate without external state help, but those groups that benefit from such support are much more viable and dangerous.

One classic demonstration of the threat of state involvement in terrorist activities is the role of Iran. On November 4, 1979, Iranian militants, with the encouragement of the revolutionary government of Ayatollah Khomenei, seized the American embassy in Tehran and held some fifty diplomats in captivity for 444 days. Currently, a quarter of a century later, President Mahmoud Ahmadinejad calls for the destruction of a sovereign state, Israel, and continues to support terrorist movements such as Hizbollah in Lebanon and Hamas in Gaza and the West Bank. What is of particular concern is Iran's apparent intention to create a military dimension to its nuclear program and if successful, the question then is when and under what circumstances terrorism might escalate to an unconventional level, thus inflicting Hiroshima-type calamity on the Middle East and beyond.

Indeed, the unprecedented catastrophe that befell the United States on September 11, 2001, regarded as the most devastating terrorist attack in history, already elevated Sun Tzu's concept of "war in the shadows" to an extraordinary threat to modern societies. That is, the hijacking of four airliners by nineteen al Qaeda operatives on that infamous day was not a "routine" act. During this attack, the suicide pilots employed "airplane missile" weapons, causing extraordinary human, economic, political, and strategic costs.

Undoubtedly, conflicts that emerge from ideological, religious, and national animosities will continue to make the challenge of terrorism a global problem well into the twenty-first century. The vulnerability of modern society and its economic infrastructure, coupled with the opportunities for the utilization of sophisticated high-leverage conventional and unconventional weaponry, require nation-states both unilaterally and in concert to develop credible responses and capabilities to minimize future threats.

Ensuring safety and interests of its citizens at home and abroad will continue to be every government's paramount responsibility in the future. Understanding the methods of operation employed by terrorists, identifying the threats and specific targets, both present and future, and becoming fully aware of the damage and consequences that may result from acts of terror will assist governments in responding effectively to the specter of terrorism nationally and globally.

It is out of these considerations that in 1998 an initiative was undertaken by a group of academics, former government officials, journalists, and terrorism experts from fifteen countries around the world to develop case studies focusing on the lessons of counterterrorism strategies. The countries selected for multinational and interdisciplinary projects were the United States, Argentina, Peru, Colombia, Spain, the United Kingdom, Israel, Turkey, India, Japan, France, Germany, Italy, Egypt, and Sri Lanka. Their inclusion was determined on the basis of the countries' experiences facing terrorist threats over many years as well as the expectation that examining the records of the responses of each country would contribute to crafting "best practices" strategies in the future.

Contributors to the project were provided with common research guidelines although it was recognized that it would be impossible to impose strict rules simply because of the different perceptions and experiences of each country studied. In general, however, the participants in the research project were asked to consider a number of factors that have an influence on the success of counterterrorism: the political environment, terrorist threats and counterterrorist policies, the legal environment, the public affairs environment, the counterterrorism organizational structure, intelligence, law enforcement, diplomatic methods, economic measures, and military responses.

In addition, the contributors were asked to focus on four questions. First, in a particular country, what are the governmental and public perceptions of the terrorist threat on the primitive, technologically advanced, and mass destruction levels?

Second, how successful were the government's policies and actions in combating both domestic and international terrorism? Success was to be evaluated in terms of the following criteria:

- reduction in the number of terrorist incidents;
- reduction in the number of casualties in terrorist incidents;
- reduction in the monetary cost inflicted by terrorist incidents;

- reduction in the size of the terrorist groups operating in a country;
- number of terrorists killed, captured, and/or convicted;
- protection of national infrastructure (e.g., transportation, communications, economic and political institutions, and security installations and units);
- preservation of basic national structures and policies (e.g., the rule of law, democracy, and civil rights and liberties);

Third, what factors influence the government's willingness and ability to cooperate with other nations in combating terrorism? And fourth, what does the counterterrorism performance record of the specific country look like?

The first product of the research project was the publication of the book *Combating Terrorism: Strategies of Ten Nations* by the University of Michigan Press in 2002. For logistical and various substantive considerations, it was decided that *Counterterrorism Strategies: Successes and Failures of Six Countries* would include not only the initial planned case studies of France, Germany, Italy, Egypt, and Sri Lanka, but also a reexamination of the experiences of the United States, particularly in light of the lessons of 9/11 that were only marginally discussed in the first research project. Finally, a third volume is presently being prepared for the purpose of integrating the "best practices" strategies of all the countries examined in the project within a single analytical framework.

It is hoped that these comparative studies will stimulate further research in the current and future struggle against terrorism in all of its conventional and unconventional manifestations.

1

UNITED STATES

Yonah Alexander

On July 4, 2001, the United States, led by President George W. Bush, celebrated its 225th birthday. The nation's strategic status as the only superpower seemed unchallenged despite extensive media reports during the spring and summer on numerous terrorism-related threats at home and abroad. Typical of this coverage were the following items:[1]

- official concerns in March that the possible reopening to the public of Pennsylvania Avenue might result in the explosion of a truck bomb in front of the White House by domestic or foreign terrorists;
- a chilling theoretical exercise dubbed "Dark Winter"— based on a realistic scenario to test the government's response to a biological terrorist attack with the smallpox virus—revealed that such an incident could bring the United States to the brink of disintegration;
- in July, the State Department issued a warning that terrorists could be about to attack American targets in the Middle East, and simultaneously the United States placed its forces in the region on the highest level of alert. It is suspected that Osama bin Laden's al Qaeda was behind this specific plot.

Yet, the foregoing "wake-up" calls, as well as numerous other warnings to American interests nationally and globally during several decades, did not prepare the homeland for the most devastating terrorist attacks in the country's history. The simultaneous, massive, and spectacular carnage that occurred on September 11, 2001, was aimed at America's key symbols of national security and economic strength.

At 8:45 a.m., American Airlines Flight 11, en route from Boston to Los Angeles with eighty-one passengers and eleven crewmembers, crashed into the North Tower of the World Trade Center. United Airlines Flight 175, also headed from Boston to Los Angeles and carrying fifty-six passengers and nine crewmembers, slammed into the South Tower at 9:03 a.m. American Airlines Flight 77, scheduled to fly from Washington Dulles International Airport to Los Angeles with fifty-eight passengers and six crewmembers, crashed at 9:43 a.m. into the northwest side of the Pentagon. At 10:10 a.m., United Airlines Flight 93, headed from Newark to San Francisco and carrying thirty-eight passengers and seven crewmembers, crashed in Pennsylvania during a struggle between the hijackers and passengers.

Nineteen terrorists on an al Qaeda suicide mission hijacked these four U.S. airliners. The cost in terms of human lives, including the passengers and crew on the planes as well as the persons murdered in New York, the Pentagon, and Pennsylvania approached three thousand dead, with thousands more injured.

Although these unprecedented attacks underscore most graphically the vulnerability of the United States and, indeed, all other modern societies, to the globalization and brutalization of sporadic and relentless terrorism, this form of violence is not new in American history. The threat and use of psychological and physical force by individuals, subnational groups, and state actors aimed at attaining political, social, and economic objectives in violation of domestic and international law have challenged the United States in the past and will continue to represent a real and present danger in the post-9/11 era.

This threat requires America, unilaterally and in concert with other nations, to undertake effective counterterrorism efforts to combat all forms of terrorism. The purpose of this chapter is to provide a historical overview of the terrorist experiences in the United States and abroad, and to analyze the American counterterrorism lessons in terms of their successes and failures.

PART I
Terrorist Threats to the United States: Historical and Contemporary

Perceptions and Definitions

Public perception in the United States, particularly since September 11, 2001, is that contemporary terrorism is a permanent fixture of life in this country and abroad. This mind-set is understandable, indeed justifiable historically; however, the term "terrorism" was not perceived "as American as apple pie."[2] Most citizens regarded the threat as a nuisance or irritant that could ultimately be managed by the established order.

The vagueness in the public consciousness about the character and meaning of terrorism is due to the diverse and protean forms and alleged purposes of the act itself, as well as to official and unofficial disagreements concerning its nature, scope, and appropriate responses. The prevailing tendency in the pre-9/11 era was to view each terrorist act as an individual incident without political pattern or strategic dimension. This attitude proved to be simplistic and naïve with dire consequences to national security interests, as demonstrated by the September 11 catastrophe.

Similarly, prior to 9/11, U.S. government officials did not consider "terrorism" to constitute a major strategic challenge to the very survival of the Republic. Indeed, the semantic, moral, and legal confusion over the precise meaning and implications of "terrorism" has hindered formulation of coherent policies and actions aimed at preventing, deterring, and decreasing the effectiveness of terrorist acts, or punishing identified terrorists after perpetrating their attacks at home and abroad.[3] The historical record indicates that the United States as a pluralistic democracy spoke with a bewildering variety of voices on the definition of "terrorism."

This section provides an overview of the evolution of perception and definitions on terrorism, particularly as advanced by state and federal entities.

State Perspectives

In the American federal system, each state determines what constitutes an offense under its criminal or penal code. States have defined terrorism generically as a crime, thus ending the need for the use of specific statutes covering other selected criminal acts that are identified as terrorism. For instance, the Arkansas Criminal Code states that "a person commits the offense of terroristic threatening if with the purpose of terrorizing another person, he threatens to cause death or serious physical injury or substantial property damage to another person."[4]

In general, state laws concerning terrorism appear under nine separate headings, including civil defense (interstate compacts and state emergency management plans), antiterrorism provisions, destructive devices, terrorist threats, enhanced criminal penalties, victim compensation, street terrorism, ecological terrorism, and taxes.[5] Regarding the first category, as an example, the authority of states to enter into interstate compacts of any kind is governed by Article I, Section IV, Clause 3 of the U. S. Constitution, which requires congressional authorization. Similarly, the Disaster Relief and Emergency Assistance Act, as amended, authorizes interstate compacts dealing with civil defense against various emergencies, including terrorist incidents.[6]

Executive Perspectives

The executive branch, partly as a result of the very nature of its jurisdictional diversities, has not developed, particularly prior to 9/11, a coordinated position on the meaning of the term. Since the 1980s, for instance, the FBI, operating domestically as a law-enforcement agency within the Department of Justice, has defined terrorism as "the unlawful use of force or violence against persons or property to intimidate or coerce a government, the civilian population, or any segment thereof, in the furtherance of political or social objectives."[7]

The FBI also made a distinction between "domestic terrorism" as perpetrated by "a group or individual based and operating entirely within the United States or its territories without foreign direction" and "international terrorism," involving acts that "occur outside the United States or transcend national boundaries in terms of the means by which they are accomplished, the persons they appear intended to coerce or intimidate, or the locale in which the perpetrators operate or seek asylum."[8]

Other executive agencies developed their own definition of "terrorism," using similar conceptual wordings but also reflecting their particular interests and concerns. For instance the Central Intelligence Agency (CIA), with jurisdiction in covert activities abroad, asserted in 1980 that "international terrorism is terrorism conducted with the support of a foreign government or organization and/or directed against foreign nationals, institutions, or governments."[9]

Similarly, the Department of Defense Commission, when reporting on the October 23, 1983, truck-bombing of the U.S. Marine headquarters at Beirut International Airport that resulted in the deaths of 241 military personnel, emphasized the "unlawful use or threatened use of force or violence by a revolutionary organization . . . considered criminal under local law or acts which violate the law of Armed Conflict."[10] In short, the Commission concluded that the attack "was tantamount to an act of war using the medium of terrorism."[11]

This linkage between terrorism and war was subsequently also underscored by the Department of State and its officials. In June 1984, Ambssador Jeane J. Kirkpatrick, then U.S. Permanent Representative to the United Nations, explained emphatically, "Terrorism is a form of war against a society and all who embody it. . . . Terrorist war is part of a total war which sees the whole society as the enemy, and all members of a society as appropriate objects for violent action."[12]

Secretary of State George Shultz, who had primary responsibility for determining the meaning of terrorism for the entire executive branch during the Ronald Reagan administration, also equated terrorism roughly with war. On October 25, 1984, he called terrorism "a form of political violence" that is "neither random nor without purpose."[13]

"But the overarching goal of all terrorists is the same," he said in his October statement. "They are trying to impose their will by force—a special kind of force designed to create an atmosphere of fear. . . . [T]hey want people to lose faith in their government's capacity to protect them and thereby to undermine the legitimacy of the government itself, or its policies, or both."

"We must understand, however," he continued, "that terrorism, wherever it takes place, is directed in an important sense against *us*, the democracies—against our most basic values and often our fundamental strategic interests."[14]

A few months later, on February 4, 1985, when speaking of defense against terrorism, Shultz declared, "Terrorism poses a direct threat not only to Western strategic interests but to the very moral principles that undergird Western democratic society. The enemies of the West are united. So too must the democratic countries be united in a common defense against terrorism."[15]

Despite the foregoing official views on the nature of terrorism and the need to confront the challenge, by the end of 1985 the United States had still not adopted a unified formal definition on the meaning of the term within the spectrum of conflict. Indeed, the public report of the U.S. Cabinet-level Task Force on Combating Terrorism, formed by President Ronald Reagan and chaired by Vice President George H. W. Bush, noted that "terrorism is a phenomenon that is easier to describe than define."[16] It further explained the absence of a definition by observing that "some experts see terrorism as the lower end of the warfare spectrum, a form of low-intensity, unconventional aggression. Others, however, believe that referring to it as war rather than criminal activity lends dignity to terrorists and places their acts in the context of accepted international behavior."[17]

This ambiguity apparently continued for the next fifteen years, ultimately leading the State Department to adopt a definition which is contained in Title 22 of the United States Code, Section 2656f(d), stating that "the term 'terrorism' means premeditated, politically motivated violence perpetrated against noncombatant targets by subnational groups or clandestine agents, usually intended to influence an audience."[18]

The term "noncombatant," according to the Department of State, is interpreted to mean, "in addition to civilians, military personnel (whether or not on duty) who are not deployed in a war zone or a war-like setting."[19] Moreover, "the term 'international terrorism' means terrorism involving citizens of the territory of more than one country"[20] and "the term 'terrorist group' means any group practicing, or that has significant subgroups that practice, international terrorism."[21]

This cautionary executive definitional approach to terrorism prior to 9/11 reflected a reality that avoided labeling the term as "war" with its legal context and implications. Rather, the U.S. government's counterterrorism conceptual framework was overshadowed by the traditional broader foreign policy objectives as linked to regional conflicts.

It was only after the September 11 attacks that the executive, under President George W. Bush, declared that "we are a nation at war" and the policy known as the "war on terror" became a top priority of the U.S. administration.[22]

Congressional Perspectives

In the legislative branch of the federal government, it is also evident that no consensus on a definition has been reached prior to 9/11. Indeed, over the past thirty-five years, the U.S. Congress has held numerous hearings, considered bills, adopted resolutions, and passed laws on terrorism.[23] Nevertheless, a comprehensive working definition that can address the different forms of terrorist attacks has not emerged from Congress for many years.

For instance, Senator Abraham Ribicoff, then the chairman of the Committee on Governmental Affairs, introduced a bill, known as An Act to Combat International Terrorism, in the Senate on October 25, 1977. The bill's definition included the following components: First, the definition builds on crimes defined under certain international conventions. Second, the definition includes descriptions of the other unlawful actions. Third, the definition concerns itself with the place—the international context. Fourth, the definition provides that to be criminal in the context of the bill, such acts must be targeted at least in part against the interests of state or international organizations. Fifth, the definition provides that essentially military operations are not to be considered acts of terrorism.

A more comprehensive definition was offered in the United States by Senator Jeremiah Denton, then the chairman of the Subcommittee on Security and Terrorism, Committee of the Judiciary, in his introduction to the Anti-Terrorism Act of 1984. He said:

> [T]errorism means the knowing use of force or violence against any person or property in violation of the criminal laws of the United States or any state, territory, possession, or district with the intent to intimidate, coerce, or influence a government or person in furtherance of any political or ideological objective.[24]

Despite the enunciation of this broad definition, more serviceable in those times than most, Senator Denton himself adopted a narrower approach under different circumstances of congressional consideration. In the Act of Rewards for Information Concerning Terrorist Acts (98th Congress, 2nd Session, H.R. 5612), the senator limited terrorism to those acts that are intended to:

> (A) intimidate or coerce a civilian population,
> (B) influence the policy of a government by intimidation or coercion, or
> (C) affect the conduct of a government by assassination or kidnapping.[25]

Moreover, Congress has tended to define terrorism mainly in terms of specific criminal offenses with an international aspect. The congressional acts include Crimes Against Internationally Protected Persons,[26] Crimes Against Aviation,[27] and Crimes Against Taking of Hostages.[28]

Since legislative authorization to conduct large and open-ended military operations against terrorism was not sought by the White House prior to 9/11, Congress continued to label the challenge as "criminal" rather than "military." It was not until al Qaeda struck the United States that Congress determined that this horrific assault must be regarded as an act of "war" against this country. The Senate Joint Resolution 23 dated September 23, 2001, cited as the "Authorization of the Use of Military Force," stated, "that the President is authorized to use all necessary and appropriate force against those nations, organizations, or persons he determines planned, authorized, committed, or aided the terrorist attacks that occurred on September 11, 2001, or harbored such organizations or persons, in order to prevent any future acts of international terrorism against the United States by such nations, organizations, or persons."[29]

It is this recognition that the battle is not a fight against "criminals" but constitutes a "war" situation that enables the president under the Constitution and with authorization of Congress to use whatever means to protect America that shifted the counterterrorism concept from past definitional confusions to national consensus and strategic clarity regarding the nature of the challenge at home and abroad.

Summary

In summary, the evolution of American perceptions has gradually emerged from traditional views that terrorism constitutes a "crime" to the view that "terrorism" is a new unprecedented form of warfare. What particularly influenced this transition in the past decade were four events attributed to al Qaeda:

First, in August 1996, Osama bin Laden, al Qaeda's founder, issued a Declaration of Jihad (holy war) against the United States and the Saudi government.[30]

Second, in February 1998, Osama bin Laden along with his senior associate Ayman al-Zawahiri endorsed a fatwah (religious ruling) stating that Muslims should kill Americans, including civilians, anywhere in the world where they can be found. The fatwah was later published in the newspaper *Al-Quds Al-Arabi* on February 23, 1998.[31]

Third, in May 1998, Mohammed Atef (bin Laden's second in command) sent Khaled al Fawwaz (al Qaeda's spokesman) a letter endorsing a fatwah issued by bin Laden and including a declaration by the "Ulema Union of Afghanistan" calling for a jihad against the United States and its allies.[32]

And fourth, in late May 1998, bin Laden issued a statement entitled "The Nuclear Bomb of Islam," in which he stated that it is the duty of Muslims to prepare as much force as possible to attack the enemies of God.[33]

Clearly, these belligerent dispositions, coupled with the tragedy of 9/11, resulted in the United States' transformation from a mind-set of terrorism perceived as "ordinary criminality" toward "warfare," or at least "irregular" conflicts against Islamist extremists and terrorists, both non-state and state actors. It is not surprising, therefore, that America and its allies used force in Afghanistan and Iraq as the "early stages" in that war. Now over four years after the September 11, 2001, attack, the United States is readying for what it calls a "long war," perhaps a generational struggle akin to the Cold War.

This emerging strategy was released by the Pentagon in February 2006 in a document titled Quadrennial Defense Review (QDR). It outlined plans for expanding the missions of the U.S. military in the next twenty years in fighting wars abroad and defending the homeland, such as preventing terrorists from obtaining weapons of mass destruction.[34]

Despite the elevation of terrorism to a "long war" level, the public seems to be still debating its political, legal, economic, and strategic implications.

Threats to the United States

The discussion in the previous section of the evolution of American definitions of terrorism in the pre- and post-9/11 periods reflects the specific realities on the ground both domestically and internationally. That is, the United States' counterterrorism policies and actions have developed in response to the nature and intensity of the dangers posed to the nation as perceived by the administration, Congress, and the public at large.

The lessons of American history indicate that terrorism was the politics of futility because the groups that adopted violence failed to accomplish their stated objectives. Radical ideologies and theologies with vested single-issue or revolutionary interests had less effect on the social order than the unmatched power of the government.

An overview of the different types of terrorist challenges to the United States at home and abroad follows.

Domestic

Before World War II, there were occasional outbreaks of terrorism perpetrated by both domestic and foreign groups in America. [35] Some of the earliest "home-grown" groups include the vigilantes, originally organized to keep law and order in the lawless Western frontier; the Ku Klux Klan (KKK) during the post–Civil War period; and the Molly Maguires, whose primary interest was vengeance against the anti-Irish-Catholic Scotch, Ulster, Welsh, and English Protestants in Pennsylvania during the 1870s.

The KKK, for example, survived since its early beginning some 140 years ago to preach and practice hatred, intolerance, and violence against their adversaries, mainly blacks, Jews, Catholics, and liberals. The most infamous Klan killing occurred in Mississippi in 1964 when three civil rights workers—Michael Schwerner, Andrew Goodman, and James Chaney—were shot dead by a lynch mob. In recent years the KKK developed alliances with other right-wing organizations such as the Aryan Nations, the Order, and Posse Comitatus. Nevertheless, none of these groups has succeeded in achieving their aims, largely because of the rejection of hate ideologies by the vast majority of the American people and the efforts of law enforcement agencies to disrupt their illegal activities.

It was not, however, until the turbulent 1960s that a proliferation of left-wing radical movements with violent tendencies occurred. The Weather Underground, the New World Liberation Front, the George Jackson Brigade, the Symbionese Liberation Army, the Black Liberation Army, and the Black Panther Party were among the most active leftist ideological groups in the United States during the late 1960s and 1970s. During the same period, ethnic and nationalist groups (e.g., the Jewish Defense League, Armenian movements, Puerto Rican Armed Forces of National Liberation, Omega 7-Cuban Nationalist Movement, and the Cuban National Liberation Front) operated within the United States and Puerto Rico.

In 1969, for example, the Black Panther Party was involved in an aborted plot to bomb a number of New York City targets, including police stations, department stores, and other public buildings. It also planned to kill police officers. Some thirteen Panther members were brought to trial the following year but were acquitted by a jury.

Although these groups have proved to be less professional and successful than their counterparts in other regions around the world during the 1970s, terrorist campaigns in the United States targeted the police, military, business, and other victims in over six hundred attacks. In justifying their operations, terrorists have communicated a multitude of rationales. For instance, in a statement claiming credit for the bombing of the Gulf Oil Building in Pittsburgh in June 1974, the Weather Underground explained that the attack was to punish the corporation for "financing the Portuguese in Angola, stealing from the poor in the United States, and exploiting the people and resources of seventy countries." The Jewish Defense League targeted Soviet facilities, residences, and vehicles as well as commercial firms or the installations of Eastern European countries in the New York area to protest the policies of the Soviet Bloc toward domestic Jewish minorities and Israel.

In addition to terrorism perpetrated by indigenous groups in the 1970s, foreign nationalist groups were also active in the United States. For instance, the Croatian group Otpor (Resistance) hijacked a TWA Boeing 727 from New York to Paris in 1976 to attract attention to its separatist goal of independence from Yugoslavia and took over the West German Consulate in Chicago in 1978 to demand the release of a Croatian leader in Cologne. The Secret Army for the Liberation of Armenia, seeking revenge for Turkey's genocide against Armenians during World War I, assassinated Turkish consular officials in Los Angeles during 1973. Also, the Black September Organization, operating within the framework of Fatah, the main group of the Palestine Liberation Organization (PLO) headed at that time by Yasser Arafat, killed an Israeli air attaché in Washington, D.C., in 1973.

During the 1980s, the United States experienced fewer terrorist incidents domestically than abroad. More specifically, terrorist acts within the United States declined drastically after the first few years of the decade. The total number of terrorist activities, both of indigenous and foreign origin, reached an estimated 220, approximately one-third that of the previous decade. The highest number of incidents was committed between 1980 and 1982 (122). Conversely, in 1989, only six cases were investigated as terrorist incidents, the lowest number in any given year during two decades of violence. A major reason for this encouraging trend was the success of the proactive operations of the FBI and its effective cooperation with other law enforcement agencies in the United States and abroad. Prosecution of terrorists, such as the 1986 indictment by a federal jury in Boston of eight radicals involved in a nine-year series of bombings, bank robberies, and murder, was also a contributing factor in the decline of domestic terrorism. Another factor was a social phenomenon—the general loss of revolutionary fervor in the United States during this period.

To be sure, some of the terrorist groups operating in the 1970s were also active to some extent during the 1980s.[36] There were left-wing groups such as the Weather Underground and the Black Panther Party, both involved in the Brinks armored car robbery in 1981 in Nyack, New York; the Armed Forces of National Liberation claimed eleven bombings in 1982. Also, the Jewish Defense League was active, engaging in violence against its perceived enemies.

In addition to these and other domestic groups, a variety of new bodies committed to ideological and political violence emerged during the 1980s. One example of a series of terrorist attacks in the United States is the letter bombs addressed to various lawyers and court officials in the southeastern United States at the end of 1989. A note claiming credit for the bombings implied racist motives. Other examples of U.S. terrorism include reactionary right-wing movements advancing anti-Semitic and white supremacist causes as well as antigovernment and antitax beliefs (e.g., Aryan Nations) and the Evan Mecham Eco-Terrorist International Conspiracy (EMETIC), desiring to preserve the ecological systems by attacking perceived despoilers of the ecology through acts of sabotage ("ecotage"). Another example is the Animal Liberation Front (ALF) and related groups, dedicated to the elimination of animal use in medical research and industry. Extremist animal rights groups in the United States have usually confined attacks to destruction of property rather than humans. An exception, however, was the attempted murder of the president of U.S. Surgical Corp. by means of a bomb.

Foreign groups also continued their sporadic operations in the United States during the 1980s. For example, the Provisional Irish Republican Army (PIRA) maintained a gun-running ring in 1982, and Sikh terrorists were prevented from destroying an Air India aircraft at Kennedy Airport in 1986 (although they had succeeded in Canada the year before). In addition, there is some evidence that foreign governments, such as Libya and Iran, have put in place in the United States an infrastructure to aid in carrying out terrorist acts. One example was the 1989 San Diego pipebomb attack on the car of the wife of Capt. Will Rogers, the commanding officer of the USS *Vincennes*, which had inadvertently shot down a civilian Iranian airliner with massive loss of life in 1988.

Between 1990 and 1999 some sixty terrorist attacks perpetrated by both domestic and foreign groups occurred in the United States, killing 182 people and injuring more than 1,932.[37] In 1990, the perpetration of only four events was the lowest number in any year since 1970. The most dramatic event was the assassination of Rabbi Meir Kahane, the Israeli leader of the Jewish Defense League (JDL), by an Egyptian immigrant to the United States. Other events included: an abortive plot by militant "skinheads" to pump cyanide gas into a synagogue; the explosion of a bomb outside a Cuban museum in Miami; and the arrest in Florida of individuals affiliated with the PIRA while attempting to purchase a heat-seeking antiaircraft Stinger missile and other sophisticated weapons.

The evolving Gulf crisis increased concern for potential Iraqi-instigated attacks in the United States in 1990–1991. Anxiety intensified as a result of specific calls by the Iraqi leadership and Middle Eastern terrorist groups to target America. Although the fear of attacks was widespread, no incidents occurred in the United States, perhaps due to the preventive security measures undertaken by the U.S. government and the private sector. These efforts included reduction of Iraqi diplomatic staff; close scrutiny of Iraqi and other nationals suspected of being linked to radical Arab causes; upgrading security at government and military installations; and beefing-up security procedures at airports and other commercial industries.

When the Gulf War broke out on January 17, 1991, security measures increased even further. These activities contributed to the absence of any Iraq-sponsored or foreign-related incidents in the United States linked to the Gulf War. Other low-level acts of terrorism in the United States were recorded during the 1990s, such as theft, arson, shooting, and bombing. These acts were undertaken mostly by domestic groups (e.g., American Front Skinheads; Animal Liberation Army; Earth Liberation Front; and Los Macheteros).

While these incidents did not seriously shake up the "American way of life," two major events influenced, more than ever before, the U.S. government's disposition as well as the public perception of the terrorist threats within the country. First, on February 26, 1993, a powerful bomb explosion occurred in the parking garage of the World Trade Center in New York, killing six people, injuring 1,042 others, and causing widespread damage. This attack, considered the largest international terrorist incident in the United States up to that time, was perpetrated by a group of foreign terrorists from Egypt, Iraq, Jordan, and the Palestinian Authority. Al Qaeda's involvement was subsequently established.

The second incident, labeled the largest act of domestic terrorism in American history, took place on April 19, 1995, destroying the nine-story Alfred P. Murrah Federal Building in Oklahoma City. This spectacular attack, perpetrated by two American terrorists, Timothy McVeigh and Terry Nichols, claimed 168 lives, including 19 children, and wounded 674 people. The bomb not only destroyed the federal building, but also severely damaged or destroyed more than twenty-five structures.[38]

Since that abominable assault and for the next ten years, the FBI aborted some sixty right-wing plots, largely because it was more successful in infiltrating these organized groups than tracking down small cells of terrorists. For instance, the FBI failed to prevent the July 27, 1996, bombing of the Centennial Park during the Summer Olympics in Atlanta, Georgia, killing one and injuring one hundred others. This act, like the Oklahoma City attack, was perpetrated by an extremist individual, Eric Robert Rudolph, rather than an established movement with inherent vulnerabilities that resulted in government penetration.

On the other hand, the historical record reveals that some large terrorist groups, such as single-issue radicals—the Animal Liberation Front (ALF) and the Earth Liberation Front (ELF)—are able to inflict considerable damage on American society over long periods. For instance, in 2003 ALF set fire to a McDonald's restaurant in Chico, California, because of the United States' "corporate dominance" and its use of animal products.[39] Similarly, in 2005, ELF, in its efforts to "protect the environment," set fire to two car dealerships in Pacific Beach, California, and perpetrated other arson attacks against property in the surrounding area.[40]

While threats posed by indigenous American groups were dealt with, the U.S. government only infrequently focused its attention on challenges to the homeland posed by foreign terrorists. For example, following the spectacular bombing of the World Trade Towers on February 26, 1993, by al Qaeda, the investigative efforts by the FBI and subsequent trials of the arrested perpetrators did successfully close that case, but the experience did not alert the administration to other potential plots planned by bin Laden's network that began to develop in this country in the early 1990s. It was sheer luck, rather than heightened concern and effective counterterrorism capabilities, such as coordinated intelligence, that aborted several major operations. One example of border security's good fortune was the December 14, 1999, arrest of Ahmed Ressam, a member of the Algerian Armed Islamic Group (GIA), an affiliate of al Qaeda, as he entered the border-crossing at Port Angeles, Washington. His apprehension occurred when U.S. customs officers at the border noticed Ressam's nervousness and referred him to additional inspection and he tried to escape. Upon examining Ressam's car the inspectors found explosives intended to be detonated at Los Angeles International Airport during the millennium celebrations on or around January 1, 2000.

A second fortunate accomplishment is the case of Zacarias Moussaoui, a French citizen of Moroccan origin, who intended to fly a plane into the White House as the twentieth hijacker of the 9/11 operation. He arrived in the United States in February 2001 and took flight lessons in Oklahoma and Minnesota. Only when a flight instructor reported to the FBI Minnesota Field Office his suspicion of Moussaoui's behavior did the Bureau initiate an investigation. He was subsequently arrested on a visa violation and was convicted in May 2006 to life imprisonment without the possibility for parole in connection with the September 11, 2001, attacks.

These two episodes illustrate, at least partially, the failure of the U.S. government in the pre-9/11 period to focus enough attention on the extent of the foreign terrorist threat to the homeland. Instead, American policymakers have been more concerned with the terrorist danger to U.S. interests abroad.

Abroad

U.S. citizens and interests have been more affected by ideological and political violence abroad than they have at home. Indeed, during the past four decades, the United States has become a major target of acts of terrorism throughout the world.[41] There are many factors contributing to this situation, including the fact that the United States maintains an extensive cultural, political, economic, and military presence abroad and that a considerable number of foreign groups and governments oppose American values, policies, and actions. This reality, coupled with other global developments such as technological advancements in weaponry and communications, has resulted in the expansion of international terrorist activities against the United States.

According to a State Department report, a total of 1,617 anti-American international attacks occurred between 1970 and 1989.[42] Out of a total of 939 incidents internationally during January–March 1991, 104 operations were directed against Americans and U.S. interests compared to 39 in 1990 and 32 in 1989 during the January–March time frame. This escalation was probably due primarily to the impact of the Gulf War.

During the 1970s and 1980s, the United States was the most popular single target of international terrorism. American citizens, officials, diplomats, and military officers have been victimized by both state-sponsored terrorism (e.g., Libya, Syria, and Iran) and substate groups, including Marxist-oriented (e.g., Germany's Red Army Faction [RAF]), Islamic Fundamentalist (e.g., Hizbollah), Palestinian (e.g., Abu Nidal Organization [ANO]), and ideological mercenaries (e.g., Japanese Red Army [JRA]).

An analysis of American victimization in international terrorist attacks demonstrates a wide range of civilian and military targets.[43] For instance, every kind of U.S. business activity abroad has been attacked, including financial (e.g., Merrill Lynch), banking (e.g., Bank of America), energy (e.g., Texaco), chemicals (e.g., Union Carbide), automobiles (e.g., Ford), communication (e.g., International Telephone & Telegraph), computers (e.g., International Business Machines), travel (e.g., American Express), and many others. In addition, every segment of the U.S. military abroad has been affected. The personnel, facilities, and operations of the Army, Air Force, and Navy have become continuing targets.

To be sure, the most spectacular incident abroad that brought home to Americans the vulnerability of the United States to terrorist attacks during the administration of President Jimmy Carter was the November 1979 seizure of the embassy in Tehran.[44] Iranian revolutionaries held some sixty American diplomats hostage for 444 days. What brutally complicated the resolution of the hostage situation were the abortive military mission to rescue the captives some six months later and the subsequent Iran-Contra Affair, in which the United States sold arms to its enemy, Iran, in an effort to release the hostages. Arguably, this incident portrayed the United States as a "paper tiger" and therefore encouraged the intensification of other significant attacks in the following decade.

American vulnerability abroad was once again dramatically demonstrated when Hizbollah, founded in 1982 in Lebanon as an umbrella organization comprised of radical Shiite groups and support by Iran, began to preach war against "Western imperialism," epitomized by the "Great Satan" (the United States). Beginning with the April 1983 suicide car bombing of the U.S. Embassy in Beirut, killing 49 and wounding 120, Hizbollah continued with other devastating attacks against American targets in Lebanon. The most spectacular operation occurred on October 23 of that same year, when a Hizbollah suicide truck bomber destroyed the U.S. Marine Headquarters and barracks in Beirut, causing the death of 241 military personnel. The Department of Defense Commission investigating this attack recommended in its report of December 20, 1983, that since terrorism is "a mode of warfare," an effective counterterrorism policy "needs to be supported by political and diplomatic actions and by a wide range of timely military response capabilities."[45]

This and other recommendations were not immediately implemented. Apparently, the administration under President Ronald Reagan still regarded attacks against the United States in Lebanon as tactical rather than strategic threats to its security interests. The American forces' pullback from Lebanon did not prevent, for example, the Hizbollah bombing of the U.S. Embassy in Kuwait in late 1983; the suicide truck bombing of the U.S. Embassy Annex in East Beirut in September 1984; and the hijacking of TWA Flight 847 in June 1985 during which 39 U.S. passengers were held hostage for 17 days in Beirut before being released. Nor were dozens of American officials and ordinary citizens immune in Lebanon from Hizbollah kidnappings and murder during the 1984–1991 time frame, two prominent examples of which were the killing of William Buckley, the U.S. CIA station chief in Beirut in 1985, and Lt. Col. William Richard Higgins, USMC (who served as a United Nations military observer) in 1991.

Americans during the 1980s were also targeted elsewhere because of the perception of terrorists around the world that U.S. responses were traditionally timid and that they could therefore strike with impunity.

During 1985, for example, numerous terrorist incidents involving U.S. citizens were recorded,[46] including the bombing by the National Front of a nightclub near Athens, injuring sixty-nine Americans; the car bombing at the U.S. Rhein-Main Air Base near Frankfurt, killing two and injuring fifteen other Americans (this attack was claimed by the German Red Army Faction and the French Direct Action); and the murder of an elderly American tourist whose body was thrown overboard from a hijacked Italian cruise ship in the Mediterranean Sea by Palestine Liberation Front terrorists. In the latter case, U.S. aircraft intercepted and forced down an Egyptian airliner flying the hijackers to a safe haven to land at a NATO airbase in Sicily where they were apprehended by the Italian authorities. But this infrequent use of American power did not deter terrorists from attacking U.S. citizens, both civilian and military, in different countries such as France, Spain, the Philippines, and Honduras.

Indeed, even when the United States once again used military force, this option proved insufficient to prevent additional terrorist attacks. A case in point is the American military retaliation against Libya in 1986 for its bombing of a West Berlin nightclub, "La Belle" discotheque, frequented by American servicemen, killing one soldier and injuring fifty others. The United States almost immediately launched air raids against Tripoli and Behghazi, killing thirty-seven people, including President Muammar al-Qaddafi's adopted daughter. Libya, on its part, threatened that "suicide squads" were poised to strike at the American homeland. Although this threat was not implemented, Libya planned and mounted the December 1998 mid-air bombing of Pan American flight 103 over Lockerbie, Scotland. A total of 270 people on the aircraft and on the ground were killed, mostly Americans.

The 1990s also recorded numerous incidents directed against American interests abroad.[47] In 1990, for example, the U.S. Embassy in Lima, Peru, was car-bombed, injuring three guards, and a U.S. general with NATO was the target of an unsuccessful kidnapping or assassination attempt in Italy. In 1991 and particularly following the start of Operation Desert Storm, Iraq and its substate supporters called for a jihad against U.S. and allied interests worldwide. Some 170 incidents were recorded against the coalition members, most of whom were Americans. For example, the U.S. Embassy in Lima was struck on January 25, 1991, by an RPG-7 rocket-propelled grenade, causing only superficial damage. The Tupac Amaru Revolutionary Movement, which claimed responsibility for the incident, condemned the United States for its involvement in the Gulf and offered its militant support for the Arab people who were being murdered by U.S. troops in Iraq.

Similar low-level attacks were perpetrated without any direct connection to Iraq itself. There were attacks on U.S. embassies and consulates (Frankfurt, Berlin, Sydney, Dhaka, Mexico City, Istanbul, and Kuala Lumpur); U.S. military personnel and facilities (e.g., Jeddah, Ankara, and Izmir); U.S. businesses (e.g., Ford, Coca-Cola, American Express, Holiday Inn, Citibank, and Kentucky Fried Chicken); and other U.S. targets (e.g., Mormon churches in America, U.S. Turkey Association, and the American School in Karachi).

The attacks against the United States abroad were once again intensified in the 1990s and through 2000 as a result of the emergence of al Qaeda.[48] Operations began on October 3, 1993, when terrorists ambushed American military personnel in Mogadishu, Somalia. Eighteen soldiers participating in the United Nations' peacekeeping mission were killed, and some of the bodies were paraded.

Al Qaeda was also involved in other attacks, including the November 13, 1995, car bomb explosion outside the American-operated Saudi National Guard training center in Riyadh, Saudi Arabia, killing five Americans and two Indians; the June 25, 1996, car bombing attack at Khobar Tower; a U.S. Air Force housing complex in Dhahran, Saudi Arabia, killing nineteen soldiers and wounding hundreds more; the two August 7, 1998, truck bombings outside the U.S. embassies in Nairobi, Kenya, and Dar es Salaam, Tanzania, killing 234 people, twelve of them American, and wounding more than five thousand others; and the October 12, 2000, suicide bombing of the USS *Cole*, killing seventeen and wounding thirty-nine American sailors in Aden harbor, Yemen.

It is noteworthy that while terrorists have mostly selected American targets, numerous attacks also involved U.S. citizens simply because they happened to be at the wrong place at the wrong time. An early example is the March 30, 1973, murder of two American diplomats, Ambassador Cleo A. Noel, Jr., and George C. Moore, chargé d'affaires in the Sudan. They were taken hostage by Black September terrorists who seized control of the Saudi Arabian embassy in Khartoum and killed the diplomats when their demands were refused during negotiations. And more recently, on October 7, 2004, an American was killed when al Qaeda-linked terrorists attacked tourist sites in the Sinai Peninsula in Egypt.

PART II
The Evolution of U.S. Counterterrorism Strategy

The historical record indicates that infrequent terrorist attacks occurred in the United States from its founding in 1776 until the 1960s. Among the dramatic acts traditionally associated with terrorism in this country are the assassination and attempted assassination of several American presidents. In 1865, John Wilkes Booth, seeking revenge for the defeated Confederacy, shot Abraham Lincoln. Leon F. Czolgosz, an anarchist idealist, murdered William McKinley in 1901. And in 1950, two Puerto Rican nationalists, Oscar Collazo and Griselio Torresola, desiring to achieve independence for their homeland, tried unsuccessfully to assassinate Harry S. Truman. Also, the assassination in 1963 of John F. Kennedy by Lee Harvey Oswald for unknown motivations, and the murder in 1968 of Robert F. Kennedy (at that time, a candidate for the presidency) by Sirhan Sirhan, a Palestinian immigrant objecting to U.S. policy in the Middle East, have been frequently cited as the more familiar cases of American terrorism, acts that sometimes were also labeled as "social" or "political crimes."

American policy to combat terrorism did not, however, begin to intensify before the 1960s and the 1970s. Several reasons account for this development. First, historical domestic terrorists did not seriously challenge the existing order in the United States; second, different administrations as well as Congress reacted to contemporary terrorism only when it became apparent that the threats eroded national security at home and abroad; and third, in the context of the Cold War, the Soviet Union utilized terrorism—"warfare on the cheap"—as a significant strategic tool in its foreign policy, thereby compelling the United States to formulate adequate responses to counter low-intensity conflict.

The following overview deals with highlights of the evolution of U.S. counterterrorism strategies, particularly focusing on the pre- and post-9/11 period. Although this presentation is not intended to be exhaustive, it does refer chronologically to a broad range of issues, including selective executive, legislative, and judicial perspectives and actions.

The Pre-9/11 Period
One of the earliest challenges to homeland security occurred in the 1970s when major race riots erupted in the country, interfering seriously with normal functioning of diverse communities. In the aftermath of these

events, the U.S. government established a National Advisory Committee on Criminal Justice Standards and Goals. This body issued in 1976 a "Report of the Task Force on Disorders and Terrorism," viewing the riots as "a tactic or technique by means of which a violent act or the threat thereof is used for the prime purpose of creating overwhelming fear for coercive purposes." The report recommended a variety of specific steps to assure greater communal stability.[49]

Similarly, in the face of increasing terrorist attacks directed against American interests abroad, the United States has undertaken initial measures to cope with the challenge.

Two events directly contributed to this development. First was the 1969 hijacking of a TWA jet by members of the Popular Front for the Liberation of Palestine (PFLP), and subsequently, the release of the hostages by Syria. And the second incident was the hijacking on September 6, 1970, of a TWA Boeing 707 from Frankfurt and a Pan American 747 jumbo jet from Amsterdam. These passenger planes were diverted to Jordan and Egypt, respectively, where they were blown up, after the passengers and crews were evacuated by the attackers.

Another incident that influenced the articulation of American policy was the spectacular 1972 murder of Israeli athletes at the Olympic Games in Munich. For instance, the United States at the United Nations vetoed a Security Council resolution because it sought to censure Israel for its subsequent raid into Lebanon as retaliation for the Munich attack, but did not mention that it was a response to terrorism that prompted the Israeli raid.

It is against this background that President Richard Nixon established a cabinet-level committee to coordinate counterterrorism efforts. A smaller Interagency Group on Terrorism, operating out of the Department of State, was established to deal with daily issues. Another body, the Interagency Intelligence Committee on Terrorism, was also set up at that time. On the basis of various presidential directives, the State Department became over the years the lead U.S. government body coordinating American counterterrorism strategies abroad.

The 1970s also marked the beginning of enactments of antiterrorism laws by the U.S. Congress. For instance, section 303 of the International Security Assistance and Arms Export Control Act of 1976 called for cutting off American help to "any government which aids or abets terrorism, by providing sanctuary from prosecution, to any group or individual which has committed an act of international terrorism." Another export control mechanism was established by Congress in 1979 that, consequently, developed into a "black list" of countries supporting terrorism and therefore was not entitled to benefit from any form of American assistance. The initial "terrorism list" included Libya, Iraq, Syria, and South Yemen. Over the years other countries, such as Afghanistan, Iran, Cuba, North Korea, and the Sudan, were added to this list.

It was, however, during the presidency of Jimmy Carter that the

United States had faced its first major terrorism challenge abroad, namely the 1979 takeover of the American embassy in Tehran by militant "students." Initially, President Carter ruled out the use of force to rescue the sixty diplomats held hostage. Instead, he blocked Iranian assets in the United States, sought sanctions against Iran at the United Nations, and brought Iran to the International Court of Justice. When none of these and other efforts resolved the crisis, the United States launched a military rescue mission in Iran. When this attempt also failed, partly due to poor planning, the United States resumed diplomatic negotiations with Iran and, ultimately, after 444 days of captivity, the hostages were brought back home and the United States faced political humiliation.

But it was not until the 1983 bombing of the U.S. Embassy and the Marine base in Beirut, killing some 270 Americans, that the U.S. government, for the first time in its history, seriously decided to develop a more coherent and proactive strategy dealing with terrorism. It immediately established two commissions to investigate the incidents and to offer appropriate recommendations to improve security for American military and diplomatic personnel abroad. The first commission was set up within the Department of Defense and was chaired by L. J. Long. Its recommendations included a major shift in national policy from reactive antiterrorism posture to proactive counterterrorism strategies. The significance of the report prepared by the Long Commission is that terrorism was regarded, at least from the Department of Defense perspective, as a form of warfare and, therefore, was elevated to a top security concern.

The second commission, headed by former CIA Director Bobby Inman, recommended massive upgrading of security at State Department embassies abroad, including personnel protection, physical improvement, and better design and structural changes of facilities. Subsequently, the position of Ambassador-at-Large for Counterterrorism was created within the Department of State for the purpose of coordinating all governmental efforts. It is noteworthy that other units at the State Department also became involved in counterterrorism activities. For instance, the 1984 Act to Combat International Terrorism (Public Law 98-533) established the Counterterrorism Rewards Program to be administered by the department's Diplomatic Security Service. Under this program, the U.S. government offered rewards (initially up to $2 million and subsequently increased to $5 million) "for information that prevents or resolves acts of terrorism against U.S. citizens or property or leads to the arrest and conviction of terrorist criminals in such acts."[50]

Moreover, in the aftermath of the hijacking of the 1985 TWA flight 847 and the *Achille Lauro* cruise ship, President Ronald Reagan appointed Vice President George H. W. Bush to chair a cabinet-level Task Force on Combating Terrorism. In its report, issued in December 1985, the Task Force recommended a broad range of actions, such as efforts to improve coordination among government agencies, creation of a full-time position on the National Security Council staff, and the establishment of a consolidated intelligence center on terrorism.

In light of numerous kidnappings of American citizens, both civilian and military, in Lebanon by Hizbollah terrorists during the 1980s, the Vice President's Task Force public report of February 1986 also established a key American policy regarding this matter. It stated: "The United States has a clear policy of no concessions to terrorists as the best way to protect the greatest number of people. However, the United States Government has always stated that it will talk to anyone and use every available resource to gain the release of Americans held hostage."[51]

This disposition was repeatedly reconfirmed by U.S. officials over the years. For instance, discussing the issue of hostages and concessions, Secretary of State George Shultz asserted on February 20, 1987:

> It's inevitable that, as a people, our hearts go out to the individuals directly affected by terrorism and to their families and friends here at home. But we cannot allow our sympathies to overshadow the pressing need for us to stand firm behind our principles and to deny international terrorism further leverage against us. Our foremost priority must continue to be to demonstrate, through word and action, that there are no rewards for terrorist violence. We have to see to it that the terrorists not only don't get rewards, they pay a price. We have to redouble our cooperative efforts with other nations in dealing with this scourge.[52]

Another tool in U.S. strategy that evolved during this period was the "long-arm statute" of the Omnibus Diplomatic Security and Antiterrorism Act of 1986 that makes it a federal crime for a terrorist to threaten, detain, seize, injure, or kill an American citizen abroad. This legislation provided American law enforcement agencies with the legal authority to conduct criminal investigation overseas. Ultimately, it resulted in the stationing of FBI legal attachés in American embassies abroad.

To be sure, during the Reagan presidency, the United States did not hesitate to project force selectively against terrorist states. For example, as a result of the April 1986 terrorist bombing of a Berlin disco club attributed to Libya, killing two American soldiers, the U.S. military launched bombing raids against Tripoli and Benghazi. These attacks killed thirty-seven people, including President Muammar al-Qaddafi's adopted daughter. The United States warned Libya that it would strike again if Tripoli was linked to further terrorist attacks against Americans.

And yet, Washington did not resort to military action in the aftermath of the December 1988 mid-air explosion of Pan Am Flight 103 over Lockerbie, Scotland, perpetrated by Libyan agents, killing 270 Americans and citizens of other nationalities. This incident, however, resulted in revived public concerns that generated calls for increased civil aviation protection. The work of two advocacy groups—Victims of Pan Am 103 and Families of Pan Am Flight 103/Lockerbie—have been instrumental in pressuring the U.S. government, particularly the Federal Aviation Administration (FAA), to take major steps to improve security and to apply political and economic sanctions against Libya.

During the 1990s, as expanding terrorist acts at home and abroad attracted increased public and U.S. official attention, American counterterrorism strategies evolved more rapidly than ever before. In 1991, for example, President Bill Clinton ordered the deployment of cruise missiles against Baghdad in retaliation for an Iraqi plot to assassinate former President Bush during a visit in Kuwait that year. In response to the bombing of the World Trade Center in 1993 and the Oklahoma City attack two years later, Clinton issued in June 1995 the Presidential Decision Directive (PDD) 39, "U.S. Policy on Counterterrorism." That designated the FBI as the lead agency for investigating acts against American citizens worldwide. The PDD also asserted that terrorist attacks, whether they occur domestically or elsewhere, will be regarded as a potential threat to national security as well as a criminal act. Such actions will result in the retaliation with appropriate U.S. force. Additionally, the PDD declared that the United States would pursue all efforts to "deter and preempt, apprehend and prosecute, or assist other governments to prosecute individuals who perpetrate or plan to perpetrate such attacks."

The White House also undertook several other counterterrorism measures in the mid-1990s. An Executive Order (E.O. 1015) established on August 22, 1996, a Commission on Aviation Safety and Security. Led by Vice President Al Gore, the White House commission final report issued on February 12, 1997, highlighted the risks of the terrorist attacks in the United States. The report references Operation Bojinka, the failed plot to bomb twelve American airliners out of the sky over the Pacific Ocean, and calls for increased aviation security. The commission reports that [it] "believes that terrorist attacks on civil aviation are directed at the United States, and that there should be an ongoing federal commitment to reducing the threats that they pose."[53]

An important law, the Anti-Terrorism Act of 1996, signed by President Clinton, provided the following measures:

- authorizes $1 billion in funding for federal antiterrorism law enforcement efforts;
- makes it easier for police to trace bombs to the criminals who made them, by requiring chemical taggants in some explosive material;
- makes it harder for terrorists to raise the money they need to fund their crimes;

- streamlines execution and expulsion procedures for terrorist aliens;
- allows the president to withhold foreign aid to countries that provide assistance to any country designated as a supporter of terrorism;
- increases the penalties for conspiracy to commit explosives violations and for specific terrorism-related crimes;
- allows victims of terrorist acts to sue foreign state sponsors of terrorism; and
- expands the use of Victims of Crime Act (VOCA) funds to include terrorism victims.[54]

Moreover, the Defense Against Weapons of Mass Destruction Act of 1996, or the Nunn-Lugar-Domenici amendment to the National Defense Authorization Act for FY97, stipulated the training of first responders to deal with weapons of mass destruction (WMD) terrorist incidents. The Nunn-Lugar-Domenici Domestic Preparedness Program began in FY97 to train first responders—fire, police, and emergency medical technicians—in 120 of the largest cities in the country.[55]

Also, in January 1997, the Federal Emergency Management Agency (FEMA) and the FBI submitted to Congress a joint report that addressed both crisis management prevention and consequence management/response activities. This report focused on capabilities and interagency roles and responsibilities to respond to an incident involving WMD. In the assessment summary, the impact of a WMD incident and significant response requirement was recognized.

Following the al Qaeda attack on the U.S. embassies in Kenya and Tanzania in August 1998, President Clinton authorized the military to launch some seventy cruise missiles at a pharmaceutical plant in the Sudan (believed to produce the nerve agent VX) and at bin Laden's camps in Afghanistan. Bin Laden himself survived the attack. However, he and his military chief, Mohammed Atef, were indicted for the East Africa embassies' bombings.

During the same year, the administration in PDD-62 established the Office of the National Coordinator for Security, Infrastructure Protection and Counter-Terrorism. The National Coordinator's role was to oversee the broad variety of relevant policies and programs, including such areas as counterterrorism, protection of critical infrastructure, and preparedness and consequence management for WMDs. The National Coordinator was placed within the National Security Council, reports to the president through the Assistant to the President for National Security Affairs, and produces for him an annual Security Preparedness Report. The National Coordinator will also provide advice regarding budgets for counterterrorism programs and lead in the development of guidelines that might be needed for crisis management.

Fearing that al Qaeda may carry out further attacks on U.S. targets around the world, the government has undertaken a number of precautionary measures at home and abroad. For example, in 1999, the FBI suspended all public tours of its headquarters in Washington, D.C., and the State Department closed numerous diplomatic posts in high-risk areas. Also, the administration on July 9 of that year imposed financial and commercial sanctions against Afghanistan's Taliban rulers in retaliation for Afghanistan's refusal to cooperate with U.S. counterterrorism efforts.

It is noteworthy that another effort, the Advisory Panel to Assess Domestic Response Capabilities for Terrorism Involving Weapons of Mass Destruction, established in 1999, headed by Governor James S. Gilmore III of Virginia, has focused attention on unconventional issues. In its second report in 2000, the panel shifted its emphasis from threat assessment to address "specific programs for combating terrorism and larger questions of national strategy and Federal organization." The Panel addressed the existence of "problems at all levels of government in virtually every functional discipline relevant to combating terrorism." This report suggested that an Office for Combating Terrorism be created, along with increased training and improved response capabilities.[56]

Similarly, a bipartisan panel, the Twenty-first Century Commission, formed in 1999 and led by former U.S. Senators Warren B. Rudman and Gary Hart, called in their report in 2000 for the creation of a Cabinet-level agency to assume responsibility for defending the United States against the increasing likelihood of terrorist attacks in the country. The commission making the recommendation included high-ranking military and former Cabinet secretaries. Their report warned that terrorists probably will attack the United States with nuclear, chemical, or biological weapons at some point within the next twenty-five years. The commission proposed a complete redesign of the National Guard to provide the proposed new "Homeland Security Agency" with U.S.-based troops to combat those who threaten a nation that for more than two centuries was isolated from attack by two oceans.[57]

The National Commission on Terrorism, another body formed by the Administration in 1999, chaired by Ambassador L. Paul Bremer III, issued its report, "Countering the Changing Threat of International Terrorism," in 2000.[58] Its executive summary contains the following key findings and conclusions:

- international terrorism poses an increasingly dangerous and difficult threat to America;
- countering the growing danger of the terrorist threat requires significantly stepping up U.S. efforts;
- priority one is to prevent terrorist attacks. U.S. intelligence and law enforcement communities must use the full scope of

their authority to collect intelligence regarding terrorist plans
and methods;
● U.S. policies must firmly target all states that support terrorists;
● private sources of financial and logistical support for terrorists must be subjected to the full force and sweep of U.S.
and international laws;
● a terrorist attack involving a biological agent, deadline
chemicals, or nuclear or radiological material, even if it suc-
ceeds only partially, could profoundly affect the entire nation;
the government must do more to prepare for such an event;
● President and Congress should reform the system for reviewing and funding departmental counterterrorism programs
to ensure that the activities and programs of various agencies
are part of a comprehensive plan.

The warnings contained in the Bremer Report did not prevent the
spectacular October 12, 2000, suicide attack by two al Qaeda terrorists in
a small boat blasting the destroyer USS *Cole* at Aden harbor in Yemen,
killing seventeen sailors and wounding thirty-nine. Out of concern for
future targeting of Americans, the United States decided to stop Navy ships
from using the Suez Canal and warned civilians not to travel to the Middle
East. In the following year, U.S. forces in the region were placed on the
highest alert, the Pentagon cancelled joint exercises with the Jordanian
Army, and American ships in Bahrain were ordered back to sea.
    During the period of July to September 11, 2001, the media recorded
the following events:

● July 10, 2001—Phoenix, Arizona, FBI agent reported to FBI
Washington Headquarters of suspicious flight students;
● July 31, 2001—FAA issued a general security alert against
hijackers;
● August 15, 2001—al Qaeda member Zacarias Moussaoui was
arrested in Minnesota;
● August 23, 2001—CIA reported to FBI that two al Qaeda
terrorists were in the United States, but a search for them was
fruitless;
● September 11, 2001—the nineteen al Qaeda terrorists struck
America.

The Post-9/11 Period: Selected Substantive Measures
    In the few years since the September 11 attacks, the country has
seen the most intensive counterterrorism efforts in its history. This development was, indeed, inevitable because the human, political, social,

economic, and strategic costs of the catastrophic attacks were unprecedented.

More specifically, U.S. government officials have estimated that more than three thousand people died or were missing and presumed dead, and thousands of others were injured. The 110-floor World Trade Center twin buildings, the symbol of American financial prowess, collapsed. All seven buildings in the World Trade Center complex fell or partially collapsed. Sixteen neighboring buildings sustained damage.

New York City closed all bridges and tunnels in the area. The Federal Aviation Administration (FAA) grounded domestic flights, and international flights to the United States were diverted to Canada. Evacuation was ordered from part of lower Manhattan. In Washington, D.C., where substantial damage was inflicted on the Pentagon, the government decided to evacuate the White House, Justice Department, State Department, Treasury Department, Congress, and the Supreme Court. Thousands of private and public offices in the area closed early on the day of the attacks.

In light of these developments, the Securities and Exchange Commission ordered the closure of U.S. stock markets. The principal U.S. stock markets reopened on September 17, 2001.

In the nation's capital a state of emergency was declared. President George W. Bush immediately placed the U.S. military on "high alert status" worldwide. He pledged to "do whatever is necessary to protect America and Americans," and promised to make no distinction between terrorists who committed the September 11 "acts of mass murder" and those nations that harbor them. President Bush also asserted that although the terrorists intended to frighten America into chaos and retreat, they failed because of the "nation's strength." Congress condemned the horrific attacks, vowed retribution against the terrorists and their supporters, and pledged its full support to the Bush Administration during this time of crisis.

Since al Qaeda was responsible for 9/11, President Bush, speaking before Congress on September 20, 2001, declared a war against bin Laden's network and terrorism worldwide. He mobilized an international coalition of like-minded countries to fight this war, and subsequently, on October 6, 2001, the United States initiated massive military operations against al Qaeda bases in Afghanistan and against the Taliban regime that provided sanctuary to bin Laden and his infrastructure in the country. This military effort, Operation Enduring Freedom, destroyed the terrorist infrastructure in the country and ultimately resulted in the overthrow of the Taliban and the establishment of a freely elected government.

In addition, the United States undertook numerous multidimensional—traditional and "out-of-the-box"—steps that were urgently required to cope with the immediate aftermath of 9/11 and critical in the campaign against future terrorism at home and abroad. These responses included various legislative, financial, law enforcement, intelligence, diplomatic, military, and public affairs measures.

A brief discussion of selected steps during the period following 9/11 suffices to illustrate the nature and scope of the U.S. counterterrorism strategy.[59]

Emergency Funding and Other Financial Support

Within days of 9/11, the administration and Congress provided a $40 billion emergency funding measure to respond to the enormous damage caused by the attacks and to support other various national security needs.

Aviation Security

Since September 11, the U.S. government has been steadily increasing the number of Federal Air Marshals by using law enforcement officers loaned from various federal agencies. During the fall of 2001, National Guard units in fifty states were called up, at federal government expense, to provide additional security at airports. Also, effective October 1, 2001, a $500 million fund was established to finance aircraft modifications to delay or deny access to the cockpit.

Public Health

In response to the various incidents of biological terrorism in the fall of 2001 involving anthrax-tainted letters, killing five people, the administration requested $1.5 billion for readiness measures and stockpiling emergency medicines.

Immigration Policies

On October 29, 2001, President Bush issued a presidential directive aimed to improve immigration policies and practices to make it more difficult for terrorists to enter or remain in the United States. This Directive created a Foreign Terrorism Tracking Task Force, which denies entry into the United States of aliens associated with, suspected of being engaged in, or supporting terrorist activity. It also provides for the location, detention, prosecution, or deportation of any such aliens already present in the United States. The Task Force consists of representatives from the State Department, FBI, Immigration and Naturalization Service (INS), Secret Service, Customs Service, and the intelligence community.

Designation of Foreign Terrorist Organizations

On October 5, 2001, Secretary of State Colin Powell redesignated, as required under U.S. law every two years, twenty-five groups as Foreign Terrorist Organizations (FTOs). This characterization enables the U.S. government to continue to take measures against these organizations in accordance with the provisions of the Anti-terrorism and Effective Death Penalty Act (AEACT). More specifically, the AEACT makes it illegal for persons in the United States or subject to U.S. jurisdiction to provide material support to these terrorist groups. The law requires U.S. financial institutions to block assets held by them and allows U.S. immigration officials to deny visas to representatives of these groups. The designation of FTO deters donations or contributions to the named organizations as well as heightens public awareness and knowledge of terrorist organizations.

On the day of the World Trade Center and Pentagon incidents, the FBI established a web site, www.ifccfbi.gov/complaint/terrorist.asp, that allowed individuals to report information about the attacks. Since then, the FBI's participation in the investigation of the September 11, 2001, attacks has been significant, involving seven thousand workers—one in four of the FBI's personnel. Between the day of the attack through October 24, 2001, the FBI gathered more than 3,700 separate pieces of evidence. Also, through the medium of the FBI's web site and 1-800-CRIME-TV, the American public contributed more than 170,000 potential leads and tips that FBI agents and support personnel are pursuing. This figure is 40 percent of the 420,000 total leads that have been generated in FBI investigations from the fateful day in September through November 2, 2001.

The FBI also established a terrorist prevention task force, which is composed of representatives from different agencies. In addition, the FBI's long-standing thirty-five task forces on terrorism gather intelligence and pursue leads to identify and apprehend terrorists and their co-conspirators.

The FBI issued its first national terrorism alert on October 11, 2001, stating, "Certain information, while not specific as to target, gives the government reason to believe that there may be additional terrorist attacks within the United States and against U.S. interests overseas over the next several days. The FBI has again alerted all local law enforcement to be on the highest alert and we call on all people to immediately notify the FBI and local law enforcement of any unusual or suspicious activity."

Financial Measures

The Bush administration has taken a variety of steps to reduce the capabilities of U.S. and foreign terrorist organizations, terrorists, and their sympathizers to raise funds for terrorist activities. For example, President Bush issued an Executive Order on Terrorist Financing (EOTF), effective September 24, 2001, that blocks property and prohibits transactions with persons who commit, threaten to commit, or support terrorism. President Bush stated, "Because of the pervasiveness and expansiveness of the financial foundation of foreign terrorists, financial sanctions may be appropriate for those foreign persons that support or otherwise associate with these foreign terrorists."

The Treasury Department has approached U.S. financial institutions to provide information that will assist in identifying patterns of terrorist financing. On October 11, 2001, the Treasury Department's Financial Crimes Enforcement Network established a Financial Institutions Hotline (Hotline) for financial institutions to voluntarily report to law enforcement agencies suspicious transactions that may relate to recent terrorist activity against the United States. The purpose of the Hotline, operational seven days a week, twenty-four hours a day, will be to facilitate the immediate transmittal of this information to law enforcement.

As a result of intensive diplomatic efforts, more than 140 countries have cooperated with the United States in tracking and blocking terrorists' access to funds. Moreover, with U.S. support, some twenty leading industrial nations have adopted a comprehensive action plan to deny terrorists access to, or use of, financial systems.

Detention, Treatment, and Trials of Noncitizens

On November 13, 2001, President Bush stated that "an extraordinary emergency exists for national defense purposes," which caused him to issue a military order which related to the detention, treatment, and trial of noncitizens suspected of being members of al Qaeda, "engaged in, aided or abetted, or conspired to commit, acts of international terrorism," or of harboring them. More specifically, the order allows for the secretary of defense to detain, either in the United States or abroad, such individuals and initiate charges against them in a military tribunal. The military tribunals are mandated to reach decisions following a two-thirds majority vote of the military commission members. The decisions cannot be appealed, although they are reviewable by the secretary of defense or president at the latter's designation.

According to White House Counsel Alberto Gonzales, the military tribunals would provide another avenue, disparate from civilian courts, by which to prosecute alleged terrorists. Critics of the presidential order proffer that the tribunals should include more procedural and substantive safeguards to suspects. It has been suggested that the U.S. action could prompt some foreign countries to charge U.S. citizens abroad with various crimes and prosecute them in their own military tribunals.

While the foregoing measures represent some of the proliferation of U.S. activities since September 11, 2001, there emerged five major pillars that deserve special consideration, namely, the enactment of the Patriot Act, the establishment of the Department of Homeland Security, the war in Iraq, the Report of the 9/11 Commission, and the restructuring of the intelligence community.

The following summary focuses on these key elements essential in understanding the current American strategy in combating terrorism:

The Post-9/11 Period: Critical Policies and Actions

USA Patriot Act

On October 26, 2001, President Bush signed into law the USA Patriot Act.[60] At that time, he underscored the importance of the legislation in that it "will give intelligence and law enforcement officials important new tools to fight a present danger." He remarked at the time, "Countering and investigating terrorist activity is the number one priority for both law enforcement and intelligence agencies."

The USA Patriot Act enables the U.S. government to be better equipped to identify, investigate, follow, detain, prosecute, and punish suspected terrorists. As today's terrorist increasingly uses sophisticated tools—advanced technology and international money transfers—the government's capabilities must be formidable as well. In essence, the USA Patriot Act aimed to significantly improve the surveillance of terrorists and increase the rapidity of tracking down and intercepting terrorists.

The main elements of the USA Patriot Act are:

- to allow for federal warrants to be effective nationwide and to no longer be limited to specific districts;
- to enable law enforcement to obtain subpoena power for alleged terrorists' communications, including fixed and wireless telephones, e-mail, web surfing, as well as unopened voice mail and e-mail;
- to attach roving wiretaps to alleged terrorists and thereby eliminate the need for the government to request wiretaps for specific telephone numbers as previously required;
- to improve coordination and cooperation, such as information-gathering between U.S. intelligence and law enforcement investigators, with respect to terrorist investigations;
- to allow law enforcement to use new subpoena power to obtain payment information, such as credit card or bank account numbers, of suspected terrorists who are utilizing the Internet;
- to create rules to counter terrorists' access to, and use of, illicit funds as well as to prevent or impede other improper terrorist activities;
- to punish those who aid or harbor terrorists.

The broad surveillance powers available in the USA Patriot Act were capped in the sense that a four-year expiration (or sunset clause) was included in order to allay fears of overextending such expansive police rights if the threat of terrorism wanes in future years.

Almost from its inception, the Patriot Act has been criticized within and outside government. Among the major criticisms of the Act and its implementation was that the legislation allows the government to spy on First Amendment–protected activities; that it diminishes personal privacy by removing checks on government power; and that it increases government secrecy while limiting public accountability.

Department of Homeland Security

President Bush appointed Tom Ridge, former governor of Pennsylvania, as the Assistant to the President for Homeland Security[61] on October 8, 2001. The Office of Homeland Security's mission was to develop and coordinate the implementation of a comprehensive national strategy to secure the United States from terrorist threats or attacks. The office objective was to coordinate the executive branch's efforts to detect, prepare for, prevent, protect against, respond to, and recover from terrorist attacks within the United States. On a daily basis since commencing his position, Governor Ridge served as President Bush's point man on domestic terrorism, although, on occasion, he was joined by other senior Bush administration representatives.

On October 29, 2001, President Bush issued his first two homeland security presidential directives: Organization and Operation of the Homeland Security Council (HSC) and Combating Terrorism Through Immigration Policies. The first directive emphasized that securing the American public from terrorist threats or attacks has become a critical national security function. As such, it requires extensive coordination across a broad spectrum of federal, state, and local agencies to reduce the potential for terrorist attacks and to mitigate damage should such attacks arise. The HSC's role will be to ensure coordination of all homeland and security-related activities among executive departments and agencies while promoting the effective development and implementation of all homeland security policies.

Indeed, the creation of the new Department of Homeland Security on July 16, 2003, involved extraordinary governmental reorganization on a scale similar to that initiated in 1949 with the establishment of the Department of Defense, and illustrates the nature of the various fresh efforts undertaken in the post-9/11 period. This integrated new department of approximately 180,000 employees in twenty-two agencies consists of four core divisions: Border and Transportation Security; Emergency Preparedness and Response; Chemical, Biological, Radiological, and Nuclear Countermeasures; and the Information Analysis and Infra-

structure Protection. It provides for effective intergovernmental cooperation on national, state, and local levels and consequently assures that
homeland security is a shared responsibility.

War in Iraq

Iraq, regarded as a state sponsor of terrorism for several decades,
became a special focal point of U.S. concern after 9/11 when the administration assessed that Saddam Hussein's regime was developing
links with al Qaeda terrorist cells and continuing with its efforts to
develop weapons of mass destruction. Although the fragmented American intelligence community could not confirm this assessment, the
United States and the United Kingdom, with a coalition of other nations, decided after months of negotiations and debates at the United
Nations to undertake military action against Iraq for the purpose of
destroying the terrorist and WMD infrastructure in the country and
removing the Saddam regime.

The war against Iraq began in March 2003. In the following month,
U.S.-led forces controlled the country. Since the defeat of Saddam and
his subsequent capture, Iraq's designation as a state sponsor of terrorism
was formally rescinded in 2004, and the country began to navigate the
difficult road of political, social, and economic reconstruction under the
guidance of American and coalition partners.

And yet, the postwar security situation in the country deteriorated
for two years, characterized by both an insurgency and classical terrorist acts undertaken by a wide range of actors, including former regime
officials, local Islamists, foreign jihadists, tribal groups, and ordinary
criminals. Despite the ongoing democratization process, as reflected by
the latest December 15, 2005, legislative elections, terrorism is escalating in Iraq with a potential danger of spreading elsewhere in the Middle
East and beyond. The notorious terrorist Abu Musab al-Zarqawi, who
pledged the fealty of himself and his group, al Qaeda in Iraq, to bin
Laden, is currently regarded as the greatest challenge in the war against
the global jihadist network.

The National Commission on Terrorist Attacks Upon the United States (the 9/11 Commission)

In the aftermath of 9/11, two lingering questions have been raised
by a shocked nation: (1) How did the tragedy happen? (2) How can the
United States avoid similar attacks in the future? To answer these and
many other related questions, President Bush and the Congress created the
National Commission on Terrorist Attacks upon the United States,[62] better
known as the 9/11 Commission (Public Law 107-306, November 27, 2002).

After examining the facts and circumstances surrounding the September 11 attacks, the Commission released the findings and conclusions on

July 22, 2004. Among the lessons that the Commission reported were the following:

> We learned that the institutions charged with protecting our borders, civil aviation, and national security did not understand how grave this threat could be, and did not adjust their policies, plans, and practices to deter or defeat it. We learned of fault lines within our government—between foreign and domestic intelligence and between and within agencies. We learned of the pervasive problems of managing and sharing information across a large and unwieldy government that had been built in a different era to confront different dangers.[63]

In its effort to make the United States "safer, stronger, and wiser," the Commission concluded:

> We need to design a balanced strategy for the long haul, to attack terrorists and prevent their ranks from swelling while at the same time protecting our country against future attacks. We have been forced to think about the way our government is organized. The massive departments and agencies that prevailed in the great struggles of the twentieth century must work together in new ways, so that all the instruments of national power can be combined. Congress needs dramatic change as well to strengthen oversight and focus accountability.[64]

With a view of improving U.S. security concerns, the Commission offered forty-one recommendations that flowed from its investigation of the September 11, 2001, attacks. Its recommendations covered a broad range of topics, including strategic policies, communications, physical security, intelligence, organizational structure, weapons of mass destruction, education, and public affairs.

To assess the status of the implementation of the recommendations, the Commission organized an informal 9/11 Public Discourse Project that issued several reports on the basis of convening a series of public panels in 2005. In its first report of September 14, 2005, for example, the Panel reported that mostly minimal progress has been made on emergency preparedness and response, transportation security, and border security. The Commission issued its final document on December 5, 2005, in which it gave a report card, asserting that some positive changes have taken place related to homeland security and emergency response, intelligence and congressional reform, and foreign policy and nonproliferation. However, the Commission pointed out too many "shocking" failures, such as the allocation of "scarce homeland security dollars on the basis of pork barrel spending, not risk." The Commission finally warned that "while the terrorists are learning and adapting, our government is still moving at a crawl."[65]

The Role of Intelligence

Although the issue of quality intelligence[66] in combating terrorism was continuously discussed by policymakers, Congress, and the public at large before 9/11, it was the September 11 attacks and the war in Iraq that moved the topic to the frontline of American security concerns. It is not surprising, therefore, that a joint inquiry by the House Permanent Select Committee on Intelligence dealt with the challenge more seriously than ever before. This body issued numerous findings, including the need to improve information-sharing within U.S. government agencies; to increase the domestic intelligence collection and analysis capability of the FBI; to implement a central counterterrorism database; to develop unilateral human intelligence resources to avoid extensive reliance on foreign intelligence services; and to create an analytical all-source center for terrorism activities that brings together intelligence from all sources in the community to produce strategic and tactical analysis.

But it was the implementation of the 9/11 recommendations on intelligence as illustrated by the Intelligence Reform and Terrorism Prevention Act that was the most extensive reform of the Intelligence Community since 1947. The Act brought together some fifteen intelligence agencies under the Director of National Intelligence. Another significant structural change is the establishment of the National Counterterrorism Center. This development already received a grade of "B" in the 9/11 Commission report card. It is premature, however, to conclude that these dramatic changes in the intelligence organization will advance the goals of the National Security Strategy of the United States, inter alia, "to defend the peace by fighting terrorists and tyrants."[67]

PART III
Summary and Conclusions

Any examination of the evolution of U.S. counterterrorism strategy throughout its almost 230-year history reveals the complexity of the debate over the definition of the term "terrorism," its root causes, and what can and should be done to reduce the risks at home and abroad. More specifically, despite its long record as a symbol, tool, method, or process of force—used intentionally by individuals, groups, and adversarial states to create a climate of extreme fear in order to obtain real or imaginary goals—this specific form of violence still evades a consensus on its meaning, implications, and "best practices" responses. As we have seen, the United States' administrations and

Congress have, for decades, spoken with many voices on these matters.

Indeed, it was not until 9/11 that the United States began shaking free from its conceptual uncertainties and moved forward to the realization that terrorism in all its manifestations will be considered war and will be fought until total victory is achieved. As one editorial observed, "For this war, the goal should be ending the use of terror against America. Winning the war . . . will require patience, perseverance, planning . . . and a steely resolve."[68]

There are no assurances, however, that this perception and approach will be universally accepted. For instance, the elected president of Bolivia, Evo Morales, recently asserted that President George W. Bush was a "terrorist" and that the American military operation in Iraq was "state terrorism."

Regardless of these and similar perceptional differences with other nations, the reality is that the strategic functions of a U.S. counterterrorism policy are currently focusing on "homeland security" or "homeland defense," consisting of a broad range of components, including an integration of missions, such as deterrence, prevention, preemption, crisis management, consequence management, and retaliation. Public debate over the utility of these and other strategies will continue into the foreseeable future.

The work of the 9/11 Commission, as well as the numerous post-9/11 congressional legislation, such as the Patriot Act, the Aviation and Transport Security Act, the National Defense Authorization Act, the Homeland Security Act, the Intelligence Authorization Act, and the Intelligence Reform and Terrorism Prevention Act, will ultimately serve as political and legal guides for any further steps to be undertaken in the future.

Debate in the policymaking community and the general public will continue due to a variety of issues currently on the national agenda four years after 9/11. These topics bear directly on making Americans safe at home and abroad and so revolve around the situation in Iraq and Afghanistan as well as the issue of balancing defense concerns with civil liberties. That is, there are rising doubts regarding the cost-benefits of the "war on terrorism" in Iraq and on the political and strategic stabilization of Afghanistan. Moreover, the government involvement in warrantless domestic eavesdropping and surveillance of American citizens by the FBI and the intelligence community; the status of suspect aliens and citizens of terrorist acts; and the use of torture of alleged terrorists in detention facilities in the United States and secret sites overseas provide a glimpse of the important policies and action placed on the U.S. counterterrorism agenda.

One issue that deserves special attention relates to the Patriot Act. It may be recalled that under section 224, several of the surveillance portions (200-level sections) of the Act were originally to expire on December 31, 2005. The date was later extended to February 3, 2006. This extension was later extended to March 10, 2006. Again, it was renewed on March 2, 2006 with a vote of 89–11 in the Senate and on March 7 with a vote of 280–138 in the House. The legislation to extend the statute will make all but two of its provisions permanent. The provisions in question are the authority to conduct "roving" surveillance under the Foreign Intelligence Surveillance Act (FISA) and the authority to request production of business records under FISA (Patriot Act sections 206 and 215, respectively). These provisions will expire in four years.

President Bush signed the reauthorization of the Act on March 9, 2006. After the public ceremony, he issued a "signing statement" to the effect that he would not feel bound to comply with some of the provisions of the law. His statement was criticized for an apparent intention to withhold information that the Act required him to provide to Congress.[69]

Thus, the meaning and interpretation of this critical legislation will have important implications, not only regarding executive-congressional relations, but also concerning civil liberties issues.

Yet, regardless of the multitude of reservations and doubts expressed already, one cardinal principle will continue to serve as a bipartisan basis in the expansion of the U.S. National Strategy for Combating Terrorism, which calls for:

- defeating terrorist organizations by eliminating their sanctuaries, leadership, finances, and command, control and communications capabilities;
- denying further sponsorship, support, and sanctuary to terrorists by cooperating with other states to take action against those who provide support;
- diminishing the underlying conditions that terrorists seek to exploit by enlisting the international community to focus our mutual efforts and resources on addressing legitimate political and social needs and by reducing security vulnerabilities in the countries most at risk; and
- defending the United States, its citizens, and interests at home and abroad.[70]

In summary, a coherent and firm U.S. strategy in responding to terrorist threats, both conventional and unconventional, will ultimately win public understanding and support at home and abroad. It is crucially important to move even more vigorously than ever before in this direction in order to gradually bring to manageable levels the emerging strategic threats not only to the United States but also to the very survival of civilization itself.

2

FRANCE

Guillaume Parmentier*

Terrorism is not a new feature in French society: in the late nineteenth and early twentieth centuries, its most spectacular outrages included Serbian terrorists killing a French president, the assassination of a Russian Czar during a visit to Paris, and the throwing of a bomb in the National Assembly's chamber by a French anarchist. The features of the more recent upsurge of terrorism in France were assembled then, with a combination of importation on French soil of foreign conflicts and a domestically grown ideological terrorism, the latter being less resilient than the former.[1]

During both periods, the French state had to contend with the contrasting requirements of democratic justice and efficiency, and this conflict led to a process of trial and error, with a significant measure of success being achieved in the end. In this process, and as is inevitable in a democracy, political differences emerged, reflected in successive and sometimes contradictory government attitudes. Even though France's experience is hardly unique in this respect, its long contention with modern terrorism since the mid-seventies can give an indication of some of the problems that other countries confronted with the same scourge will encounter, and the story of the successes and failures of French policy might be of interest to its partners in this difficult and inevitably lengthy process. The so-called riots that affected parts of France in November 2005 (and which in fact for the main part were car arsons) cannot be identified with terrorism. This is why they will not be mentioned in this chapter. They fit in the category of "civil unrest," not terrorism properly understood.

After describing the magnitude and variety of the threats encountered by French society and French leaders for the past thirty years, this chapter outlines the main features of French counterterrorism policies. Cooperation between the French and American authorities on fighting terrorism has been exemplary, as has been described in a number of recent articles.[2] A discrete international counterterrorism intelligence center codenamed "Alliance Base" was set up in Paris by the CIA and French intelligence in 2002 and has remained functioning even at the height of the French-American crisis over Iraq in 2003.

Terrorism in France:
Its Main Features and Its Evolution Since the 1970s

The Most Significant Terrorist Attacks in France Since the 1970s

The Rise of Terrorism in the 1970s

In the 1950s and 1960s, mainland France experienced a wave of terrorism that was closely linked to the war in Algeria. The Algerian independence movement made wide use of terrorism against Frenchmen and Algerians alike from 1954 to 1962. L'Organisation armée secrète (OAS), a French anti-independence group with strong links to the French population in Algeria and some elements in the French armed forces, carried out its most famous operation at Petit Clamart near Paris on July 22, 1962, when it came close to killing General Charles de Gaulle.[3] A lull of nearly a decade and a half followed. From 1974–1975 onward terrorism committed by separatist movements, international networks, and ideological groups emerged in France. In 1976, a total of 480 attacks were carried out while in 1979, more than 605 attacks were blamed on foreign organizations (e.g., Fils du sud Liban, PLO), extremists, left and right wing (e.g., Honneur de la police), and separatist movements.[4] Separatist groups began to make their mark in 1969. The first to appear was the Liberation Front of Brittany (FLB), which deprived Brittany and Normandy of television in 1974 and 1976 by blowing up several television transmitters, and partially destroyed the Hall of Mirrors at the Château de Versailles in 1978. The FLB limited itself, however, to material damage of symbols of the so-called French colonial state. Taken into custody at the beginning of the 1980s, the members of this group ceased all activity at this time.[5] In 1973, the Marxist-Leninist Basque group of Iparretarak commenced operations.[6] Less violent than the Euzkadi Ta Azkatasuna (ETA), the Basque Freedom Party and main Basque terrorist grouping, its target was state property alone. Finally, the Corsicans in the form of the National Liberation Front of Corsica (FLNC) emerged in 1976, carrying out bombings of public and private sites, arson, and political assassinations. Attacks in 1974[7] and 1975[8] blamed on the famous international terrorist Carlos, who was linked to the Palestinian cause, marked the arrival of international terrorism on French soil. The worst of this form of terrorism would not come until the following decade, still the bloodiest and most destructive one in the history of France's experience of terrorism.

Bloodshed in the 1980s

This decade opened with the attack of Rue Copernic in Paris, which killed four and wounded twenty-two and was blamed on Abou Nidal, the head of a splinter group of Palestinian terrorists. The violence continued to get worse the following year, with four bombings for which no responsibility was claimed, a hostage taking, a double assassination, and four explosions in Paris in December that were attributed to *Action Directe*. This Marxist-Leninist group with anarchist leanings, directed by Jean-Marc Rouillan and Nathalie Mérignon, had made itself known two years previously for having gunned down the minister of cooperation in Paris. Captured, then amnestied by President Mitterrand, these leaders were responsible for radicalizing the movement and defining as its targets the military, industrial, and political apparatus of the West. In 1982, *Action Directe* shot up a bank, shot at the car of an Israeli diplomat, bombed a shop, and bombed the headquarters of the extreme right-wing newspaper, *Minute*. This year would be remembered for being particularly violent, with attacks blamed on Carlos on the Paris–Toulouse train (five dead, twenty-seven wounded) and in Rue Marbeuf in Paris (one dead, sixty-three wounded). Abou Nidal's shootings in the Jewish neighborhood of the Rue des Rosiers also in Paris (six dead, twenty-two wounded), and the assassination of an Israeli diplomat were linked to the Palestinian question. There were also anti-American attacks on the occasion of Ronald Reagan's visit in June, and two bombings in Paris in July linked to the Orly Group, the other name of ASALA (Secret Armenian Army for the Liberation of Armenia), not to mention the more than eight hundred attacks committed in Corsica that the newspaper *Le Monde* tallied. Total for the year: thirteen dead, 185 wounded.

The three years that followed were punctuated by attacks committed by ASALA (Orly Airport: eight dead, sixty wounded), *Action Directe*, which had moved into "Euroterrorism" with the German Red Army Faction (twenty-three explosions and one assassination),[9] the attack at the main Marseilles railroad station on December 31, 1983, blamed on Carlos (five dead, fifty wounded), an Islamic jihad attack on the British department store, Marks & Spencers, in Paris, on February 23, 1985,[10] and, finally, a number of attacks on Paris restaurants and the Paris Bourse for which no responsibility was ever claimed.

An unprecedented terrorist campaign, in terms of its violence, intensity, and form, kicked off in December 1985 with explosions in two Paris department stores. In close succession came the assassination of Georges Besse, chief executive of Renault and the attack on Interpol, both committed by *Action Directe*, and the kidnapping of twelve French nationals in Lebanon between May 1985 and January 1987. Three waves of terror, in February, March, and September of 1986, saw more than twenty attacks that targeted large Paris bookstores, shopping centers, public buildings, high-speed trains, subway stations, and the Rue de Rennes in Paris, causing 230 wounded and thirteen deaths. Those responsible for the attacks, the Council for Solidarity of Arab and Near Eastern Political Prisoners (CSPPA), demanded the liberation of three terrorists imprisoned in France: Anis Naccache, Waroud Garbidjian, and Georges Ibrahim Abdallah. After following up leads that implied a Syrian connection, the antiterrorist investigators turned to Iran, the real coordinator of the attacks, following the arrest and turning of a Tunisian, Lofti Ben Khala, by the DST (*Direction de la Surveillance de la Territoire*). Infiltrated, the Fouad Ali Saleh network, which gave logistical support to Hizbollah in France, was dismantled in 1987–1988.

After 1986, terrorists no longer targeted French territory directly for almost a decade, though internal terrorism linked to the Corsican independence movement was recurrent. Following the arrest of its leader, the Iparretarrak movement ceased its activities in the Basque country. Still, France remained a target, as demonstrated by the attack perpetrated by Libya on the DC-10 of French carrier UTA traveling between Brazzaville and Paris on September 19, 1989, causing the deaths of 170 people, of whom fifty-two were French.

The Rise of Radical Islamist Terrorism in the 1990s

In 1994, during which twelve French nationals living in Algeria were killed by the Algerian Muslim fundamentalist terrorist group Groupe Islamique Armé (GIA), the security services alerted the government to the growing unrest of extremist Islamists, not only in Algeria but also in a number of European countries, and to the growing threat weighing over France. On December 24, the GIA took over an Air France Airbus at Algiers airport, demanding the liberation of two Islamic Salvation Front (FIS) leaders imprisoned in Algeria. At the request of the French authorities, the plane was directed to Marseilles, where the special intervention group of the French gendarmerie (GIGN) intervened. In the end the terrorists killed three hostages in Algiers before they were themselves killed during the assault of the plane, with four gendarmes injured. The inquiry would reveal that the terrorists had intended either to crash the plane on Paris or explode it over the French capital and destroy the Eiffel Tower. In the meantime, from November onward, the Chalabi network, the largest support post for Algerian fundamentalists, was dismantled in France and Europe.

The threat of a jihad against France materialized on July 25, 1995, with the explosion of a gas cylinder at the St. Michel subway station in Paris, followed by seven other attacks or attempted attacks[11] which caused the deaths of twelve people and wounded 173. The main operative in these summer attacks, a young Algerian living in France, Khaled Kelkal, was killed in a gunfight during his attempted arrest the following September.

The man responsible for coordinating the attacks, Boualem Bensaïd, was arrested in November. The presumed financier and the person who gave the go-ahead for the attacks, Rachid Ramda, an Algerian living in London, was imprisoned only after September 11, 2001, but has still not been extradited. The attack of December 3, 1996 at the subway station, Port Royal, killing seven and wounding eighty-two, brought the terror campaign of the GIA to a close. France has not suffered another Islamist attack since, even if many threats have been made, especially during the 1998 soccer World Cup matches. In 2000, a network of GIA commandos was dismantled as it prepared to undertake an attack in Strasbourg intended for either the Christmas outdoor market or the Cathedral.

Terrorism linked to independence movements has reemerged in Brittany and the violence has intensified in Corsica. On February 6, 1998, a small Corsican independence group known for its ultra-violent ways, Sampieru, assassinated the Prefect of Corsica, Claude Erignac. Explosions and attacks have come in succession since, though most of these have been directed at other Corsican groups for the purpose of settling scores rather than at the French state. In Brittany, around fifteen attacks on public buildings occurred in 1998, for which responsibility was claimed by the ARB, the Breton Revolutionary Army, the armed wing of the Breton Liberation Front of the 1970s. On September 28, 1999, logistical support was provided by Breton militant nationalists to the ETA for their theft of eight tons of explosives from the Côtes d'Armor factory in Plevin. After the death of an employee of a McDonald's restaurant in Quevert in a bomb attack in 2000, members of the Breton group Emgan, suspected of being members of the ARB, were arrested and charged with conspiracy.

Thus France has suffered not one but several types of terrorism, in which the players, demands, means, and modus operandi were different. From the 1970s through to the middle of the 1980s, the tradition of France as a haven for refugees and its policy of openness confronted it with exported terrorism, where foreign interests in France (such as ASALA against Turkish interests) and opponents of certain regimes became targets. At the same time, separatist movements began to target French interests and have continued to do so to this day, as has a terrorism with a revolutionary and anarchic tendency that *Action Directe* exemplified in the 1980s and an international terrorism that has emanated from the Middle East. These Middle Eastern groups have linked their activities to the Palestinian cause, the Lebanese crisis (attacks carried out between 1980 and 1982), the Iranian revolution, the Iran–Iraq War (the 1985–1986 campaign), and Libyan foreign policy (the attack on the UTA DC-10). Terrorism was used as a "pseudo-diplomatic weapon" to put pressure on Paris, whose foreign policy upset many people in France.

In effect, by supporting Lebanese integrity, France ran counter to Syria's interests, the maintenance of troops in Chad stymied Libya's aims in that direction, and military assistance to Iraq in its conflict against Iran could only foster hostility from Tehran. "Carried out by professional transnational groups, Carlos, Abou Nidal, CSPPA, on the payroll of Middle Eastern states,"[12] state-sponsored terrorism began to benefit more and more from European logistical bases in the households of Muslim immigrants, which in the case of France means primarily North Africans.

The wave of attacks in 1995 exemplified a hybrid type of terrorism, between classical international terrorism and twenty-first-century terrorism, which is ever changing. In effect the primary motivation for these attacks was to put pressure on France to stop its financial and political support for the Algerian government. This development was international, but not state-sponsored, terrorism because it was the Algerian GIA that organized it, a group that reflects "nationalistic Islamism" and religious extremism.

Another innovation was the apparent implantation all over France of GIA networks with links to correspondents in a number of foreign countries. Nonprofessionals, furthermore, train the fighters, some of whom are recruited directly from radical areas in French suburbs to combat for what they think is Islam. This recruitment, organizational, and ideological motivational framework correspond to a new form of terrorism that is inspired by a fundamentalist view of Islam, and which today seriously threatens France.

New Forms of Terrorism

Organized Terrorism: A New Configuration of the Threat

Since the fall of the Berlin Wall, terrorism has undergone significant mutations. Terrorism during the Cold War was essentially "controlled," an instrument of indirect foreign policy, or of demands for recognition of identity, or to alter policy. Terrorism today has become popularized, democratized, structureless, and linked to organized crime. Its methods and organization are unprecedented, changing, fluid, and disconnected from states.

Recent terrorism in France fits in perfectly with this new configuration. New participants have emerged, such as employee organizations, sects, and ecologists, for whom terrorism is the only way to make their messages heard. This assumption implies spectacular action, in either their extreme violence or other means employed. In 2000, for example, employees of the Cellatex factory in the Ardennes, which was due to close, poured 1,500 gallons of sulfuric acid into a tributary of the Meuse, and threatened to use 56,000 tons of chemical products in their possession unless a plan to restructure the factory was presented. Similar tactics were used the next year when employees of a brewery and a Moulinex factory threatened to blow up the machines and buildings unless their union demands were met. This act was evidence of a difficult economic situation in which "socialist" terrorism demonstrates the profound changes that terrorism in general has undergone, and where amateurs, with many different motivations, use a form of terrorism to publicize their economic, social, and cultural ill-being. Recent Breton terrorism is another illustration of this mutation. Whereas in the 1970s, this activism was the preserve of young intellectuals who demanded recognition of their identity, today, the ARB and its presumed political wing, the extreme left-wing group, Emgann, recruit young, unemployed, and low-paid workers (on the minimum wage or on short-term contracts), for whom demanding recognition of the rights of the Breton people is a way of underscoring their own precariousness. This dubious recruitment explains to an extent the amateurism of the operations since 1996: more than half of the explosives planted failed to detonate. In 1999, Irene Stoller, a judge in charge of antiterrorist enquiries at the Paris courts, stressed that "although this terrorism has not resorted to the same degree of violence as the IRA [Irish Republican Army], ETA, or Islamist terrorism is capable of, it is still in our interests to beware"[13] because of the stated will of these groups to use increasing violence to be heard,[14] or even to, as shown on April 19, 2000, cause death and thus lose the local support that they depended on.

It is possible to identify today an evolution, a complete change of direction even, of separatist movements in the Basque country and, especially, in Corsica. Basque terrorism, which still takes its inspiration from Marxist-Leninist thought, remains very limited in France, essentially being involved in the destruction of property. The ETA considers that France is a sanctuary worth preserving. France is used as a base, a base for explosives, bought or stolen, a refuge for militants and for arms dumps. For five years now, the political implantation of ETA in France has become a reality as the official location of Spanish independence syndicates and their political wing, the Eskual Batasuna party.

Another change is on its way, which could presage the coming of the armed struggle in France: the growth of operations against private property, blamed on young Spanish militants, who are second-generation "combatants." Basque terrorism, however, remains limited in France, with around twenty attacks a year being the norm. And if, in the Spanish Basque country, there is the so-called revolutionary tax, such practice has not yet come to France. In Corsica, on the other hand, this "tax," which is levied under duress on all economic activity on the island in exchange for "protection," has gone hand-in-hand with break-ins and attacks on cash transports. But this racketeering situation, transformed into pillage, has brought the independence movements into a degenerative impasse, with numerous factional splits, and this has led to a continual raising of the violence stakes to increase profits. According to Marianne Lefevre, the fifteen-odd revenge operations of 1995–1996 are the consequence of "rivalries pertaining to the control of lucrative activities,"[15] such as racketeering, gaming, arms, and drugs smuggling.

The result in Corsica is the criminal degeneration of separatist terrorism. Money from racketeering, kidnapping, and smuggling is laundered in the financial circles with Mafia-type operations. This collusion between the terrorist and criminal worlds is more and more pronounced, either because the quest for profit has replaced that of political aims, or because it provides greater means and represents a significant financial attraction for recruitment, which the players who have broken with society see as a sign of power.

Radical Islamist terrorism, which today represents the greatest threat for France, brings together all the characteristics of this "new terrorism." Taking in "amateurs" who are undergoing identity crises, its secret networks, which form a flexible structure to anticipate international action, combine Islamic militancy with all manner of trafficking. For some fifteen years now, France has experienced the rise of Muslim fundamentalism on its territory. It is now a recruitment center and target for these "new religious terrorists."

Radical Islam and Terrorism

Because of its historical links with and former colonial role in the Maghreb, and, in particular, with Algeria, France has seen large numbers of immigrants arrive from northern Africa since the 1960s. Often among the least well-off social classes and living on the outskirts of large towns, some of these Muslim immigrants, now the second generation, are confronted with an identity crisis, whereby they are comfortable neither with their home country, France, nor with their parents' country. A rejection of values and an economic crisis make these youngsters, known as "Beurs"[16] in France, prime targets of fundamentalist recruiters, essentially those of the GIA who have been present in France since the beginning of the 1990s. In effect, the Islamic Salvation Front, which has been banned since 1991 in Algeria, has taken root in France, which is considered by the heads of the movement to be a natural rear base. The fundamentalists move into immigrant suburbs with the help of educational and social associations that chosen militants lead. Proposing classes for Arabs, financial help to families in distress, and school help, these associations, by claiming to fight against delinquency and drug smuggling, impose the Islamic model and values, with an undercurrent of anti-French and anti-Zionist dialogue. They also support jihad. The rapid increase in mosques, 23 in 1974, 550 in 1984, and 1,480 in 2001, often financed by Saudi Arabia, exemplifies the growth of Islamic activity in France. And another new trend since the mid-1990s has been that terrorists direct their recruitment efforts not only at young Algerian, Moroccan, and Tunisian immigrants of French nationality like Kaled Kelkal, head of the Lyons network, which was responsible for the 1995 attacks, but also at native French people. This confuses even more the identification of future militants.

According to France's top terrorist judge, Jean-Louis Bruguiere, Iraq has become a black hole which has provided a training ground to radicalize some young Muslims and has drawn them into violence. They are receiving training in Iraq before returning to Europe to carry out jihad in their home countries.[17] In a recent television interview, the French Interior Minister called the terror risk for Paris "very high," adding, "We know that there are about ten young Frenchmen in Iraq, ready to become suicide terrorists."[18]

Just recently, a terrorist plot was uncovered by the French police: on September 29, 2005, Groupe Salafiste pour la Prédication et le Combat (GSPC) issued a call for action against France, which it described as "enemy no. 1." Nine people detained in a series of raids west of Paris were suspected members of the GSPC. One of them allegedly admitted that the suspected cell was plotting attacks against the Paris metro, an airport, and the headquarters of a police intelligence and a counterterrorism agency.[19]

Often marginalized and engaging in delinquent activities, many young Muslims are converted to radical Islam during a stay in prison, which has become a major proselytizing center, especially for Tabligh, the Salafist movement. Tabligh, a member of the French Council of the Islamist Faith, played, in effect, an ambiguous role, which was revealed during the inquiries into fundamentalist circles between1995 and 2002. Former members of Tabligh include Kaled Kelkal and Zacarias Moussaoui. According to the DST,[20] at least 80 percent of European recruits into the Salafist grouping have gone through the Tabligh,[21] which has become a medium for recruitment into terrorist movements such as al Qaeda or the GIA. Kaled Kelkal followed a by now classic path: an Algerian who arrived in France as a child, he was approached by the Tabligh in prison while he was doing time for a robbery. The GIA then recruited him following his liberation. Many youngsters have followed the same path—first delinquency, then terrorism.

This recruitment embodies a double threat. Not only are the young recruits indoctrinated during stays in Afghanistan or Pakistan, where they are trained in the art of guerrilla warfare and then used as a jihad strike force as happened in Bosnia,[22] but they also do not hesitate to use extremely violent methods, borrowed from serious delinquency. The Roubaix gang, named after a town in Northern France, illustrates the collusion between delinquency and Islamist terrorism. Seven young Muslim extremists, including native Frenchmen who had fought in Bosnia, formed the gang, which specialized in the robbery of cash transport vans and car theft in 1996, financing, thus, the GIA guerrillas and the jihad in Bosnia. Two members of the gang were killed during the Recherche Assistance Intervention Dissuasion (RAID) operation against it; the others were arrested or managed to flee.

In addition to these new "Islamist-delinquents," organized into cells by the fundamentalists, there is another dangerous phenomenon that has been on the scene for five years now: delinquents who call them-selves "sons of Allah" and who identify themselves with suicide terrorists and the Palestinian cause. The murderous cell of Safir Bghioua of Béziers in Southern France in 2001 follows this pattern. Possessing heavy weap-onry that is either sourced from Kosovars or a branch of organized crime, this young man of Arab descent was killed by the special intervention group of the national gendarmerie (GIGN) after having attacked a police station with a rocket-launcher, killing the chief of the Béziers police.

Synergies between the fundamentalist and criminal circles are wide-spread. In dismantling some networks, links to mafia-type criminal orga-nizations were revealed. The Chalabi network, which was undone from 1995 onward, financed its activities, which included shipments of arms to Algeria, forgery of official documents, the hosting and rescue of GIA "combatants," and even arms bunkers on French soil, through drug traf-ficking between France and the Netherlands (where drugs are readily available) and illegal gaming machines. The far reaches of this organiza-tion were uncovered in Belgium, Germany, and eastern Europe, revealing a structure of autonomous, secret cell-groups, hidden behind bogus com-panies. This type of organization, which breaks with the hierarchical structures of 1970s and 1980s terrorist groups, is a perfect example of the organizational charts of the new Islamist terrorism.

Using dubious fund-raising techniques and organized into autono-mous, flexible small groups, hard to notice among the Muslim population, these Islamist networks are becoming more and more transnational and intertwined. The Islamist networks of the GIA are somewhat indistinguish-able from bin Laden's evil empire. Financial links between the two organiza-tions are said to have been uncovered when terrorist Rachid Ramda was arrested in connection with the 1995 attacks. These links underscore the French concerns. These groups no longer have to do anything to convince the authorities of their powers of organization and resolve since September 11. There is the fear of new attacks in France, which is under a GIA fatwa since 1994,[23] and, more insidiously, of a vast internal destabilization op-eration, taking the form of insurrectional terrorism.

Ten percent of the French population belongs to the Muslim faith. There are suburbs of large cities where 50 or even 60 percent of the people living there are Muslims of Maghreban descent (Dreux, Roubaix/Tourcoing/Lille, north Marseille, and the outskirts of Lyons). In these unstable suburbs, where the fundamentalists are gaining in power, "the possibility of an outbreak of violence spreading from suburb to suburb to the whole of the country must be seriously envisaged, especially if cer-tain foreign elements find it in their interests to put pressure on the governmental apparatus or to destabilize the state. In this scenario the police and the gendarmerie could be quickly overwhelmed."[24] Since the summer of 2001, more and more urban violence has been taking on ter-rorist shapes, particularly with the use of heavy weaponry.

To counter these modern terrorists, France has a prevention and repression setup that has been molded in reaction to these waves of attacks, adapting itself reasonably quickly and effectively as new threats were appearing.

French Antiterrorist Policies: Trials, Errors, and Successes

The Operational Antiterrorist Structure in 2002

Specialization, *coordination*, and *centralization* are the three keywords of the antiterrorist setup in France: specialization of the services that form a complex whole; coordination at ministerial and operational levels; and centralization of the police and magistrates.

Administrative Organization: Coordination and Centralization

Presided over by the prime minister, the Council for Home Security drives the political process. The ministers of the interior, defense, foreign affairs, justice, and finance participate in the meetings. The council evaluates threats and then considers the means to deal with them. Resolutions for countering terrorism at the ministerial level are confirmed within the Interministerial Committee for Antiterrorist Liaison (CILAT), the overall coordinating committee. The minister of the interior presides at this committee, which brings in heads of ministries and antiterrorist services in a flexible and reactive setting. This structure has been active since 1982. Finally, the coordination, operation, and orientation of the operative services (information services and police) are carried out within UCLAT, the Group for the Coordination of Antiterrorist Action, which reports to the minister of the interior. A purely administrative body, which the director-general of the national police directs, it centralizes information, rules on the responsibilities of each service, and is responsible for rolling out the Vigipirate contingency plan.

Vigipirate is a uniquely French feature. It mobilizes the police, gendarmerie, and armed forces to ensure the protection of sensitive sites in France. It reinforces border checkpoints, increases the incidence of searching, adds greater numbers of patrols, protects schools, and conducts increased surveillance of airplanes. Introduced in January 1991, it has never been disbanded, though certain measures are periodically reinforced or rolled back depending on the seriousness of the threat.

Operational Structure: Intelligence Services and Police

The principal services that are responsible for antiterrorist measures are, for the most part, answerable to the minister of the interior, within the General Directorate of the National Police (DGPN). The gendarmerie, which assures the policing of nonurban zones of France, used to be under the Defense Ministry.[25] It was formally transferred from the Defense Ministry to the Ministry of the Interior after the presidential election in 2002. However, it is still managed by the defense minister as it is comprised of military personnel.

The intelligence services that are involved in antiterrorist matters are those of the interior ministry: the DST, the Central Directorate for Intelligence (DCRG). Then, but to a lesser extent, there are those that report to the defense minister: namely, the General Directorate for External Security (DGSE), the Directorate for the Protection of Defense Security (DPSD), and the Directorate for Military Intelligence (DRM).

Set up in 1941, the DCRG looks after research into, and the centralization of, interior information matters. It is primarily responsible for dealing with home-grown terrorism, but has some responsibility for countering terrorist threats that are linked to separatist factions (ETA, FLNC) or to political extremists (*Action Directe*). It also takes an interest in foreign communities in France, particularly those of the Islamic fundamentalist groups. Three thousand eight hundred people work within a very hierarchical structure, with outposts in the regions and a centralized command. They can, depending on their clearance, handle informants, carry out surveillance, or plant monitoring devices. One of the advantages of the DCRG is its regional outposts. It is also highly reactive and has greater judicial latitude than the other services. As a result, information is gleaned that is not available to the DST, which has insufficient agents on the ground, as was demonstrated during the operations against *Action Directe* in 1980 and 1987, and the dismantling of the Islamist networks in Lyons and Lille in 1995, in which the DCRG played a leading role. The DCRG posts of the Paris region,[26] which are integrated into the police headquarters in Paris, have a specific statute that makes them quasi-independent of the rest of the service. Under a dual command, of the DCRG and the police chief, and with ten times as many personnel as any other DCRG post (seven hundred civil servants), the Paris service is practically independent of the central directorate. And, within Paris, each case is allocated between the DCRG and the Paris service without any particular guidelines, rather according to the availability and competence of each.

Established on November 16, 1944, the DST was designed to research, prevent, and neutralize, on French soil, "the activities inspired, engaged, or supported" by foreign powers that could threaten the security of the country. DST missions are threefold: domestic counterespionage; protection of industrial, scientific, and technological goods; and the fight against terrorism. Since 1986, it also exerts a degree of judicial responsibility. This means that it can proceed with inquiries or interrogations concerning spying or terrorism. On an organizational level, the DST is comprised of its central service in Paris, seven regional directorates,[27] and several other subunits in France and in France's overseas possessions. Furthermore, the DST has several liaison officers on foreign soil, thus strengthening bilateral links with certain foreign intelligence services.

Within the defense ministry, three other services can be relied on for providing essential intelligence in antiterrorist matters. The first of these, the DGSE is responsible only for overseas missions, in which its mandate is to collect intelligence on political, economic, scientific, and military activities on the one hand, and to detect and counteract any operation that foreign secret services might carry out against French interests on the other. The fight against terrorism, however, is not one of its priorities as its personnel and technical means are not suited to breaking up terrorist networks. Intelligence on terrorist activities overseas is gleaned by DGSE.

The second service is the DSPD, which is responsible for the security of military installations, material, and personnel. It has no judicial authority. It acts in permanent liaison with the DST.

Finally, there is the DRM, which was created following the Gulf War. It has a small military structure with a general mission. It gathers and uses information that the military have uncovered in their work. This surveillance makes it possible to follow movements of people, for instance between Afghanistan and Bosnia.

There is also the essential support that such diverse services, such as the gendarmerie, and the Airborne and Frontier Police,[28] can give. Thanks to their comprehensive coverage of the territory and the surveillance of the frontiers, they are able to bring not only logistical support but also, and especially, first-rate intelligence on the ground.

Another major part of the antiterrorist setup is repression, implemented by the Central Directorate of the Judicial Police (DCPJ), dependent on the DGPN of the ministry of the interior. The DCPJ has divisions that are specialized in each area of intervention. The sixth division (6th DCPJ) is responsible for terrorist matters. Also known as the division responsible for the repression of threats to state security and of subversive elements, it was given increased status in 1998 when it became the National Antiterrorist Directorate (DNAT). Its role is twofold: to undertake judicial investigations into terrorist activities within mandated commissions, and to collate intelligence centrally on criminality for the entire territory. DNAT is made up of some fifty-odd police officers, inspectors, and commissioners, who are grouped into a "separatist" section, which looks at the Basque, Breton, and Corsican questions, and an "international" section, which takes a close interest in Islamic fundamentalist and Near-Eastern terrorism, European terrorism (excluding the ETA), as well as the Kurdish problem and extreme left-wing groups. It relies on the criminal bureaus of regional judicial police services (SRPJ), especially at Pau and Ajaccio, as well as on the Criminal Brigade of the Paris police headquarters. It also has the authority to call in the RAID, the search, assistance, intervention, and dissuasion unit of the interior ministry, which, like the defense ministry's GIGN, is a specialized intervention force made up of highly technical specialists. RAID distinguished itself in particular with the GIGN, when it apprehended members of the ETA during the Airbus hijack in 1994.

Legislative and Judiciary Powers and Counterterrorism

There is legislation in France that targets terrorism specifically. A law passed on September 9, 1986, which is part of the new penal code, defines an act of terrorism as an infraction that is intentionally "linked to an individual or collective effort that intends to disturb public order through intimidation or terror." Such infractions include: murder, degradation of a person's well-being, kidnapping, sequestration, the hijacking of any form of transport, robbery, extortion, destruction, partial destruction, some forms of computer hacking, and finally, the making, storage, and use of explosive devices, and biological or chemical weapons. French legislation also prohibits conspiracy to commit terrorism[29] and ecological terrorism.

The September 9, 1986, law, which was strengthened with laws passed on July 22, 1996, December 30, 1996, and November 15, 2001, establishes a special procedure. It allows certain exemptions to the body of general law, such as an extension to the legal detention period to four days, the delay of the right to see a lawyer to the 72 hours of detention, the possibility of searching and seizing the accused's dwelling at any time and without the authorization of the owner, the deciphering of ciphered messages (in particular those sent via the internet), and the granting of reduced sentences to persons that cooperate with the authorities. As a distinct and well-defined offense, a terrorist act is punished with severe sentences that are derived from the general legal code. These range from banishment for a foreigner, removal of civic and family rights, fifteen years of imprisonment, 200,000 euro fines for ecological terrorism, to life imprisonment in the gravest cases.

Since 1986, the legal proceedings on matters pertaining to terrorism are handled centrally by the high court (*Cour d'Appel*) of Paris, where the Central Antiterrorist Service (SCLAT) is based. The 14th antiterrorist section, the generic name of SCLAT, is comprised of five prosecuting magistrates and four investigating judges, who have "total and general knowledge"[30] of terrorist groups. With responsibility for the entire territory, the prosecutors can demand to examine any affairs that it considers sufficiently sensitive to be judged on a national level. In practice, it is difficult to strike a good balance between the 14th section and the local prosecutors, who traditionally prefer not to relinquish their inquiries, though more and more regions are asking that Paris take over. Even if officially judges are no more versed in the activities of one terrorist group than another, a certain specialization is taking place: for instance Judge Jean-Louis Bruguière examines cases of international terrorism, and Judge Laurence Le Vert looks at Basque terrorism. The choice of which police service to bring in is at the discretion of the magistrate. And as there is closer and closer collaboration between the 14th section and the DNAT, often an affair is examined jointly,[31] which creates a certain amount of confusion and rivalry.

A criminal court delivers the judgment. It is "specially constituted," in other words, without a civilian jury. There are in fact a president and six professional assessors, all professionals, but not specialists in terrorist affairs.

The law is tailor-made for terrorism, but never inconsistent with other legislation. The legislative arsenal is just one part of the French antiterrorist setup. The reason it is specialized, centralized, and coordinated is, in fact, because the emphasis has been placed on simplicity. This does not mean that the French setup is not in fact extremely complex, and it still suffers regularly when different work practices or rivalries between the services cause friction. For the last thirty years the French antiterrorist setup has evolved in step with political priorities and the degree of the threat. Structures have been put in place, some of which are complementary, some of which compete with each other, while some, like the UCLAT, have taken several years to prove that the organization is finally finding its way and that France has moved from a policy of reaction and response to events during the 1970s and 1980s, to one of genuine prevention in the 1990s.

Antiterrorist Policies, 1975–2002

Because of its electoral and security stakes, French antiterrorist policy cannot be compared with other public policy. It must anticipate the next move of a phenomenon whose origins, demands, methods, and means are constantly mutating. In order to reassure the population, governments have been forced to find and adjust responses rapidly. The ineffectiveness of these has sometimes been quickly shown when the same terrorist acts have continued or new types of terrorism have emerged. The decision process has thus been reversed: instead of the state driving change, it is compelled to respond to the dysfunctions on the ground. For thirty years now, the conceptions held by the terrorists have dominated the reaction of the authorities. In view of the intensity of the threat, governments have tried to reconcile two conceptions: criminalizing the act, in other words, reducing it to an ordinary criminal offence, or bringing it up to the level of an act of war. Finding the right balance between creating exceptions and using the existing criminal code when democracy faces extraordinary attacks, governments have eventually managed to put in place an effective anti-terrorist operation that is the result of compromises between policies of negotiation and repression.

From the 1970s to the Late 1980s: The Growing Involvement of Public Authorities

From the 1970s to the Turning Point of 1982

At the beginning of the 1980s, France began to suffer from separatist and international terrorism. But this terrorism was sporadic, either limited to some regions (Corsica, Brittany, and the Basque country), or limited to foreign interests.

The population at large did not at this time really appreciate the reality of the threat. Even the attack on the synagogue on the Rue Copernic by Middle Eastern terrorists in 1980, which did make such a mark on public opinion because of the bloodshed, was perceived by the authorities as a grave accident, a criminal act that should be considered as a particularly serious crime. The intention was not to ignore what was happening, but to deny the importance that the terrorists craved and to avoid scaring the population through a specific mobilization of the police and judiciary. By acting in a reasoned manner without dramatizing terrorism, the authorities hoped to discourage further attacks. From the first attacks of 1974–1975, the then right-wing government chose this approach notwithstanding the use of tough repressive policy with rapid responses to contingencies. For this, the government used instruments and methods that had been used in the early 1960s in the fight against the OAS: infiltration of potential terrorist cells, surveillance of high-risk targets by the information services, mass arrests and convictions, and increased specialization of the police. In Paris, the judicial police of the Paris police headquarters extended the authority of its criminal brigade to include terrorist attacks and set up the antiterrorist section (SAT). The anticommando brigade (BAC) was created in 1972, specialized for intervening quickly on the prefect's orders in the event of a hostage-taking or kidnapping.

For its part, the gendarmerie, which reports to the defense minister, had carefully studied the Munich Olympic Games attacks and developed an appropriate response: the first intervention unit specialized in violent activity, the special intervention group of the national gendarmerie (GIGN). The outcome of this policy was mixed: while the State Security Court (*Cour de Sûreté de l'Etat,* established during the Algerian independence war), a special court whose make-up was half military, half civilian,[32] successfully convicted members of the FLB and *Action Directe,* whose members were arrested respectively in 1978 and 1980, repression in Corsica only resulted in the radicalization of the separatist movements.

When groups were deemed to pursue genuine grievances, with no ability to obtain redress in their country, France had a policy of toleration, which had the added advantage of protecting France and French interests. This policy was considered part of the "rules of the game"[33] agreement between secret services and the police of the countries concerned. It was established under President Charles de Gaulle, continued under President Georges Pompidou, and followed by President Valéry Giscard d'Estaing, as evidenced by the arrest and rapid expulsion in 1977 of Abou Daoud, an important PLO figure. It meant leaving alone those terrorists who were residing in the country, protecting them from extradition requests, as long as they broke no French law or, in the case of those combatants of the Near East who were arrested for minor infringements, leading them back to the border as long as they had committed no attack on the national territory. In the same spirit, Basque separatists also benefited from special treatment, at least when Spain was under Franco's dictatorship. In spite of repeated requests of the Spanish government, they were not extradited but were instructed to leave the Basque country. The error of the government was to send some of them to Brittany where they were able to forge links with Breton separatists, who have provided arms caches and refuges to this day.

1982–1986: Hesitation

When the Left won power in May 1981, there was to be no change to this general policy of not using special legislation and of allowing sanctuary, merely a change in the way the problem was managed. The Socialists' perception of security involved a structural reform of society and no longer a policy of repression. The terrorists fit into this scheme as the "refuse of modern society who cannot find their place."[34] So as to fit them into society and to defuse the violence, the government of François Mitterrand immediately put into action a policy of "openness" with a regional assembly for Corsica, the removal of the State Security Court, the abolition of the death penalty, the opening up of frontiers, and the generous use of the presidential amnesty. This applied to the FLB terrorists as much to those of *Action Directe,* who had nevertheless received lengthy sentences from the State Security Court. At the same time, secret negotiations were started with the FLNC and ASALA.

In a first, very brief, period this policy would bear fruit: separatist terrorism died down. But, from spring 1982, the resurgence and fast escalation of the attacks showed the limitations of the policy. Attacks on the Rue Marbeuf in April, on the Rue des Rosiers in August, further action in Corsica, and the return to the scene of *Action Directe* and ASALA angered the public, and, under intense pressure from the population and the opposition, the Left put in place a policy of repression that no government has swayed from since, simply adjusting the policy depending on events. This policy change saw the president of the Republic take over the antiterrorist brief. After having opted for amnesties and openness, François Mitterrand took a firm line in summer 1982. The president announced that it was essential to "to cut back terrorism where it takes hold, to yank it out by the roots."[35] An emergency unit was set up. The Airborne and Frontier Police (PAF) increased the number of its operatives and undertook greater surveillance of frontiers, backing up a general crackdown and further tightening of migration flows. A major innovation was the creation of a minister responsible for public security, an antiterrorist unit that reported directly to the president, the Interministerial Committee for Antiterrorist Coordination (CILAT), and a central databank of intelligence on terrorists. This databank, which had information on the identities and habits of suspected terrorists, called "Violence-Attack-Terrorism" (VAT), was established in September 1982. The files of the general information services, the judicial police, the DST, and the DGSE were thus centralized. The minister for public security, based on the Italian model, had for a mission the coordination of the activities of the services so as to discharge his function to his chief minister, the minister of the interior.

Finally, the antiterrorist unit of the Elysée brought together, under the commandment of a "gendarme," an information group comprised of gendarmes, police officers of the general information services and the DST, and an action group comprised of GIGN members and the police. Authorized to proceed with secret investigations, this unit had to centralize antiterrorist operations at the Elysée, clear any blockages between the services, and discern significant threats.

But these measures, apart from providing a reassuring presence, quickly came up against difficulties: the Elysée unit, operating secretly, was discredited following the Irish affair at Vincennes[36] and attracted the hostility of the police officers who were not included in the Elysée meetings; the VAT file only partially centralized intelligence, with each service preferring to hold on to its own important information; and the new minister came into rapid conflict with the DGPN. To deal with the information blockages and the exacerbating of rivalries on the ground between police officers and gendarmes, the new government of 1984 readjusted its antiterrorist policy. On the one hand, the president took a back seat, leaving to the then interior minister, Pierre Joxe, the responsibility of carrying out the operations. M. Joxe continued an offensive policy along the same lines as his predecessor, but distinguished himself by making more use of traditional police forces, which the Elysée had previously shied away from. The state security minister and the Elysée unit were removed, and the Group for the Coordination of Antiterrorist Action (UCLAT), which has a flexible and nonhierarchical structure, was used to drive the coordination of the existing groups. The UCLAT framework, which relies on the confidence and mutual comprehension of each player in antiterrorist work, did not have immediate success.

In fact, for each service to learn the role of the others and to know of their intentions in a particular affair in order to avoid mess-ups, it was necessary to wait a whole decade. Then, in a break with the previous policy of allowing sanctuary, M. Joxe decided to extradite ETA terrorists to Spain beginning in September 1984. He also placed an emphasis on intelligence gathering, allocating more resources to the DST, which, like the general intelligence services, had been following terrorism for more than ten years. The DST had been following several affairs linked to Palestinian terrorism at the beginning of the 1970s.

A structure that was dedicated to gathering information on Middle Eastern groups was set up in 1974, which was then reinforced one year later after the attempted arrest of Carlos. But its activity remained limited, terrorism remaining a secondary priority until 1982, when the DST took it over officially at the request of the government. Two years later, the "manipulation"[37] group, a part of the antiterrorist section, was able to claim several successes. The "Vulcan" source gave it two years of important intelligence on Middle Eastern terrorist habits and financial resources. The turning of Jean-Paul Mazurier, Georges Ibrahim Abdallah's[38] lawyer, provided information on Abdallah and his contacts. For their part, the general intelligence services were put in charge from 1976 with "researching intelligence on internal terrorist matters."[39] Through their specialization on separatist and extreme left-wing ideological terrorism, they were behind the apprehension of FLB members in 1976 and of the *Action Directe* network in 1980. Between the two services, as between the DST and the DGSE, little dialogue would take place, with each service working alone and in secret.

The Left's policy was concentrated on the operational level. It sought to improve the organization of the services, but not to specialize them. Not much progress, aside from within the intelligence services, had been made since 1980. The police force, which is by no means a monolithic bloc, was divided by hierarchical and territorial authority squabbles that were aggravated by the policy choices in 1981–1983. The partitioning of the services meant information simply did not circulate. And, on the ground, it was not unknown for several services to intervene at the same time, in the same sector, and on the same affair. For example, in the Basque country the growing role of the PAF in antiterrorist activity provoked the opposition of the general intelligence services as well as of local gendarmes. Suspicion was rife between intelligence services and magistrates, police officers and magistrates, police officers and intelligence services, and within the services themselves. Judicial affairs, since the removal of the State Security Court, were spread around according to the criminal matters to which they were connected. Information on one group could be sourced in as many places as there are crimes committed. For example, four different proceedings were initiated against Georges Ibrahim Abdallah, in four different courts, preventing the overall perspective that is essential for acting against a terrorist group.

At the end of 1985, the antiterrorist setup was in a shambles. Because there was no planning, none of the services was ready to face the wave of attacks that hit France between December 1985 and September 1986.

1986–1991: Outcry and Repression

In the legislative elections of 1986, the right-wing opposition made much use of the inability of the government to stop the attacks and arrest the perpetrators. When in power, it had to quickly put in place the security principles that it had been advocating for years. With continuing attacks, popular outrage grew, demanding immediate results. Putting an end to the principle of describing and treating terrorists as criminals, the new government, more clearly than its predecessor, compared terrorist acts to ones of war, unacceptable on the national soil. Virulent speechmaking followed: Prime Minister Jacques Chirac talked of the "leprosy that is terrorism;"[40] Charles Pasqua, his minister of the interior, upped the stakes with a call for the need to "terrorize the terrorists." The fight against terrorism became a major political preoccupation.

The government opted for offensive policies and made the resources available to lead the fight. First, there was legislative innovation. The law of September 9, 1986, not only defined a terrorist act and established specific legislation to deal with it, but also created the SCLAT and the 14th antiterrorist section at the Paris prosecutor's office. By ensuring a national scope for the 14th section, files were no longer scattered. The police were given a specific pool of magistrates to work with, specialized in antiterrorist enquiries, to ensure that thinking would take place along the same lines. Furthermore, so as to prevent the withdrawal of jurors, as happened in the Schleicher *Action Directe* trial in 1985 because of intimidation, a special appeals court without popular jury was instigated.

After these events, the minister of the interior took over the direction of all the antiterrorist files, while hostage-taking in Lebanon aggravated the threat in the eyes of the population. Energetic measures were taken: multiple arrests, the expulsion of thirteen activists, reinforcing surveillance in public areas, the introduction of a six-month visa for any non-European Community citizen (not including Switzerland). Unfortunately, on the ground, the competition and rivalry between services continued to slow down enquiries. None of the services knew how (or wanted) to work with the others on matters that, nevertheless, needed multiple skills. It was observed in hindsight that each service (DST, general information services, judicial police, and 6th DCPJ) had a piece of information that might have helped to identify those responsible for the attacks more quickly. Giving back to the 6th DCPJ its specialized repressive service in antiterrorism, through the law of September 9 did not help the situation, with the 6th DCPJ competing with the Criminal Brigade, which also had authority to enquire into the Paris region. To free up these blockages Interior Minister Charles Pasqua initiated and directed new organizational efforts. At the ministerial level, he brought together again the Interministerial Committee for Antiterrorist Coordination (CILAT), while the Council for Internal Security was created, making sure that coordination was taking place at the highest level. The arrest of the perpetrators of the 1986 attacks confirmed the important role of the Criminal Brigade in Paris (PJPP), and of the DST, whose infiltration[41] made it possible to stymie the Islamic terrorist Fouad Ali Saleh. For this operation, the DST was given extra judicial powers.

On the political level, the interior minister had to respond to the security demands of the population, which was calling for the liberation of French hostages detained in Lebanon. In view of the Iranian link to the attacks and hostage-taking, the interior minister took the "gray diplomacy" route, launching secret negotiations with Tehran. The expulsion of the Lebanese citizen Wahid Gordji, who was suspected of having played a part in the 1986 attacks, which preceded by only a short period the release of the first two hostages,[42] bears example of this. The liberation of the last hostages in May 1988 was the culmination of this policy motivated in part by the upcoming presidential election. The mismatch between public statements (making war against terrorists) and the action undertaken (negotiation) continued, as illustrated by the liberation in January 1990 of the Lebanese terrorist leader Anis Naccache.

The return of the Left to power in 1988 did not prompt the abandonment of the repressive policies that had been put in place under the Right from 1986–1988. A sort of Right-Left consensus became the rule, not only on the need to fight terrorism, but also on the means made available for the combat, with the sum of previous measures considered as given. Further modernization of the police was undertaken, as well as specialization and coordination efforts. Genuine coordination became a reality with the services recognizing UCLAT. This first success of the unit was the capture of the *Action Directe* leaders, which was the result of a joint operation attributed to the DCRG, Versailles SRPJ, 6th DCPJ, Paris criminal brigade, and RAID, the specialized intervention corps that reports to the minister of the interior. An indication of UCLAT's increased power was the installation of an antenna in the Basque country to facilitate relations between the gendarmerie, the PAF, and the Spanish police, with which France was by then cooperating in combating separatist terrorism, even if this was only a secondary priority at the time.

The outbreak of the Gulf War in 1991 heightened fears of Iraqi reprisals on French territory. For the first time ever, the antiterrorist setup took a preventive approach. The Council for Internal Security, which had been inactive since 1986, began to meet regularly. Then, also for the first time, the defense minister and the armed forces were fully involved in the antiterrorist setup. In effect, the authorities, in order to ensure maximum protection of the territory and its sensitive points, decided to activate a civil defense plan, the Vigipirate contingency plan, which mobilized the police, gendarmerie, and armies in concert under the prime minister's authority. Beyond its operational effectiveness, it also played a reassuring psychological role in the minds of the French people. Its activation confirmed the utility of UCLAT, which managed, in times of crisis, to ensure close coordination between the services.

In the 1980s, succeeding governments tried to strike a balance between, on the one hand, repressive measures that were a response to the demands of a population that, deeply affected by an indiscriminate and bloody terrorism, put constant pressure on the authorities and, on the other hand, conciliatory gestures to terrorist states because of French interests. Foreign policy went through some turbulent years: normalization of relations with Syria, negotiations with Iran, and a complete break with Libya. The "sanctuary" policy was slowly abandoned, with a repressive standpoint adopted in its stead. The 1990s confirmed this trend, which was as much due to political choices as to the work of strong-willed magistrates.

On the ideological level, the Left-Right divide had ceased to be significant, resulting in an emphasis on a management of terrorism stressing, on the operational level, greater use of military-type handling of the problem. The general structure for combating terrorism had been set in place. The only thing left to do was to find a balance between a collective and individual approach. Any equilibrium found to date has been weak, being severely put to the test during the 1995 attacks.

1990–2005: Better Coordination of Scattered Efforts

The Early 1990s: A New Concentration of Government Attention

In 1994, a white paper on defense was published, illustrating the evolution in perceptions of the terrorist threat by the public authorities. Terrorism became the "main nonmilitary threat capable of affecting" security. Religious extremists and nationalists represented another destabilizing threat, with radical Islam being considered as "most concerning." The previous prevention policy was pursued, with emphasis placed on reinforcing the intelligence services. In 1992, the Directorate of Military Intelligence was brought in to complement the setup, bringing information on the movements of certain extremists who had been spotted in Algeria, Bosnia, and Afghanistan. The surveillance of Islamist fundamentalists became the absolute priority for the services, which, at the end of the Cold War, had to reposition themselves to deal with a complex threat, complex in its transnational organization as much as in its obscure, even irrational, motivations. Adapting themselves quickly, in 1991 the general intelligence services put in place two units to look at some of these closed communities: "Urban Violence," and "Towns and Suburbs." Another special group was dedicated to analyzing the culture, society, and implantation of radical Islam in France. The general intelligence services of the Paris police centralized all infiltration and information work in a 13th section, called Radical Islam, which includes a group that monitors what the imams say.

With globalization, any internal/external division of the threats disappeared, bringing about a confusion of territorial responsibilities and, therefore, an upheaval in the missions of the DST and the DGSE. The activities of the various networks abroad caused the DST to place agents abroad, which was until then the privileged domain of the DGSE. Carlos's arrest in 1994, which happened thanks to the contacts of the DST with the intelligence services of the Sudan, confirmed the standing of the DST in this area. On national territory the DST was watching certain suburbs closely because of possible connections with the upheaval in Algeria, thus complementing the work of the general intelligence services and the Paris police, who are themselves interested in the suburbs because of the potential presence of Islamist extremists. Because the work of the two services overlapped, close cooperation was the rule, with information swapping and total transparency.[43]

In the face of the rise of the radical Islamist threat, which the information services have often underscored, the government has opted for offensive and preventive policies. In 1994, the newly created Antiterrorist Bureau of the ministry of justice gave instructions to try to dismantle any structure with activist radical Islamist connotations. To carry out these orders, the 14th section and the police used an article of the new criminal procedure code that covers terrorist conspiracy. The police must check whether, when investigating any activity involving arms smuggling or document forgery, there is a terrorist network behind it. These instructions resulted in the discovery and dismantling of the Chalabi network[44] in a very short time. Not long after, on August 31, 1994, in spite of the risk of reprisals from the GIA, twenty radical Islamists were expelled from France as a direct response to the killing of five French nationals by the GIA in Algiers. By February 1995, the "Islamist" threat was considered so serious that France called for an urgent meeting of all European antiterrorist authorities. For the first time, the threat was assessed as soon as it emerged, which, even if it could not prevent attacks from occurring, did allow repression operations and future prevention to become more effective.

Nevertheless, when the July 1995 attacks by the GIA came about in Paris, the antiterrorist setup was in crisis. Far from reuniting the services around the common goal, which was to identify and arrest terrorists, competition and mistrust became exacerbated.

1995–1996: A Political Adjustment

The arrival on the scene of strong personalities, such as Judge Jean-Louis Bruguière and commissioner Roger Marion, the head of the 6th DCPJ from 1990, brought about the personalization of the combat against terrorism. This caused friction and rivalry. The intelligence services often perceived Judge Bruguière's intervention in Libya and his demand that the DGPN hand over secret DST files in the context of his investigation into the DC-10 affair as exceeding his jurisdiction. Furthermore, the services considered that the magistrate allowed journalists too much latitude, blaming the failure of several operations on his indiscretions. "Justice is conducted in the town square, in complete indiscretion," lamented a senior official of the intelligence services. Relations were similarly fraught between the police and the magistrates. The police criticized the 14th section for wanting to direct the inquiries, while the magistrates complained of a lack of cooperation from the police, who on occasion advised of major antiterrorist operations the day before they happened.

In 1995, the geographic spread of the attacks (Paris, Lyons, and Lille) raised the prospect of competition between the local services and the 6th DCPJ, which tried to dominate the hierarchical management of the whole operation. Like ten years before, this rivalry brought about the nonsharing of information, which resulted in unfortunate loss of time, as demonstrated the dispatch by the gendarmerie to the 6th DCPJ of a file that showed similarities with the Port Royal attack, fifteen days after its discovery. This lack of coordination was just as blatant between the justice and interior ministries who piled on contradictory statements. For example, when the minister of justice affirmed that the threat came from a "variety of groups and interests," the minister of the interior announced that a single group was responsible. This confusion destabilized public opinion and meant that the response lost credibility.

These operational and policy dysfunctions plagued the inquiry. This would lead President Chirac to intervene publicly for the first time, first calling for a return to public order, then having to take a personal interest in the running of the antiterrorism setup, much as François Mitterrand had done in 1982. Jacques Chirac's public pronouncements at the outset of the attacks gave a feeling of a return to the 1970s. The emphasis was put on playing down the attacks. The gravity of the attacks was not forgotten, but the publicity that the terrorists were demanding was refused. President Chirac would rail against the media frenzy in the face of the events. On September 5, 1995, he announced that "the barely believable media runaround, with which there is nothing to compare elsewhere in the world, that has characterized these attacks has, without any doubt, surpassed all the hopes that the terrorists had in their campaign to destabilize French society."[45] From the first attack on the St. Michel metro station, the police and rescue forces were instructed not to make any declarations to the media. Promoting the crisis to a national priority, only the president, prime minister, and interior minister made speeches to the media. Three main points dominated their speeches: a call for calm, an involvement of the public in the face of the threat, and repeated explanations on how the threat would be handled. Since 1986, a defensive approach had been usurped by an approach that explained the threat, and outlined the setup to deal with the threat and the role that the population was to play. But, in 1995, the approach was amplified and generalized. Incessant appeals for vigilance and mobilization were made in the subway, on trains, and in public buildings in order to develop a security reflex.[46] Moving beyond its victimhood, the population became a part of the antiterrorist combat. This approach bore fruit: a bomb was defused in the summer of 1995 thanks to the vigilance of a passenger. An offer of one million francs was made by the interior minister following the St. Michel attack to any person who could help identify those responsible, a feature that French law had hitherto made impossible.

The role of managing the antiterrorist setup was taken up by the president and the prime minister, whereas, in 1986, the interior minister had looked after matters. Jacques Chirac's call to order of the services involved in the inquiry in the above mentioned speech had the effect of a cattle prod, reinforced, it is true, by the removal of the head of the Paris PJPP and of the second-in-command of the DCPJ. Alain Juppé, the prime minister, took over some responsibilities from the interior minister, personally presiding over meetings of the CILAT. To the interior minister went the job of coordinating the police and the intelligence services, whose rivalry diminished in the face of the threat. The emergency, the spread of information, and the mobility of the terrorist networks dictated the need for shared thinking and intelligence. With the director of national police taking over the direction of UCLAT, his authority was better respected and genuine coordination was brought about by the fall of 1995. Preventive and repressive measures were intensified: the Vigipirate plan was rolled out, the Schengen common-visa zone was suspended, publications inciting racial hatred were seized, and there were numerous arrests among radical Islamists. The earlier groundwork that the general information services and the DST had done proved invaluable, as the speed of the inquiry demonstrated, in spite of the many false trails.

On the operational level, the success with which the GIA networks were dismantled in France confirmed the UCLAT in its coordinating role in times of crisis. The complementary work, based on reciprocity of exchanges, continued to be reinforced. The crisis also signaled the rise in the authority of the 6th DCPJ, which was now recognized as the service, par excellence, for forming a specialized double-team in combating terrorism with SCLAT. The antiterrorist judges saw their role enhanced within the setup with additional financial and personnel resources, but also with the introduction of better exchanges between magistrates and police officers, a consequence of the progress of inquiries during periodic meetings.

The 1996–1998 period can, therefore, be seen, in the light of years of rivalries, as a time when complementariness and mutual involvement of all the actors in combating terrorism became the norm. The Vigipirate plan's effective use in 1996 confirmed it as a lynchpin of preventive policy.

In 1998 for the soccer World Cup matches, the government brought back the preventive measures used in 1994: Vigipirate was strengthened, and there were mass arrests in radical Islamist circles in the whole European Union in cooperation with the Belgian, British, German, and Spanish police forces. A joint operation between France and Belgium led to a fledgling European GIA network being dismantled.

Post-9/11: Prevention and International Support in the Face of the al Qaeda Menace

After September 11, 2001, because of the new degree and form of the threat, the antiterrorist setup was reinforced, with additional involvement from the armed forces and the adoption of specific measures. It was also extended with the integration of the health and medical chains into the alert mechanism and further measures to combat the funding of terrorism.

Antiterrorist policy in 2001 could be distinguished first by its specific legislative characteristics. In a break with all the measures that had been adopted since 1981, a specific law was passed on November 15, 2001, on "everyday security and combating terrorism." Adopted under an emergency, this law was comprised of specific measures relating to terrorism that, unusually, were applicable temporarily up until December 31, 2001. This law added to the number of terrorist offenses (extension to offenses involving money laundering and other organized criminal activities, and creation of a new separate terrorist offense: the financing of terrorist activity). It also lightens the procedural requirements in the combat against terrorism: authorization of car searches on application to the attorney general; the possibility of setting up flying squads for frisking persons and searching luggage in and around airports and harbors; the possibility of officially using information services techniques to decipher messages (e-mail, etc.). The official recognition of deciphering goes some way toward establishing a new legal basis for the activities of the intelligence services. Responding to the bombings in London in July 2005, France's interior minister Nicolas Sarkozy recently presented an anti-terrorism bill to the Cabinet.[47] The bill stiffens prison sentences for convicted terrorists, allows police to monitor citizens who travel to countries known for terror training camps, and broadens the use of surveillance cameras. The bill was adopted by parliament on December 22, 2005.

This legal arsenal allows increased surveillance of areas considered dangerous. Furthermore, the preventive measures that proved their worth in 1998 are brought back: the DST and the DNAT (former 6th DCPJ) have proceeded with preventive arrests, which have led to the preliminary hearings of twenty-four presumed members of the radical Islamist group Takfir, while the Vigipirate plan was reinforced and reactivated. Furthermore, the armed forces were brought in to reinforce the protection of sensitive sites. Thus, in the face of the risk of air strikes, Crotale land-air missiles have been deployed to cover the nuclear attack submarine (SNLEs) base at l'Ile Longue and the COGEMA's plant for radioactive waste reprocessing at La Hague in Normandy. For the first time, the antiterrorist prevention mechanism was brought up a level to include the nuclear, biological, and chemical weapons threat and, in particular, the bioterrorist threat. France was somewhat behind the efforts of other countries in dealing with this threat, especially Sweden and the United States.

In the wake of concerns relating to the anthrax scare in the United States and false alarms in France, the government has now launched a plan of action. For the reinforcement of the detection network, a national alert mechanism has been put in place, which reports to the National Watch Institute (INV). Any pathogenic germs are placed under high surveillance in French laboratories, and two sets of bylaws have been issued that stipulate in strict terms the use, storage, purchase, and transport of samples of infectious diseases such as measles, anthrax, plague, and botulism. Within the Vigipirate plan, the government has put in place a new combat and prevention plan, the Biotox plan, which includes the surveillance of water networks, the transformation of hospitals into contamination centers, etc. In another innovation, the government has admitted to the existence of this plan that had heretofore been classified as a defense secret, as well as other plans that the SGDN[48] had established, such as Piratom (against nuclear attacks) and Piratox (chemical threats, established following the Gulf War) whose existence had previously been known only unto a small group of people. As in 1996, the government chose to explain in order to reassure, especially through the interior minister, who allowed the media to mention the possibility of simulation exercises involving attacks.[49] These measures signify a turning point in combating terrorism: no longer limited to a group of three involving information services, the police, and the justice system, the fight also involves the health and medical authorities, which were involved for the first time and brought to the fore.

As to repression, France has been targeting the nerve center of the war by fighting against the financing of the international terrorist network. France has proposed an international convention on this subject at the United Nations. It has created a special unit to fight money laundering, the FINTER unit, at the ministry of economy and finance, and it has frozen the equivalent of 4.7 million euros of the funds of persons and organizations suspected, or known to have supported, al Qaeda.

CONCLUSION

A new period was ushered in on September 11, 2001, with an unprecedented international mobilization against terrorism, and a concentration of public and political attention upon it that will inevitably lead to greater international cooperation in this respect, and it is to be hoped better effectiveness as a result. France, which with its European partners has launched the Schengen process of European cooperation in this field, and the Trevi group that directs the European fight against terrorism and other major threats to society, has thus acquired invaluable experience of international cooperation in this field, and has welcomed the post-9/11 American emphasis on cooperation.[50] French authorities have also remained convinced that fighting terrorism involved much more than a purely military, or indeed a purely repressive stance. Dismantling international terrorist networks requires the deployment of a variety of means as well as a considerable amount of patience. The long "war" against terrorism in which all civilized countries are now engaged may benefit from the experience gained by France in its longer fight against terrorism.

3

GERMANY

Ulrich Schneckener

For thirty-five years, Germany has experienced different forms of terrorism. The various groups involved in terrorist activities differ largely in their ideological background, political ambitions, organizational structures, operational profiles, use of violence, and, last but not least, scope of activities. In particular, the former West Germany had suffered from both homegrown left- and right-wing terrorism as well as from activities by foreign terrorist groups.

For some groups, Germany was the key battleground. In other cases, Germany has been primarily used as a sanctuary, meeting point, or preparation ground for propaganda and violent activities elsewhere. It is precisely this latter aspect that connected Germany with the attacks of September 11, 2001: Three of the four pilots, among them ringleader Mohamed Atta, studied in Hamburg. They were radicalized in Germany and joined Osama bin Laden's al Qaeda before they finally entered the United States in early summer of 2000 in order to prepare themselves for the attack.

Immediately after September 11, German security authorities started one the most extensive investigations ever: The Federal Criminal Police Office (BKA) set up a special task force with about six hundred police experts focusing on the al Qaeda network; more than two hundred bank accounts of individuals and organizations have been frozen; and, as of early 2004, no less than 190 investigations with Islamic extremist backgrounds are being conducted nationwide. Those steps were accompanied by various changes in law enforcement and in strengthening the security apparatus, laid down in two "security packages" as well as in other measures.

Before September 11, however, the most troubling period for (West) Germany was the mid-1970s when the country was shocked by a whole series of violent acts against prominent political and economic figures committed by the left-wing extremists of the Red Army Faction (RAF). The spectacular high peak was reached in the fall of 1977 (the so-called

Deutscher Herbst) when nationally and internationally operating groups linked their activities. RAF members kidnapped Hanns-Martin Schleyer, the then-president of the BDA (Federation of German Employers' Associations), and few weeks later a commando from the Popular Front for the Liberation of Palestine (PFLP) hijacked the Lufthansa airliner *Landshut*, killing the pilot Jürgen Schumann. Both operations were aimed at forcing the German government to release eleven RAF prisoners.

The showdown took place on October 18, 1977, when the German antiterror unit GSG9 stormed the hijacked plane in Mogadishu, Somalia, and killed most of the Palestinian terrorists. During the same night, three key RAF prisoners committed suicide, and Schleyer was finally executed by his kidnappers.[1] Despite a number of arrests in the 1970s and 1980s, the RAF was still able to recruit new "generations" and to continue its "struggle" until the early 1990s.

Past and Present Terrorist and Extremist Activities

In order to systematize groups and their activities in Germany, various types of terrorism should be distinguished (Table 1, next page). Here the differentiation between *national*, *international*, and *transnational terrorism* is used since each type poses a different challenge for the security authorities and has presumably to be combated with a different mix of countermeasures.

National or Domestic Terrorism

National or *domestic terrorism* challenges explicitly the political order of a particular state. The groups involved fight for a radical change of the political system at the center or, in cases of ethno-nationalism, the separation of a region or a subnational entity. As a rule, assassins and victims are both residents of the same state. Typically, these groups act mainly within the borders of their home states. However, they may have some international contacts with like-minded groups elsewhere. For example, the RAF kept links not only with Palestinian groups, but also with other West European leftist militants (such as *Action Directe* in France, *Brigate Rosso* in Italy, or Combatant Communist Cells in Belgium) for ideological, operational, and logistical purposes.[2]

In the past, Germany was mainly affected by this type of terrorism. The most prominent groups were radical left-wing, self-styled revolutionary organizations, such as the RAF, the smaller 2 June Movement (which later joined the RAF), or the Revolutionary Cells (RZ). Both had their sociocultural and ideological origin in the student revolt of the late 1960s, which spread across Western Europe and the United States. In particular,

Table 1: Major Terrorist and Extremist Groups in Germany		
	National terrorism	*International terrorism*	*Transnational terrorism*
Left-wing groups	Baader-Meinhof-Group, later Red Army Faction (RAF) (1970– 92/98) 2 June Movement (1971–80, joined the RAF) Revolutionary Cells, RZ (1973–mid-1990s) Anti-Imperialist Cells (1992–96)	Group Carlos, including RZ members (1973–mid-1990s) Revolutionary People's Liberation Party-Front, DHKP-C (since 1994) Mujahedin-e Khalq, MEK (1990s)	
Right-wing/ neofascist groups	Military Sports Group Hoffman, WSG (1973–80) German Action Group, DA (early 1980s) Militant Skinhead and Neo-nazi groups (since 1990s, e.g., Kameradschaft Süd, Skinheads Sächsische Schweiz)	"Grey Wolfs," MHP (1990s)	

Table 1: continued		
	National terrorism	*International terrorism*	*Transnational terrorism*
Secular ethno-nation-alist groups		Palestinian Groups, i.e, PFLP, PFLP-GC, Black September (1970s) Kurdistan Workers' Party, PKK (1990s) Tamil LTTE (1990s)	
Religious-motivated groups		Hamas Hizbollah	al Qaeda (e.g., Hamburg Cell, Frankfurt Cell) Al-Tawhid Ansar al-Islam Hizb-ut-Tahrir Caliphate State

the protest against the U.S. war in Vietnam, the insufficient dealing with the Nazi past, and the conservative restoration of postwar Germany shaped the anti-imperialist and anticapitalist ideology of many Marxist-inspired groups.

The use of violence started with firebombs in department stores and bank raids. It ended with explosive attacks, hostage taking, kidnapping, shooting, and executing people.[3] In 1992, the RAF command declared the "temporary suspension of the use of violence"; finally, in 1998, the group officially announced its dissolution. In total, the RAF alone was responsible for the death of at least thirty-five persons, among them four U.S. soldiers who were killed in May 1972 when the group attacked two U.S. army bases in Frankfurt and Heidelberg.[4]

Another form of domestic terrorism is represented by right-wing extremists and Neo-nazi groups. The first prominent case was the *Wehrsportgruppe Hoffmann* (WSG, Military Sports Group Hoffmann). In 1980, WSG members were responsible for an explosive attack at the Octoberfest in Munich (thirteen people dead) as well as for the killing of a Jewish publisher and his wife. The WSG was banned in 1980 by the Ministry of the Interior and its leader Hoffmann was arrested in 1981 (released in 1989). Another case was the *Deutsche Aktionsgruppe* (DA, German Action Group), led by the Neo-nazi Roeder (arrested in 1980, released in 1990), which launched various arson and explosive attacks: one against a home for foreigners in Hamburg (two people dead).

Shortly after German unification, right-wing extremism increased rapidly, most notably in the former East Germany. Until today, Neo-nazis are involved in criminal activities as well as in violence against Jewish or U.S. institutions, suspected "leftists," asylum seekers, or other foreigners. According to its 2003 report, the Federal Office for the Protection of the Constitution counts roughly 160 of the so-called *Freie Kameradschaften* (free comrade associations) in which right-wing extremists and skinheads tend to organize themselves.[5] The most militant groups have been outlawed by the state authorities, the most recent case being the *Kameradschaft Süd–Aktionsbüro Süddeutschland* (founded in 2001), whose members are accused of planning an explosive attack at a ceremony at the building site of the new Jewish Community Center in Munich in 2003. In total, fourteen members have been arrested on charges of "formation of a terrorist organization" (according to article 129a Penal Code).[6]

International Terrorism

International terrorism (a better term is *internationally operating terrorism*) is essentially a strategy of "internationalizing" a local conflict. Similar to internal terrorists, the overall goal of international terrorists is to change the political system in a particular state. However, they use a different strategy in order to attract the attention of a wider public and to put their demands on the international agenda. They, therefore, deliberately choose and attack targets abroad. Thus, typically assassins and victims are not residents of the same state.

According to a common definition, international terrorism implies "incidents in which terrorists go abroad to strike their targets, select victims or targets that have connections with a foreign state . . . , or create international incidents by attacking airline passengers, personnel or equipment."[7] The paradigm cases for this kind of terrorism involved Palestinian groups, such as the PFLP, Palestine Front for the Liberation of Palestine-General Command (PFLP-GC), or Abu Nidal, which in the late 1960s consciously decided to undertake spectacular operations abroad in order to make the world aware of the Palestinian cause.

Germany was affected by this strategy for the first time in 1972 at the Olympic Games in Munich when the Fatah-related group Black September took Israeli athletes hostage and demanded the release of more than two hundred "comrades" in Israel. Another example would be the Group Carlos, led by the Venezuelan terrorist Ilich Ramirez Sanchez and composed of key members of the German Revolutionary Cells.[8] Carlos started to act on behalf of the PFLP. Later, he also established links to secret services in Libya, Syria, Romania, Hungary, and East Germany. In West Germany, the group was responsible for attacking Radio Free Europe in Munich (1981), apparently on behalf of the Romanian secret service, and the French Culture Center in Berlin (1983).[9]

Other foreign groups also occasionally chose targets in Germany or deliberately attacked German citizens abroad. During the 1990s, the country suffered mostly from activities of Turkish and Kurdish groups, such as the extreme right-wing and anti-Kurdish party Grey Wolfs (MHP), the radical left-wing Revolutionary People's Liberation Party-Front (DHKP-C), and the ethnic Kurdistan Workers' Party (PKK). They launched several arson and explosive attacks, mainly against Turkish/Kurdish officials, restaurants, shops, and businesses in Germany. Moreover, in 1993 PKK members occupied the Turkish General Consulate in Munich taking twenty persons hostage.[10] A well-known example for targeting Germans abroad is the kidnapping of a manager and a technician in Beirut by members of the Hizbollah (1987) in order to put pressure on the German government to release an arrested "comrade." Other militant groups of different ideological background, such as the Tamil Tigers (LTTE), the Iranian Mujahedin-e-Khalq (MEK), or Hamas, have so far not been involved in terrorist acts in Germany, but use opportunities for fund-raising (often via different organizations), for recruiting supporters and activists in diaspora communities, and/or for engaging in propaganda.[11]

Transnational Terrorism

Transnational terrorism differs from the other two types of terrorism with regard to political ambitions and ideology, the composition of its membership, and its organizational structure.[12] First of all, transnational terrorists aim at changing the global or, at least, a regional political order. They are not primarily involved in a local struggle, but fight a global or regional one. To some extent, European left-wing terrorism as well as the Group Carlos also showed a degree of transnationalism because of its anti-imperialist and anti-American rhetoric, and its (largely failed) attempts at joint operations. However, the prime case for this "new" type of terrorism is clearly the al Qaeda network.

Since 1996 at the latest, bin Laden's Islamist movement has been directly targeting U.S. and Western influence, or "imperialism," in the Islamic world, which in its view has to be defeated first in order to "liberate" Muslim populations from their "corrupt" rulers and install a "true" Islamic order under the rule of the Caliphate. In its ideology, al Qaeda has successfully linked local conflicts with Muslim involvement (e.g., Palestine, Bosnia, Chechnya, Mindanao, or Indonesia), with the mission of a global jihad against the "Jewish-Christian crusaders." Moreover, in contrast to most conventional terrorist groups, al Qaeda works as a multinational enterprise, which—despite its Arab origin—comprises persons of different ethnic, national, or linguistic backgrounds bound together by a common transnational Islamic ideology.

While many traditional terrorist groups are organized as centralized and hierarchical organizations, al Qaeda operates via a decentralized, flexible network structure that has links and contacts with a variety of cells and different associated groups—ranging from Northern Africa and the Gulf region to Central and Southeast Asia.

Germany, like other West European states, has also been affected by this network and related groups. Most crucial, the above-mentioned "Hamburg cell" was the core group of the 9/11 plot. It largely planned, prepared, and implemented the operation; its members had close links with the masterminds of the plan and with the leadership of al Qaeda. The multinational cell was composed of the three pilots, the Egyptian Mohamed Atta, Marwan al Shehhi from the Arab Emirates, and the Lebanese Ziad Jarrah; as well as of the Yemenite Ramzi Binalshibh, one of the key organizers of the plot who was arrested in Karachi, Pakistan, in 2002.

Organized and advised by the Mauritanian businessman Mohamedou Ould Slahi, the four went to Afghanistan in late 1999 to receive training and orders. Two Moroccans, Said Bahaji and Zakariya Essabar, were also part of the group; both left Germany before 9/11 and are still at large. Two other Moroccans, Mounir el-Motassadek and Abdelghani Mzoudi, were arrested by German authorities. Both attended training camps in Afghanistan in 2000. They allegedly provided logistical support for the hijackers and are accused by the German Federal Prosecuting Attorney General of membership in a terrorist organization. In both cases, however, it proved to be difficult to find sufficient compelling evidence that the two men indeed had been involved in the 9/11 plot.[13] In addition, the two German-Syrians, Mohamed Haydar Zammar and Mamoun Darkanzanli, are suspected of being involved in logistical and financial activities for al Qaeda's European network. German investigators linked both also to the 9/11 plot.[14]

Before and after September 11, German authorities, often in cooperation with others, detected various Islamic extremist cells and, thus, prevented potential attacks. Back in 1998, the German police arrested the Sudanese Mamduh Mahmud Salim, a suspected key financial operative of al Qaeda, and extradited him to the United States. Another prominent case was the "Frankfurt cell," or the so-called Meliani Group, comprising five Algerians who, together with conationals in France, planned to bomb targets in Strasbourg. They were put in custody in December 2000 and sentenced to ten to twelve years in prison in 2003.

Another example is the arrest of eleven Al-Tawhid members, mainly Palestinians, in April 2002—a group linked to the Jordanian extremist al-Zarqawi, who has acquired worldwide notoriety because of his brutal terrorist activities in Iraq after the U.S. invasion.[15] In December 2003, the police crushed a cell of Ansar al-Islam in Munich, another al Qaeda-related or -inspired group, which according to official sources, set up several cells, particularly in the southern part of Germany. Another serious incident happened in December 2004 when the Iraqi Prime Minister Ijad Allawi visited Germany. Based on information acquired via phone-tapping the police arrested three Iraqi Kurds, all suspected members of Ansar al-Islam, who apparently planned to attack Allawi during his stay in Germany.

In addition, the minister of the interior has forbidden the activities of other Islamic extremists, such as the radical pan-Islamic Hizb-ut-Tahrir, which has about two hundred supporters who have so far not been involved in any violent acts, but are engaged in disseminating anti-Semitic and anti-Western propaganda. This transnational network aims at establishing an Islamic Caliphate, which should cover at least the Muslim world. A similar goal is pursued by the Cologne-based Turkish Islamic group Caliphate State (Kalifatstaat), led by the Turkish extremist Metin Kaplan (imprisoned in 1999 and extradited in October 2004). The group, including its foundation Servants of Islam and nineteen other suborganizations (in total eleven hundred members), were banned in December 2001, and about 1,200 objects of their members have been searched by the police.[16]

These cases exemplify the fact that after 9/11, the focus of German security authorities has clearly shifted toward Islamic extremism and foreign militant groups abusing civil liberties and trying to infiltrate Muslim communities in Germany. In total, the Federal Office for the Protection of the Constitution (2004) estimates that roughly thirty-one thousand people are members of radical Islamic organizations and that three thousand to four thousand militant Muslims ready to use violence live in Germany.

Domestic Security Institutions in Combating Terrorism

Until today, Germany's domestic security architecture was largely shaped by the historic experience of the Nazi period between 1933 and 1945. The word *terror* in German public discourse, therefore, refers often to the Nazi state and its inhumane and criminal activities. Thus, in order to prevent a strong central security apparatus, domestic security in post-1945 West Germany—initiated and supported by the U.S. occupation regime—was based on the following principles: first, police and other security authorities had to be organized along federal lines. The result is that each of today's sixteen German *Länder* (states) has its own police, intelligence service, and law-enforcement institutions. Germany has no federal police force or an equivalent to the Federal Bureau of Investigation (FBI); the only federal institutions are the Border Guard and the Federal Criminal Police Office. Second, there had to be a clear legal and political distinction between police and intelligence services. This "separation clause" (*Trennungsgebot*) was explicitly enforced by the Western allies after the Second World War.[17] And third, German authorities distinguish strictly between internal and external security matters, which is exemplified by the separation of the police and the military. In general, the military cannot be used for domestic purposes (e.g., in cases of violent demonstrations or social uprisings).

According to articles 35 and 87a of the German constitution (Basic Law), the German army (*Bundeswehr*) can only be employed in a supportive manner in cases of a catastrophe (e.g., natural disasters), for humanitarian purposes, for technical assistance, and in a declared state of emergency (*innerer Notstand*)—in other words, when the democratic order of the Republic or of one state is challenged and when police and border guards are not sufficient to solve the crisis.[18] It is only very recently that the German police forces and experts have been sent abroad to support peace missions (e.g., in Afghanistan, Bosnia, and Kosovo) and thereby play a role in international security.

Based on these principles, the institutional setting is rather complex. In total, at least thirty-nine distinct authorities plus various ministries hold responsibilities in counterterrorism:

- *Federal Office for the Protection of the Constitution (Bundesamt für den Verfassungsschutz*, BfV) as well as sixteen *Länder* offices (LfVs) working independently from the Federal Office. Together, they constitute the German domestic intelligence service. The Federal Office (twenty-four hundred personnel), however, has only a coordinating role and cannot give orders or supervise the *Länder* offices. The offices are responsible for observing and monitoring groups and persons who may threaten the constitutional order of the Federal Republic. They are subject to their respective Ministry of the Interior and publish a general report every year.

● *Federal Criminal Police Office (Bundeskriminalamt, BKA)* as well as sixteen *Länder* LKAs, again each linked to its respective Ministry of the Interior. The BKA with its fifty-three hundred people coordinates the work of the LKAs, provides for information exchange (e.g., information boards) and for central databases (e.g., for criminal records, fingerprints, photographs, or DNA analyses), and has the right to conduct criminal investigations in cases of national and international interest. In 1975, a special unit for antiterrorism was established. In the 1980s, the office gained additional powers for dealing with international drug trafficking and transnational organized crime. The BKA is also responsible for European and international cooperation in combating crime (e.g., Interpol, Europol). For that purpose, several liaison officers are deployed abroad.[19]

● *Federal Intelligence Service (Bundesnachrichtendienst, BND)*, was officially established in 1956. The "German CIA," with its approximately six thousand people, is responsible for gathering and analyzing information from abroad. As most secret services in the world, the BND relies also on open sources, human intelligence, and analyses of satellite pictures and of signal intelligence. The BND reports regularly to the government, and its president is part of the so-called security cabinet (committee of the security-related ministries).

● *Military Counterintelligence Service (Militärischer Abschirmdienst, MAD)* is a department of the Federal Ministry of Defense and also a part of the armed forces. Its responsibilities include the gathering and evaluation of information on activities within the German army or directed from outside against the army with the aim of threatening or undermining the constitutional order (e.g., by espionage or extremist propaganda).

● *Federal Border Guard (Bundesgrenzschutz, BGS)*. Its key tasks are, among others, border protection, railway-police duties, protection against attacks on the security of air traffic, police duties in the case of emergency or national defense, as well as protection of German diplomats and missions abroad. The special antiterror squad *Grenzschutzgruppe 9* (GSG9) with its two hundred thirty police officers, established in 1972, is also part of the BGS.

● *Customs Criminal Office (Zollkriminalamt, ZKA)*, replaced in 1992 the former Customs Criminal Institute (ZKI), works as the central office for the Customs Investigation Service (*Zollfahndungsdienst*). The ZKA has to coordinate and direct investigations in customs crimes (e.g., document forgery and smuggling). It controls exports, and it cooperates with police and fiscal and trade authorities. Since 1990, the office has been responsible for recording, coordinating, and evaluating all information related to the proliferation of weapons of mass destruction as well as for initiating corresponding investigations. The ZKA also acquired powers in investigating drug trafficking, the illegal transfer of technology, and money laundering.

● *Office of the Prosecuting Attorney General*, attached to the Federal High Court of Justice, is responsible for investigation and prosecution in cases of severe criminal activities directed against the internal and external security of the Federal Republic, among them, espionage, politically motivated crimes in general, and terrorism in particular.

The federal institutions are politically supervised by different ministries. The Ministry of the Interior is responsible for BfV, BGS, and BKA; the Ministry of Defense for the MAD; the Ministry of Finance for the ZKA; the Ministry of Justice for the Attorney General; and the Chancellor's Office for the BND. In addition, the Federal Coordinator for the Secret Services, based at the Chancellor's Office, has to oversee and direct the work of all intelligence services. The day-to-day business is further complicated by the fact that these institutions are not based in the capital of Berlin, but are, rather, spread across the republic. The BKA is located in Wiesbaden, Meckenheim (near Bonn), and Berlin; the BND near Munich; the MAD close to Bonn; the BfV and the ZKA in Cologne; and the Attorney General in Karlsruhe.

Counterterrorism Policy Prior to 9/11

As the overview on past experiences indicates, before 9/11 German counterterrorism was largely shaped by the threat of homegrown groups. Therefore, the fight against terrorism was almost entirely understood as a domestic affair and treated in a manner analogous to that against organized crime. Based on this assessment, law-enforcement and police measures were developed.

In the 1970s, three antiterrorism acts were adopted (1974, 1976, and 1978), which criminalized the "formation of terrorist organizations" (section 129a, Penal Code) as well as the support and encouragement of serious violent crimes;[20] strengthened the powers of prosecution authorities; and limited the rights of the defense, in particular, restricting contacts between prisoners and lawyers.[21] Additionally, the 1977 *Kontaktsperregesetz* (contact ban law) stipulated that orders can be made to prevent contacts between detained and convicted terrorists and with anyone else, including written and oral contact with their defending lawyers. This act was passed during the Schleyer kidnapping.

These legal changes and instruments led to an intense debate over whether they challenged or even violated fundamental rights and freedoms. In particular, the supposedly inhuman incommunicado detention even led to some degree of sympathy and even solidarity with RAF prisoners among leftists and liberals. The Constitutional Court, however, ruled that the law did not contradict the German Basic Law (1978).

Another measure introduced into criminal law was a special regulation for principal witnesses (*Kronzeugenregelung*, 1989) which allowed exemptions from prosecution and punishment for those suspected terrorists who offer crucial information to the authorities and who help to prevent major criminal acts or lead to the arrest of other members of terrorist groups. This regulation expired in 1999. It was criticized by experts as a "dirty deal" with criminals, and was largely seen as ineffective in combating terrorism or organized crime. Nevertheless, after 9/11, politicians and security experts, including the Minister of the Interior, called for a renewal in order to obtain information from Islamic extremists. So far, the ruling coalition of Social Democrats and Greens, however, has not decided to reintroduce this controversial measure.

Beyond new legal instruments, the fight against left-wing terrorism led to a modernization and computerization of police and intelligence work. In the 1970s, German security authorities developed new forms of investigation and set up various databases with information about tens of thousands of Germans. The "trawl net search" (*Schleppnetzfahndung*) based on section 163d of the Code of Criminal Procedure, for example, made it possible to keep personal data or other information about people checked at borders and other control points, which may lead to the arrest of suspected terrorists or the solving of a severe crime. For example, during the Schleyer kidnapping the police established that all letters from the terrorists were posted at the Gare du Nord in Paris and apparently were taken by a courier from Cologne to Paris. Therefore, the police with the aid of the railway office checked all passengers aged between twenty-five and thirty-five on the night trains to Paris.[22]

Most databases were used primarily for identifying overlapping clusters of suspicious traits in parts of the population. These clusters were deduced from the typical behavior and profile of RAF members. As illustrated by Katzenstein,[23] this so-called grid search or scanning method (*Rasterfahndung*) worked as follows: "[T]he police used the files of utility companies to identify customers who paid their bills in cash or through third parties. This group was narrowed down further by running data checks on lists of residence and automobile registrations as well as receipts of social security and child-care payments. The people remained in this 'drag-net' were potential suspects. . . . If they lived in large apartment complexes with underground garages and unrestricted access to four-lane highways, . . . changed their look as soon as they moved in, kept their curtains closed, and received little or no mail, they were put under direct police surveillance."[24]

After 9/11, the same method was used on the level of the *Länder* in attempts to detect Islamist "sleeper" cells in Germany. Contrary to its former usage, the method was now not implemented under the condition of an "imminent danger," but, rather, for the first time, as a preventive measure, in other words, the search started no matter whether there had been the concrete suspicion of persons having committed or planning crimes.[25]

The results, as many experts and practitioners admit, were not impressive.[26] First, it was not until March 2002 that the scanning process started properly; therefore, possible suspects had had enough time to leave the country before the necessary regulations were enacted. Second, it turned out to be very difficult to come up with a precise cluster or "grid" in order to reduce the number of hits. Based on the profile of the Hamburg hijackers only, the following key factors were used: male, Arab background, aged between twenty and thirty-five, students of engineering or another technical education, and without a criminal record. This "grid" was far too general for producing any reasonable results—not a single "sleeper" was identified. Third, the whole exercise could only cover persons about whom some basic information existed (e.g., registered addresses). It did not, for instance, cover illegal migrants, travelling business people, or occasional visitors. Fourth, considering the scant results, it required disproportionately high resources within the security authorities. Finally, taking all these points together, the question arises whether it is justified and appropriate to scan the data of millions of innocent people. This example underlines that the nature of the "new" transnational terrorism differs largely from conventional forms of terrorism. This type of terrorist does not usually stick to a particular pattern or set of clusters. Consequently, traditional methods are not always conducive for successful investigation in such cases.

Counterterrorism Policy Since 9/11

A few days after September 11, the Federal Government approved the first "security package," followed shortly afterwards by a second one. In addition, various domestic and international measures and policies, including special budget lines, have been adopted. According to the official government documents, they shall address five key objectives: destroy terrorist structures through comprehensive search and investigations; repel terrorists before they can launch attacks in Germany; enhance international cooperation in combating terrorism; protect the German population and reduce the vulnerability of the country; and remove the causes of terrorism.[27]

In most cases, the decisions were supported by the overwhelming majority of the German *Bundestag*. This result, however, does not imply that the parties agreed easily on each and every detail. In particular, when debating the second package, legislators clarified the differences. On the one hand, for the Greens and the Liberal Democrats (FDP), certain proposals of the Federal Minister of the Interior Otto Schily went already too far in limiting the scope of civil liberties. Even in his own party, the Social Democrats (SPD), he was confronted with some resistance.[28] On the other hand, the main opposition party, the conservative Christian Democrats (CDU/CSU), called for more substantial changes in favor of domestic security. Consequently, until the new elections in September 2005, the key decisions were based on a compromise within the ruling SPD-Green coalition, sometimes including the opposition parties.[29]

The most dramatic step, however, was not related to domestic security, but to the use of military force for counterterrorism purposes elsewhere. This brought the government almost to the brink of collapse in November 2001 when Chancellor Gerhard Schröder and Foreign Minister Joschka Fischer pushed for German participation in the military Operation Enduring Freedom with troops and special forces.

According to German law for sending armed forces abroad, the government always needs the approval of the parliament. Because of a number of SPD and Green dissidents, the government was short of a parliamentary majority of its own, thus requiring the consent of the opposition. The chancellor considered this situation unacceptable and linked the German commitment to Operation Enduring Freedom with the question of whether he and his cabinet should stay in power. Thus, he was able to bring most dissidents into line—otherwise, coalition reshuffle or general elections would have taken place. In the following sections the main aspects of Germany's post-9/11 policies will be presented in more detail.[30]

Additional Financial and Human Resources

Responding to September 11, the Federal Government earmarked for 2002 a special budget of 1.47 billion euros for the fight against terrorism. To finance the additional funding, the parliament increased the tax on cigarettes by two cents and the tax for accident and damage insurance by one percent in 2002. The money was mainly used to provide the security authorities with additional capabilities and to allow ministries and other bodies to hire new personnel (e.g., Arabic-speaking persons, Islam experts, and infrastructure security experts). The 2002 budget was divided in the following way:[31] 767 million euros for the Army to improve crisis management capabilities; 251.7 million euros for the Federal Ministry of the Interior to strengthen border control, homeland security, and the security apparatus (BKA and BfV); 102 million euros each for the Foreign Office and the Development Ministry to address the root causes of terrorism, for special aid programs, and for interreligious and intercultural dialogues; 25.6 million euros for the Federal Ministry of Justice and the Federal Ministry of Finance to support the attorney general and the combat against money laundering and terrorist financing; 25.1 million euros for the German Intelligence Service; and ten million euros for the establishment of an emergency fund in order to support the victims of terrorist attacks and their families.

First Security Package

This package, in part already prepared before 9/11, focused primarily on two issues: First, it led to the abolishment of the "religious privilege" (*Religionsprivileg*) in the Act Governing Private Association (section 2, paragraph 2 [3]). In the past, this provision guaranteed religious organizations special rights and protection. Now, it became possible to ban them if their purpose or activities run counter to the provisions of criminal law, are directed against the constitutional order, or disregard the "idea of international understanding." This amendment, which entered into force in December 2001, relates in particular to fundamentalist Islamic organizations that do not reject the use of violence as well as to purely profit-making organizations that claim for themselves a special status of a religious group in order to obtain special tax treatment. Based on this decision, German authorities were finally able to ban the organization Caliphate State (December 2001); the Hamas-related, fund-raising association Al-Aqsa (August 2002); and the network Hizb-ut-Tahrir (January 2003).

Second, a new paragraph was included in the Penal Code that criminalized the support of or membership in criminal or terrorist organizations based in other countries (new section 129b).[32] After some parliamentary controversies, this new provision finally came into force in September 2002. Until then, it was not possible under German law to be convicted for membership in a foreign terrorist group as long as this group had not established some kind of formal base in Germany. As with earlier antiterrorism legislation, this new provision again does not provide a legally binding definition of the term *terrorism*. The German law (section 129a) refers only to particular crimes and activities that are considered terrorist acts. There is, however, no reference to the subjective intention of the perpetrators, i.e., whether they, indeed, aim at creating an atmosphere of panic and shock within the population in order to pursue political goals.[33]

Second Security Package

The second package entered into force in January 2002 and covered a broad range of issues since it contained changes in seventeen laws and a number of administrative decrees.[34] The main goal was to strengthen the rights and capabilities of the security authorities. According to the Ministry of the Interior, the amendments should give security agencies the necessary legal powers and improve information exchange between them. They should prevent terrorists from entering Germany and should improve identification measures in visa application procedures. The amendments allow for the use of armed sky marshals from the Federal Border Guard and authorize the use of firearms by security officials on civilian airliners. They should improve border controls, in particular as regards coastal border areas, and the chance to detect extremists who are already in the country. Especially with respect to the last issue, federal police institutions, intelligence services, and law-enforcement agencies were granted the power to obtain information from various public and private services and to access, for example, telecommunication and mail, air traffic, bank accounts, and money flows as well as employment or university records of organizations and individuals who may bear threat to the "idea of international understanding" or the peaceful coexistence of the peoples.[35]

These expanded rights for information gathering are, however, subject to special permissions by the government and controlled by a parliamentary body. Other new provisions are related to extended security checks on employees in sensitive areas (such as airports, railway services, military bases, energy and water supply facilities, chemical companies, and banks). Changes in passport and ID card regulations now provide the legal basis for introducing biometric features other than photographs and signatures. Through this measure, personal documents should become more forgery-proof and, thereby, permit identification beyond doubt.[36]

Many amendments affect, in particular, foreigners and immigrants. A key issue is the extended option for prohibiting foreigners' associations (*Ausländervereine*).[37] They can now be banned if they promote activities outside Germany that are incompatible with basic values respecting the dignity of human beings; if they support, advocate, or encourage the use of violence for political objectives; and if they support groups inside or outside Germany that promote or threaten attacks against persons or other targets.

Correspondingly, the new sections of the Alien Act stipulate that persons who constitute a threat to democracy and freedom or to the security of the Federal Republic or who engage in acts of violence in the pursuit of political goals, who incite the use of force in public, or who are proven members or supporters of an organization that supports international terrorism, shall not be granted entry visas or residence permits.[38] For that reason, the cooperation and data exchange between domestic security authorities and German missions abroad that are responsible for granting visas will be intensified. Laws have also been changed in order to introduce forgery-proof ID cards for persons whose residence is tolerated and for asylum-seekers to provide for the storage of personal data and for the use of these data by security authorities.[39]

Immigration Law

In addition, outside the security package, the new immigration law (entered into force in January 2005), initially aiming at enabling and regulating immigration to Germany, contains some provisions related to the fight against extremism and terrorism. Depending on an "evidence-based threat prognosis," federal or *Länder* institutions have the possibility of issuing a deportation order against persons with a suspected terrorist background or persons who may threaten the public order, including people who publicly propagate hate and violence. In other words, it is no longer necessary to prove the involvement in a planned or committed crime. According to the new rules, these persons can be deported more quickly and more easily than before, because they can only appeal to the Federal Administrative Court and no longer rely on lengthy appeal proceedings.[40] A deportation is not possible if that person is threatened by torture or the death penalty in his/her home country; however he/she has to live under certain restrictions (e.g., regular reports to the authorities, and limited freedom of movement).

Aviation Security Law

In June 2004 the parliament adopted the "Act for the New Regulation of Air Security Tasks" (entered into force in January 2005). It provides the legal basis for the use of military force in cases of hijacked or suspicious civilian planes inside the German airspace that either might attack buildings or sites or could cause serious accidents. In extreme cases, the Minister of Defense can now order combat aircraft to force these planes to land, threaten to deploy weapons against them, or, if these attempts fail, shoot them down (article 14). Previously, the Army was responsible for securing airspace and air traffic since it is the only institution that possesses the necessary means.[41] The law essentially clarifies the rights of the *Bundeswehr* in cases of an extreme emergency situation.[42] The reason for this addition was an incident in January 2003 when a sport airplane flew over Frankfurt and the pilot threatened to crash into the banking towers. He was, fortunately, convinced to land safely and turned out to be a mentally disturbed person without any terrorist background.[43] In February 2006, however, the Federal Constitutional Court declared article 14 of the Aviation Security Law unconstitutional.

Homeland Protection

Closely linked to the issue of air security are other aspects of homeland protection. Similar to the field of domestic security, in cases of emergencies, civilian protection, and the protection of physical infrastructure, various institutions at the federal, *Länder*, or district level hold different competencies. For that reason, the Federal Government pushed for some degree of centralization. For example, in October 2001, it decided to establish a new central information office for biological weapons and a center for biological security at the Robert-Koch-Institute (Berlin), a federal institution under the responsibility of the Federal Ministry of Health for infectious and noninfectious diseases. The office shall gather information on biological weapons, analyze possible dangers, and elaborate proposals for better protecting the population.[44]

In March 2004, the Federal Minister of the Interior and his respective *Länder* colleagues finally agreed to set up a new Federal Office for protecting the population and for assisting in case of catastrophes (*Bundesamt für Bevölkerungsschutz und Katastrophenhilfe*), which replaces the former Federal Office for Civilian Protection (*Bundesamt für den Zivilschutz*). In addition, an information system in cases of greater emergencies (*Deutsches Notfallvorsorge-Informationssystem*, deNIS), a new Joint Communication and Situation Center of federal and *Länder* authorities (*Gemeinsames Melde- und Lagezentrum*, GMLZ), and a satellite-based warning system (*Satellitengestütztes Warnsystem*, SatWas) were established.[45] The governmental and nongovernmental technical services got more capabilities and equipment for rescue and protection measures (e.g., enhanced protection against nuclear, biological, or chemical agents through the Federal Border Guards, and the storage of medicine against smallpox).

Combating Terrorist Financing

The Federal Ministry of Finance issued new regulations for credit institutes and banking systems in order to combat terrorist financing and money laundering.[46] Germany then implemented the recommendations made by the Organization of Economic Cooperation and Development (OECD)-based Financial Action Task Force (FATF). For example, banks and credit institutes are now obliged to create "adequate internal security systems for combating money laundering and fraudulent activities detrimental to the institutions themselves" as well as to implement a strict "know your customer" policy.[47] Stronger regulations and control mechanisms also exist for credit card companies, estate agents, business and tax consultants, as well as for owners of banks and insurance companies. In addition, a Financial Intelligence Unit (FIU) was established at the BKA, which shall coordinate and evaluate the information in cases of suspected money laundering and terrorist financing, and work closely together with police and law enforcement authorities.

Foreign, Security, and Development Policy

Combating terrorism did not only become a domestic priority. It also became a key objective in German foreign and security policy. First of all, Germany strongly supports multilateral institutions and international organizations in combating terrorism, in particular within the North Atlantic Treaty Organization (NATO), EU, United Nations (UN), the Organization for Security and Cooperation in Europe (OSCE), and the Group of Eight (G8).[48] In order to coordinate these activities, the Foreign Office appointed a special ambassador post-9/11 for "international combat and prevention of terrorism" and expanded the respective unit. These merely diplomatic efforts include the drafting of counterterrorism charters and resolutions, the establishment of monitoring bodies and task forces (e.g., UN Anti-terrorism Committee and G8 counterterrorism action group) formulating recommendations for governments (e.g., in combating terrorist financing), agreeing on action plans (e.g., EU Action Plan of 2001), and more generally, strengthening international law with regard to combating terrorism.

With regard to the last issue, Germany had already ratified ten of the twelve UN counterterrorism conventions before 9/11 (adopted by the UN between 1963 and 1999). In July 2002, the *Bundestag* ratified the two latest conventions in order to underscore Germany's support for the UN counterterrorism regime. Germany is also in favor of a new UN convention on nuclear terrorism and a global antiterrorism convention, including a binding definition of terrorism, which has been debated at the UN level for several years.

A major shift in German policy was marked by the deployment of military force for counterterrorism purposes. Up to 9/11, the fight against terrorism was understood as a strict nonmilitary issue left to police and law-enforcement. The challenge of the al Qaeda network, however, proved that under certain conditions, the use of military force might be necessary in order to destroy a larger terrorist base, to hunt groups of terrorists and fighters, or to observe transit and escape routes. Here, the most relevant aspect is Germany's commitment to the international, U.S.-led counterterrorism initiave, Operation Enduring Freedom.[49]

The original German participation with up to 3,900 soldiers was subdivided into six components:[50] NBC (Nuclear, Biological, Chemical) reaction teams (approximately eight hundred soldiers), medical service (approximately two hundred and fifty), special forces (so-called KSK forces, approximately one hundred), air transport forces (approximately five hundred), maritime forces (approximately one thousand and eight hundred), as well as general supporting forces (approximately four hundred and fifty). The German contingent was active in different ways: The NBC teams were placed in Kuwait (February 2002 to July 2003) to assist local authorities and the deployed U.S. forces in cases of a terrorist attack with weapons of mass destruction.[51] From winter 2002 to fall 2003, the German KSK Special Forces were active in Afghanistan and worked jointly with antiterror squads from other countries. Finally, the German Marines, based in Djibouti, observed the Gulf of Aden, the Horn of Africa, and the coast of Eastern Africa in order to deter or to stop Taliban or al Qaeda associates moving from Afghanistan to the Gulf region or to failed states like Somalia.

Step by step, these tasks were reduced: In November 2003, the German parliament renewed the mandate for Enduring Freedom for another year, but reduced the overall contingent to a limit of 3,100 soldiers.[52] In practice, however, only three hundred soldiers were still engaged in December 2003. A year later the number went down to ninety involved in the maritime operation at the Horn of Africa.

Beyond that immediate response, German foreign and security policy necessarily addresses a number of long-term issues, which could have an impact on the future opportunities for transnational terrorist networks to grow and to expand. The most crucial undertaking is the broad German military and civilian engagement in Afghanistan after the defeat of the Taliban regime. Germany hosted the first peace conference in Bonn in December 2001, which brought all relevant parties (excluding the Taliban) to the table and established rules and timetables for the establishment of an interim government, the drafting of a new constitution, and the preparation of elections (Bonn Process).

In order to safeguard the political process, Germany supports the UN-mandated International Security Assistance Force (ISAF) mission with 2,200 soldiers (November 2004) and established two Provisional Reconstruction Teams (PRTs) in Kunduz and Fayzabad, both under ISAF mandate (together up to four hundred fifty soldiers).[53] The security presence is backed up by a whole range of civilian activities—such as the rehabilitation of the energy sector, supporting schools and education, fostering of nongovernmental organizations (NGOs) and civil society, as well as assisting institution-building and state structures.

Within the international community, Germany serves as "lead nation" for the establishment of an Afghan police force and, thus, provides police training facilities in Kabul, Kunduz, and Herat. Since 2002, Germany has spent 80 million euros each year for Afghanistan (cost of the military forces not included). At the Afghanistan Conference in Berlin (2004), the Federal Government agreed to provide another 320-million-euro aid package for the years 2005 to 2008.[54] Clearly, the overall goal is to stabilize Afghanistan and to prevent a return of Taliban or other extremists.

Another key aspect became the policy toward Islamic countries in general. After September 11, the Foreign Office quickly appointed a special envoy for the "Dialogue with the Islamic world." He and his staff keep contacts with governmental and nongovernmental organizations in Islamic countries, try to identify possible cooperation partners, and evaluate the development in these countries. Within the program "European-Islamic Culture Dialogue," directed by the Foreign Office and implemented by various organizations (e.g., Goethe Institutes and German Academic Exchange Service), civil society projects in Islamic countries are financed, in particular with regard to media, education, and young people.[55]

In order to prevent terrorism in particular and the spread of political extremism in general, Germany pursues other more general objectives via diplomatic, security, and development measures—such as supporting international initiatives for solving regional conflicts (e.g., Israel/Palestine, Kosovo, and Chechnya), fostering democratization processes, protecting human rights and the promotion of the rule of law, emphasizing poverty reduction and the fight against HIV/AIDS, as well as supporting state-building projects and security-sector reforms (e.g., Balkans, East Timor, and Georgia). In April 2004, Germany started also to train Iraqi criminal police officers in the United Arab Emirates; by the end of the year, more than 400 officers have benefited from this education conducted by BKA trainers.

For connecting these instruments and activities, the government finally adopted the Action Plan, *Civilian Crisis Prevention, Conflict Resolution and Post-conflict Peace-Building* (May 2004). This whole-of-government document attempts to develop German capabilities further and to ensure a greater coherence among ministries—in particular between the Foreign Office (AA), the Ministry of Defense (BMVg), and the Ministry for Economic Cooperation and Development (BMZ). It comprises more than 160 specific initiatives for conflict management and prevention, which are explicitly seen as an "integral part of efforts to combat international terrorism."[56] The Action Plan, thereby, points to the complex interplay between combating terrorism and other activities in foreign and development policy: "On the one hand, attributing the growth of terrorism merely to poverty and bad governance is a dangerous oversimplification. On the other hand, however, it is indisputable that the highly hazardous mix of fundamentalism, smouldering regional conflicts, the danger of deployment of weapons of mass destruction (WMD) and the threat of terrorist attacks can only be defused through a system of global cooperative security. Without the resolution of fundamental political and societal conflicts, which are often the breeding ground for terrorism, this task cannot be mastered."[57]

Dilemmas and Open Questions

The post-9/11 counterterrorism measures led to new dilemmas and shed light on old, well-known problems of Germany's domestic security architecture. The range of issues comprises a number of interrelated legal, administrative, and political problems, which are disputed among the different political parties and within the German public. Therefore, the debate about internal and external security policy is still ongoing, and the process of adjusting structures and instruments to the new challenge of transnational terrorism has so far not been concluded. The most pressing open questions and disputes are the following:

- *Civil liberties versus security concerns*: As in other Western democracies, for Germany, one first key controversy arises about the appropriate balancing of civil liberties and security. On both sides of the argument, the German past plays a crucial role. On the one hand, most parties would agree that guarantee of internal and external security is a necessary precondition for assuring civil liberties. This idea is by and large acknowledged in the German context by the concept of *wehrhafte Demokratie* (democracy capable of defending itself), which implies that democracy should be defended against its enemies and that civil liberties and democratic principles should not be abused by groups that ultimately want to destroy the democratic order. Thereby, post-1945 Germany drew one lesson from the Weimar Republic and the fact that the Nazi party had been able to gain power by legal means. On the other hand, the yearning for security should not become a threat for civil liberties and the rule of law, which one wants to protect in the first place. Also due to the Nazi period, today's German political culture, as enshrined in the German constitution, is largely shaped by a strong emphasis on human rights, fundamental rights, and personal freedom, among them in particular the right to privacy, personal data protection rights, freedom of religion, as well as the rights to freedom of expression, association, and assembly. According to critics, these rights are now challenged by the extended power for the security authorities and by certain counterterrorism measures, e.g., surveillance, grid search, gathering and storage of personal data, phone-tapping, or eavesdropping.[58] In particular, rights for foreigners and asylum-seekers are reduced and restricted significantly. Most notable are the possible ban of religious organizations, the extension of expulsion grounds, the limited access to appeal proceedings, or the restriction of the "non-refoulement" principle for asylum-seekers as enshrined by international law which gives refugees under certain conditions safeguards against deportation to their home country.[59] One way to manage the general dilemma is reflected in the decision of the government to introduce "sunset provisions" into the most disputed laws and regulations, which have to be evaluated and renewed after five years.

● *Conflicting objectives in domestic and foreign policies*: Another debate concerns conflicting objectives between the imperatives of domestic security on the one hand and the underlying goals of external policies (e.g., trade, development, and foreign policy) on the other hand. While the former is concerned with controlling and restricting access to Germany, the latter is concerned with promoting, generally speaking, freedom of trade, communication, and travelling. While the Ministry of the Interior is interested in labelling terrorist groups as such, the Foreign Office has to take into account that some of these groups are needed in order to solve regional conflicts (e.g., Hamas/Palestine, LTTE/Sri Lanka). While the domestic security authorities put foreign students, in particular from Islamic countries, under special surveillance, development policy promotes programs in various countries for higher and professional education in Germany. These somehow unavoidable tensions became rather obvious when in 2004 the Ministry of the Interior and the Foreign Office clashed over the visa policy. The discovery of corruption and fraud scandals in some German embassies was seen a "security risk," since not only organized crime but also potential extremists may have profited from those practices.[60] In addition, in November 2003, the German embassy in Algiers gave a visa to an Algerian citizen who is apparently a member of a group that is mentioned on the EU list of terrorist organizations. After these incidents, the Minister of the Interior demanded a more restrictive visa regime, and the opposition called for a special parliamentary investigation. Indeed, the Foreign Office had to revise its general visa policy, which, since 1999, has favored explicitly the freedom of movement and the opportunities for travelling to Germany.

● *Questioning the distinction of internal and external security*: Related to the former issue is the question whether the distinction of internal and external security is still relevant vis-à-vis a number of transnational threats, such as terrorism, organized crime, trafficking of drugs and human beings, or the proliferation of materials for WMD. In particular, the legal, administrative, and political separation of civilian protection, police, border guards, special forces, military, diplomats, and intelligence is questioned by experts and politicians. They point not only to problems of information-sharing and coordination, but also to operational questions in preventing or reacting to emergencies. Therefore, some favor a closer linkage and networking between police, military, and civilian protection services, including joint analysis, exercises, and training.[61] One interesting aspect is the fact that in missions abroad (e.g., Kosovo or Afghanistan), both German police and military have to work closely together on a day-to-day basis; the same would not be possible inside Germany. In particular, the Christian Democrats would like to blur the line between police and the military; they call for the legal possibility for the *Bundeswehr* to be active domestically in cases of terrorist attacks or terrorist threats.[62]

● *Fragmentation of the security apparatus:* As described earlier, the security apparatus in Germany is fragmented in two ways. At the horizontal level, Germany is divided into various agencies (e.g., police, border guards, law-enforcement, and different intelligence services). At the vertical level, Germany is characterized by the sharing and division of powers between several federal and *Länder* institutions. This fairly decentralized structure has certain advantages since it relies heavily on institutions with intimate knowledge about extremist or criminal structures at the local or regional level. The crucial problem, however, is not about information gathering but about information sharing, information management, and common analysis. In other words, while searching for information and investigations could be done in a decentralized manner, the evaluation and analysis of them have to be done in a more centralized and coordinated manner. Since 9/11, a number of steps have been taken in that direction. For example, in 2001 the Federal Criminal Police Office set up an "information board" as a coordination mechanism between various institutions. In June 2004, after lengthy debates, the Minister of the Interior and his *Länder* colleagues finally decided to establish a joint database on Islamic extremism at the BKA that should contain all information gathered by the police and the intelligence services. In addition, a Joint Counter-Terrorism Center was established by the end of 2004 which is subdivided in two physically separated, but interacting branches: One comprises of the BKA and *Länder* Police Departments, the other of representatives of the intelligence community. Still debated are other decisions, such as strengthening the central role of the BKA in counterterrorism, the establishment of a central database on suspected terrorists and known Islamists, and the restructuring of the BfV and *Länder* Offices that make these offices dependent on the BfV. All these issues, however, are very much contested because of the political rivalry between federal and *Länder* governments, which are ruled by different parties and coalitions.[63] The decisions necessary can only be taken by consent of the two levels, and the *Länder* would have to accept a transfer of competencies to the federal government.

● *Multilevel governance in Justice and Home Affairs*: The former problem becomes even more complex when one takes the European dimension into account. The EU with its intergovernmental policy in Justice and Home Affairs adds a de facto third layer to the two German levels. Because of the internal market and the dismantling of border controls between member states (so-called Schengen system), more and more decisions on domestic security issues are made in Brussels, and the amount of coordination necessarily increases. This development concerns, inter alia, the control of external borders, visa policy, immigration and asylum regulations, fight against transnational organized crime, and, certainly, counterterrorism measures. The integration process in this area is far from smooth since the twenty-five member states bring different legal traditions, security architectures, and threat perceptions as well as differing experiences in dealing with terrorism to the table. Despite these difficulties, the implications for Germany are already manifold: At the operational level, the German structure needs to be more transparent and accessible for foreign security authorities in order to foster close cooperation and information-sharing among EU member states. At the political level, EU institutions, bodies, and instruments (including Europol, Eurojust, European Police Academy, Task Force of the Chiefs of Police, or EU arrest warrant) have to be strengthened and, therefore, the German government would have to agree to some kind of transfer of competencies, which is not an easy task considering the divisions of power within the German system. At the legal level, German law, including constitutional rights and appeal proceedings, may conflict with EU law, regulations, or directives and may hinder closer cooperation among member states. An illustration for that is the failure of the EU arrest warrant in Germany when the Federal Constitutional Court decided in July 2005 that the implementation of the EU legislation into German law did not meet constitutional requirements—in particular concerning the question under which circumstances German citizens can be extradited to other EU member states.[64]

Conclusion

Similar to the situation in other Western countries, 9/11 and the threat of transnational terrorism also resulted by and large in a *securitization* of the political agenda in Germany, in other words policies usually not related to security matters became "securitized." In public discourse, many issues and policies are now indeed linked directly or indirectly to internal and external security concerns (e.g., alien law; immigration and visa policy; association law; reforms in banking systems; interreligious and intercultural dialogue; and economic, humanitarian, and development aid). Ranging from home affairs and justice to financial and economic policies, and from defense and intelligence to foreign and development policies, various ministries and agencies associate and legitimize their activities with counterterrorism efforts. Indeed, 9/11 called into question long-standing approaches and beliefs on security with regard to both German domestic and foreign policy. Despite the range of activities and changes, still no cross-governmental strategy exists for counterterrorism (e.g., governmental White Paper), which systematically links the various issues and measures.

One key aspect is the question of how to integrate *operational* as well as *structural* counterterrorism policies. On the one hand, many changes in law and policies, in particular in home affairs, refer to operational counterterrorism, i.e., measures that primarily focus on actively combating and arresting terrorists, destroying their bases, prohibiting terrorist financing, and preventing their acts. On the other hand, Germany is undertaking various efforts in diplomacy, security, and development policy in order to address structural counterterrorism, in other words, focusing on the societal and political causes of terrorism, preventing the establishment of groups, and aiming at the prevention of existing terrorist groups from growing and becoming manifest. Both approaches should reinforce and not contradict each other. This is not an easy undertaking, since operational counterterrorism, in particular when military force is used, is necessarily repressive and may even trigger terrorist reactions and the formation of terrorist groups. Waiting for successes in structural counterterrorism, however, is equally dangerous because of imminent threats that have to be tackled in the first place.

Against this background, German counterterrorism policy indeed aims at balancing these approaches. Therefore, at the international level the German government argues that counterterrorism has to be understood as a *multidimensional* and *multilateral* endeavor that cannot be reduced to a certain set of instruments (e.g., the use of military force) and should not be carried out by unilateral actions that would be counterproductive in combating terrorism. For exactly these reasons, the government of Gerhard Schröder and Joschka Fischer (in line with the overwhelming majority of the German public) opposed the U.S. invasion in Iraq. While the U.S. government, at least in its rhetoric, saw the war against Saddam Hussein as an integral part of its "global war on terror," in Germany most decision-makers and experts distinguished strictly between the two issues. For them, there was no link between Saddam Hussein's regime and the transnational network of al Qaeda—as later admitted by prominent members of the U.S. government. Moreover, already months before the war, German intelligence and security experts issued several warnings that a U.S.-led war in Iraq might even make the fight against transnational terrorism more difficult and would put at risk the emerging international consensus on terrorism.

4

ITALY

Germana Tappero Merlo and Sergio Marchisio

PART I
by Germana Tappero Merlo

This section deals with the governmental counterterrorism strategy in Italy from the beginning of the 1970s to the beginning of the new millennium. During this long period, the strategy has radically changed as terrorist activities in Italy have been modified. In order to fully understand this evolution, it is necessary to take into account the specific nature of Italian terrorism in its two-fold aspects: left-wing terrorism, during its initial period, aimed at fighting so-called capitalist society, while right-wing terrorism aimed at pushing the state in an authoritarian direction. In this sense, one can observe that the two components of Italian terrorism have always had antithetical aims, making it difficult for anti-terrorism strategies to succeed. Counterterrorism strategies adopted two fundamental operative tactics: infiltration and repentance. The first was directed at penetrating terrorist groups and was based on wide coordination among counterterrorism units; the second used the testimony of repenting terrorists who, in order to obtain some judicial advantages, revealed information about names, places, hideouts, logistics, and ideological supporters.

The elucidation of a counterterrorism strategy was complicated by two elements: first, the behavior of Mafia organizations that, at the beginning of the 1980s, began to collaborate with terrorist organizations or carried out terrorist attacks themselves; second, at the end of the 1990s, a worrying social uneasiness triggered new outbreaks of violence, strongly supported by imported foreign terrorists. These developments meant that totally new forms of counterterrorism policies had to be devised.

Now, at the beginning of the third millennium, Italian terrorism presents specific new traits. The end of competition between the two superpower blocs—the West, founded on the free market, and the East,

founded on a communist and centralized system—has certainly attenu-
ated the ideological foundations on which terrorist activities were based
during the post–World War II period. After the fall of the Berlin Wall and
the end of the communist experience in Europe, right-wing terrorism has
radically changed its targets as the communist threat has vanished. Violent right-wing terrorism in Italy is now directed at fighting the loss of
national identity as a consequence of lax immigration policies. In this
case, counterterrorism measures adopted to combat left-wing subversion,
such as the repentance of terrorists, have not been successful against
these movements that have often been confused with *skinhead* groups or
soccer supporters. Left-wing terrorism, in turn, seems to be more linked
to fighting against globalization and powerful economic interests, both
private and institutional, and to supporting the infiltration of foreign terrorism, mainly belonging to Muslim fundamentalism.

The existence of increasing international links among Italian terrorists and foreign subversive organizations has made it difficult to define
a winning counterterrorism strategy. In order to better understand the
nature of these new terrorist threats in Italy and to specify future
counterterrorism policies, we need to understand how the successful
measures used against terrorism during the 1970s and the 1980s can help
against terrorism in the new millennium.

Historical Background

As we indicated previously, the terrorist phenomenon in Italy, born
at the end of the 1960s and vitalized through the following decade, had
two main ideological connotations: extreme right and extreme left. In
this sense, it was fundamentally close to the terrorist experience in other
European countries like France and Germany. It was not however a struggle
of an ethnic or religious group, as with Euzkadi Ta Azkatasuna (ETA) in
Spain or the Irish Republican Army (IRA) in Northern Ireland.

Left-wing terrorism in Italy started with the ideological assumption of extraparliamentary political groups that acted in the spirit of a
proletarian revolution in order to weaken and even destroy the democratic society. This action rapidly degenerated into armed struggle,
both political and economic, against some of the most prominent leaders of the existing political groups. At the beginning of the 1970s,
many terrorist groups in Italy were identified by government agencies. Among them were *Gruppi di Azione Partigiana* (GAP, Partisan
Action Groups), *Brigate Rosso* (BR, Red Brigades), *Nuclei Armati
Proletari* (NAP, Armed Proletarian Groups), *Prima Linea* (PL, First
Front), and *Partito Comunista Combattente* (PCC, Fighting Communist Party). Their supporters were usually young people who had either a factory or university background.

The extreme-right subversive groups, however, had the common objective of directing Italian institutions in an authoritarian way and fighting communism. In the 1970s, this clearly identified movement engaged in bloody indiscriminate massacres of civilians, which had a strong psychological impact in Italy. Among several groups, the most active were *Ordine Nuovo* (ON, New Order), which concentrated its activities among young people, and *Avanguardia Nazionale* (AN, National Vanguard). They had common ideological roots coming from the historical tradition of fascism and the *Repubblica Sociale Italiana* (Italian Social Republic), created by Benito Mussolini during the last half of World War II. Both tried and succeeded in involving not only private individuals, but also members of state institutions. In this sense, the extreme right-wing groups were mainly responsible for the so-called strategy of tension, an escalation of violent actions against Italian citizens and institutions.

In the 1970s, both extreme left-wing and right-wing groups started to demonstrate violently in city squares. It was a matter of Italian students demonstrating in the wake of the French 1968 protests, with the trade unions increasing tension by adding their distinctive voice. Later these demonstrations exploded into violent urban guerrilla attacks involving the militants of the left- and right-wing extremist groups. As time passed, the terrorist opposition assumed more and more violent tones with bomb attacks on party offices or newspaper agencies, and the killing of people active in other movements who did not agree with such strategies.

Subversive groups in Italy adopted different operative tactics during a second phase, in the 1970s, when left-wing groups began to be responsible for crimes such as violent robberies, the killing of police officers, and the kidnapping of industrialists and judges. These acts were not aimed at getting money in exchange for hostages, but were justified as a form of political propaganda or as a way of freeing militants. The kidnapping of men, who were considered to be representatives of the "capitalist" system that the extreme left-wing groups (in particular the BR) wanted to destroy also served to undermine political institutions. Through "political" trials of their victims, the terrorists were able to manipulate public opinion and humiliate the highest public authorities.

The most significant among those kidnappings was that of Judge Mario Sossi, who had inflicted heavy punishments on left-wing terrorists, in May 1974; but the BR's most aggressive act, and one that even today is shrouded in mystery, was the kidnapping in 1978 of Aldo Moro, the chairman of the Christian Democrats, Italy's largest political party. This kidnapping should have led its perpetrators to gain the support of other more extreme movements of left-wing subversion, but the popularity of the BR decreased after the killing of its hostage. This act cancelled the limited support received by terrorists up to then and failed to achieve the declared aim of attracting wider popular support.

After the tragic end of the Moro case, a split developed in the BR organization, which was followed by a proliferation of various-sized groups that had a variety of targets: the *militarist wing* on one side and the *political activist wing* on the other. Left-wing subversive groups then passed on to more violent and bloody actions that upset most Italians in the years between 1979, when Judge Emilio Alessandrini, one of the most active judges in investigations on terrorism, was killed, and 1981, when Ciro Cirillo, a Neapolitan politician, and Gen. James Lee Dozier, a U.S. officer responsible for North Atlantic Treaty Organization (NATO) logistics in Italy, were kidnapped. The handling of Cirillo's case revealed, for the first time, shady links between terrorists and organized crime. The counterterrorism strategy in the Cirillo case was clearly inadequate: the state authorities accepted negotiation with the terrorists, and the hostage was released following the payment of a sum of money. The role of the so-called Camorra (criminal organization active mainly in Naples and in the southern regions) was not clear, even if an indirect support to the liberation of the hostage was confirmed.

The end of the Dozier kidnapping was completely different: the action carried out by the Italian special forces to free the hostage was so brilliant that their reputation, so greatly harmed after the failure of the Cirillo case, was fully restored. The liberation of the American general was a turning point for the terrorist organization: the terrorists publicly declared that the organization as it had been created by the historical leaders in the 1970s was now outdated and that, following the ignominious end of the Dozier case, their new policy would be one of "strategic retreat."

The last kidnappings made by the BR were acts of intimidation, designed as propaganda to exert psychological pressure on society.[1] They were the last attempts of a decimated organization, divided in its political aims and in its tactical strategies, to carry out the armed struggle.

On the opposite side, the right-wing terrorist groups were responsible for bomb attacks that assumed aspects of indiscriminate massacre of civilians on trains and in banks, public squares, and stations. The most famous attacks were at the Piazza Fontana in Milan (1969), followed by Peteano (1972), Piazza della Loggia in Brescia (1974), the "Italicus" train (again in 1974), and finally the Bologna railway station (1980).

The investigations into those massacres and the trials that followed did not lead to the identification of those actually responsible. In fact, it is well known that the Italian judicial system has not yet been able to completely unveil the mysteries of the bloodiest slaughters. From the analyses made by the investigation committees, which were set up by parliament to throw light on those destabilizing events, it can certainly be said that subversive activities of all kinds during the 1970s could have been stopped once and for all, if more resolute and immediate repressive action were taken by Italian political and judicial authorities. This assessment emerged clearly from the investigations made by several parliamentary commissions on terrorism. A stronger intervention by the Italian institutions would have been able to prevent disorganized, embryonic, and immature cells of extreme left-wing and right-wing organizations from becoming effective instruments of armed struggle that would find strong support from foreign terrorist organizations.

Counterterrorism Activities in the 1970s and 1980s: Infiltration and Repentance

In 1974, the first Italian counterterrorism agency was set up. It succeeded in centralizing and integrating the efforts of all the police corps in the country to fight terrorism. The practice of security forces infiltrating terrorist groups was adopted in order to obtain a complete picture of subversive underground activities. In a short time, the founders and historical heads of the BR were captured; the terrorists' logistical bases (so-called dens) were found; and support from nontraditional groups, militants still in prison, trade unions activists, and cells in industry and universities, was identified.

In 1975, parliament approved an emergency bill, the so-called Legge Reale,[2] which was strengthened in 1980 by the Cossiga Law. These two sets of rules legitimated police intervention, suspending the release from jail of those charged with the most serious crimes, such as homicide, kidnapping, extortion, bombings, and massacres, and extending the terms of pretrial detention. The laws gave wide powers to the police, allowing them in urgent cases to search premises without a search warrant.

This counterterrorism strategy relied on tactics and legal instruments already tested in the fight against the Mafia. It did not inflict a final blow to the subversive movement, but offered remarkable support to the work of operational units and represented a turning point in the struggle against armed subversion. Still today, it contains a remarkable means to fight terrorism effectively.

The success achieved by the counterterrorism units in the 1970s was not yet complete because of the "stop and go" policy imposed by political authorities on repressive action. That is to say that there were periods of tight control, interspersed, with periods when pressure was relaxed. On more than one occasion, this easing of pressure allowed terrorist groups to reorganize and to reach more dangerous levels. The most evident case showing the uneasiness of the police forces occurred in 1976, when the BR killed the prosecutor of Genoa, Francesco Coco, and his escort. It was the first case of the BR attacking with the intention of killing its victim in a period when the state's response was clearly disappointing.

The limiting factors of antiterrorist activities in Italy in the 1970s consisted mainly in a lack of coordination among the investigations and operations carried out by intelligence agencies and by different police forces throughout the territory. The problem of subversion was often not clearly understood. There was inopportune institutional interference as well as the dismantlement of efficient security units, which unavoidably led to an excessive and bloody extension of a phenomenon that could have been circumscribed and dismantled at its origin.

It was only toward the end of the 1970s that the so-called phenomenon of repentance of some terrorists arose, and it was destined to inflict a blow on left-wing subversion in Italy. In fact, it was by using the testimony of some terrorists that both the police forces and judicial authorities collaborated in the destruction of terrorist organizations. As a reward for their collaboration, the repentant terrorists, or *pentitos*, obtained short sentences, early release from jail, and even the chance to start a new life abroad. Their revelations of names, places, political links, and financial support stopped all subversive activities. This measure, together with efficient counterterrorist units and, above all, clear political will to act resolutely against terrorism, were effective weapons. The repentance of terrorists also opened the road to the *dissociation*[3] of those militants who, although not convinced of any possible further evolution of the terrorist movements to which they belonged, did not wish to disown their origin, but publicly renounced the armed struggle, repudiating violence as a political instrument. Although frequently these people admitted their own responsibility, they did not denounce their companions.

The repentance and the dissociation by some of the terrorists of the subversive groups was an exclusively Italian phenomenon that marked the turning point, at the end of the 1970s, in the struggle against terrorism. The so-called die-hard terrorists, who were determined to support the armed revolution to its bitter end, launched threats of retaliation against repentant former companions; and so, a new phase of the struggle began, defined as transversal revenge. This phase was characterized by the murder of relatives of the informers. However, these murders did not stop some terrorists from declaring their repentance and dissociation.

The state's vigorous response, strongly supported by the rejection of subversive action by the public, brought about the political and military defeat of the original armed party. Between 1981 and 1983, the security forces identified and arrested 54 percent of those people who were in some way involved in terrorism. They uncovered about half of the hiding places and logistic bases, and confiscated about 60 percent of the arms and munitions in the hands of subversive groups. By the end of 1987, about four thousand people—militants and supporters—had been arrested, with one-third of them belonging to right-wing subversive groups.

The repentance system was widely successful again in the 1990s, in the fight against the Mafia, which increasingly forged hidden links with terrorist activity. With the collaboration of high-ranking members of the Mafia, the inquiry authorities obtained outstanding results that led to the total destruction of some sectors of Italian criminal activities. At the same time, the repentance of members of the Mafia raised the heated debate about the credibility of *pentitos* and whether it was appropriate for the state to guarantee them not only early release and protection through reduced sentences but also substantial financial support. In this latter case, the success of this strategy against criminal organizations was not so brilliant as the success against terrorism.

International Connections and Increasing Difficulties in Counterterrorism Strategies

The counterterrorism strategy based on repentance brought some immediate results, such as the dismembering of operative structures, the so-called columns, set up in many Italian towns; and the imprisonment of the most active and dangerous militants, responsible for the most bloody actions of subversive groups. But, in spite of these positive results, the BR, with the help of detailed support offered by foreign organizations, such as the French *Action Directe* (AD) and the German *Rote Armee Fraktion* (RAF, Red Army Faction), reorganized itself and set up new bases. It is not yet possible to give a detailed description of those international relations during the Cold War period, but we can say the climate of ideological conflict between Western and Eastern blocs, subversive movements in the Middle East, and revolutionary groups in Latin America influenced the terrorist struggle in Italy, guaranteeing different groups financial and logistic support, and supplying them with arms and appropriate training.

In the middle of the 1970s, Italian terrorists were equipped with war materiel that usually came from Arab countries. Those were the years during which Libya heavily armed the Palestinians of the so-called Front of Refusal. It was a group that already had close ties with the Soviet Union and was very active in Lebanon, the country in which many Italian terrorists were trained. Both men and weapons for the BR, PL, and other groups belonging to extreme left-wing subversive movements were ferried along the Italy–Cyprus–Lebanon route. During their trials, the BR repentants spoke about this connection, which lasted for a long time, and also about the involvement of East European intelligence agencies, especially the Soviet KGB. Also during the inquiries into the main bloody episodes at the end of the 1970s, testimony was collected on the hypothesis that a central agency of subversion was situated outside Italy.[4] The close network of international links existed for both "red" (left-wing) and for "black" (right-wing) terrorism. For the latter, the international links endured at least as long as the three dictatorships in Spain, Portugal, and Greece survived in Europe.

Certainly, Italian terrorism of both colors had an origin, evolution, and identity that were, above all if not exclusively, Italian. But international connections started with the crisis and tensions between East and West, such as when the Atlantic Alliance asked member nations in Europe to re-arm with missiles. In this case, terrorist action was directed against NATO bases in West Germany and in Italy, and was carried out partly under the guise of a pacifist movement.

The international terrorist network, although divided in its goals, evolved into a loose coalition to protect wanted militants. It later favored the creation of other, less important groups. Already in 1979, following the police policy of stepping up the fight against both left-wing and right-wing subversion, the number of terrorist groups operating in Italy multiplied until it reached 269, its all-time peak. Of this number, 217 were left-wing subversive groups and 52 were right-wing. The division into so many groups prevented them from operating efficiently and carrying out the "long-term war," which they often proclaimed in their propaganda. But at the same time, the counterterrorism forces found greater difficulty in uncovering and fighting the subversive movements than they did when the number of subversive groups was smaller.

Some key members of Italian terrorist organizations emigrated clandestinely to other European countries, particularly to France. In general, no extradition was allowed for "political" crimes under the 1957 European Convention on extradition, and terrorism was too often defined by French authorities as a "political crime." This is why, in the middle of the 1980s, France gave hospitality to two hundred Italian terrorists who were on the wanted list. Only toward the end of that decade did this official attitude change, even if only slightly.

During the 1980s, in spite of the international support given to terrorist movements, the fight against subversion was having some deterrent effects and, after the imprisonment of the BR leaders, generated a strategic retreat. Nevertheless, terrorism was not completely defeated: the work of recruitment continued actively and successfully, thanks to this international support. The new targets for terrorist outrages testified to how fast the new BR adapted its strategies to the new changes in the political and international economic situation in those years. In the 1980s, terrorism turned to those individuals whom it called "imperialist leaders" and the leaders of the "new reformism," in other words, the representatives of universities, trade unions, government, and the entrepreneurial world, who were considered to be responsible for their work in the economic and social field. Documents were found in the hiding places identified, showing agreement on joint actions among Italian terrorists, the French AD, and the German RAF.

From that time, people began to speak of *Euroterrorism* being based in France and made up of Italian refugees, with new militants arriving from Italy and Germany. If the joint claims were not irrefutable evidence of joint responsibility for the attacks, they revealed a change in the climate compared to the past when the BR defended its national ideological roots. Because of the logistic problems caused by the highly complex organization of an underground network, and the fact that there were few new recruits, the remaining members of the BR also tried to establish links with European and Middle Eastern terrorist groups in order to find a new and more effective ideological classification. In those years, in fact, there was no efficient coordination among European police, who were impeded by a lack of cooperation laws among the majority of the countries. As seen above, national security forces were successful only because terrorist repentance became increasingly widespread. Also the Italian intelligence agencies ("Servizi segreti"), even when reorganized at the end of the 1970s, were not efficient in counteracting international cooperation among subversive movements.

The difficulties in organizing successful, international counter-terrorism action served the interests of the terrorists.

Subversion in the 1990s: Mafia Terrorism and New Fighting Strategies

To better understand the evolution of the terrorist threat in Italy in the new millennium, it is necessary to clarify terrorist links with the Mafia. The two phenomena, terrorism and Mafia, seemed to be historically in opposition, although there is evidence of sporadic, dramatic collaboration between them during the 1980s and 1990s. The few remaining members of the former left-wing terrorist organization, in fact, tried and succeeded to establish links with organized crime in the south of Italy in order to finance the reorganization of the movement. This collusion was confirmed at the beginning of 1986, when, during an important trial against Sicilian crime, the former mayor of Florence, Lando Conti, was killed by the BR as a diversionary action. In the statement made by the BR after the assassination, it was claimed that prosecuting the Mafia diverted "public opinion from the real problems of the country." In the mind of the BR, the Mafia was not the real danger the country had to face. The inquiry committees that investigated Conti's killing agreed that both the Mafia and the heads of the terrorist organization wanted Conti's murder in order to divert attention from the Palermo trial.

This link between terrorism and organized crime was the impetus behind a new wave of hideous terrorist actions. Such actions began to hit Italy in 1992 with the fatal attacks on judges Giovanni Falcone and Paolo Borsellino, two men who were very active in the struggle against organized crime. Shortly after, in the summer of 1993, centers of art in

Florence, Milan, and Rome were the targets of some of the most spectacular terrorist acts.

This phenomenon has been described as *Mafia terrorism*. It has been proved, in fact, that the massacres of civilians carried out by the Mafia, from the middle of the 1980s onward, were warning signs indicating its new operative strategy. The investigation into the dynamite attack on the train *Rapido 904* (the so-called Christmas Massacre) in December 1984 revealed that the attack was organized by one of the Sicilian Mafia gangs.[5] The Mafia action in 1984 was inspired by terrorist activity in order to "divert the nation's attention" from the positive results that were being achieved in the fight against organized crime through the collaboration of repentant members of Mafia gangs.

From the trials that followed, it clearly emerged that the Mafia acted "with terrorist aims and to subvert constitutional order." Traditionally, Mafia organizations have no interest in overthrowing governments and weakening the social order of a nation; they need a solid economy that makes it easy for illegal trade to prosper. Public institutions became targets for Mafia attacks as soon as the measures taken by public authorities began to undermine the Mafia's structure. It was a real war during which the state went through alternate successful and unsuccessful phases, and the Italian Mafia had to make some radical changes to its organization.

Thus, two very different realities came together, as a result of this situation.

At the beginning of the 1990s, the Mafia adopted terrorist tactics. The counterterrorism policy leaders decided to fight back, using the same strategies that had been adopted against subversion, for example, repentance of its members and the establishment of specific police agencies, such as the *Direzione Investigativa Antimafia* (Anti-Mafia Investigative Agency, DIA), created in 1991. This strategy marked the first important step to counteract Mafia actions as if they were subversive activities. The DIA is still operating successfully by using a three-pronged approach: local analysis, repression, and, above all, relations with foreign police agencies.

This approach has been strengthened by a series of measures including: the introduction, in the Italian legal system, of a new type of crime, the "Mafia criminal conspiracy," in order to incriminate those with illicit links with the Mafia; the adoption of counter-kidnapping strategies; the protection of repentants; and the establishment of a system devised to uncover suspected operations in order to identify self-financing mechanisms, such as money laundering.

The DIA's activity has been successful against Mafia terrorism, considering that those responsible for bomb attacks in the 1990s have been identified and imprisoned. But at the beginning of the new millennium, the Mafia in Italy has much more international connotations and links than before, making its objectives stronger and more subversive.

Moreover, during the 1990s, the threat to the security and stability of the country also derived from the rebirth of the ideological terrorism of the so-called Autonomy groups and groups from community centers (*Centri sociali*). These factions of opposition to every institution, public or private, were signs of a certain failure of the traditional economic and social policies and of a more general lack of values among young people.

Marginalized social groups offered fertile ground in which the terrorist seed could take root. The risk of dangerous elements or professionals of subversion infiltrating such groups had already been pointed out by the inquiry authorities. It is worrying that such a danger continues to exist today.

In fact, there were further bomb attacks against selected institutions by terrorists active in the military wing of the old BR. The terrorists used acronyms, such as *Nuclei Territoriali Antimperialisti* (NTA, Territorial Anti-Imperialist Groups), *Nuclei Comunisti Combattenti* (NCC, Fighting Communist Groups), *Comitati di Appoggio alla Resistenza per il Comunismo* (CARC, Support Committees to the Communist Fight), and *Associazione Solidarietà Proletaria* (ASP, Proletarian Solidarity Association). Those terrorist groups have never been fully defeated and they are still acting in Italy, as the murders of two eminent academics, professors Massimo D'Antona in 1999 and Marco Biagi in 2002, clearly demonstrate. Both victims were government advisors for social and labor affairs. In this respect, one can say that the danger of a new spread of BR traditional terrorism is open yet.

The New Threats: Islamic Fundamentalism, Foreign Immigrant Terrorists, and Their Collusion with Local Criminals

In the meantime, globalization led to a widening in the range of attack, thus creating conditions in which further contradictions in the international context became evident. In the written claims of responsibility for terrorist outrages during the last decade, the supranational aspect of the new struggle of Italian terrorism has been emphasized more than in the past. The continuous exaltation of the "anti-global" character of the new terrorist struggle favored collusion with other subversive groups outside Italy.

At the beginning of the new millennium, new terrorist groups began to operate in Italy in two strategic directions: on the one hand, conducting attacks on state institutions, and, on the other, engaging in attacks on the structures which the terrorists considered to represent the ruling powers, both at the international and national level. The new terrorism would use and trigger tensions in those social sectors suffering from the employment crisis and the worsening situation in some urban contexts, particularly in the south of Italy.[6]

Messages from die-hard terrorists still in prison are addressed first to militants, but also to those active in the area of pacifism, anarchism, and "eco-terrorism".[7] These die-hards have continued to draw up detailed but unrealistic subversion plans, aware that they can still play a destabilizing role. The only common element among many new groups seems to be that their revolutionary raison d'être rests on their action being part of an international plan.

Another element to be carefully taken into account is that, already during the 1990s, the Italian security forces indicated the presence of "cells" of Muslim revolutionary radicalism, which were using the country for terrorist operations in other Western nations and against American diplomatic and NATO military sites. In this sense, the terrorist threat in Italy in the new millennium can more than ever claim to be international.

In fact, thanks to the mass media and communication networks, the demands made by Islamic religious extremists or the ultranationalists of different political groups go beyond the borders of regions in the Middle East, North Africa, the Balkans, or the Caucasus, and reach the large foreign communities in Europe and the Western hemisphere, which are all nourished by illegal migratory flows. The greatest risk to Italy is the presence of terrorist and criminal groups hidden in these large flows of immigrants into its territory from the Balkans and from the Middle East.

Because of its strategic geographical position in the Mediterranean, Italy is an important meeting point for many international subversive groups from North Africa, and above all, from the Balkans and from the Caucasian region. For these groups who are fighting for ethnic or religious reasons, it is not a question of identifying targets in this country, but rather of exploiting the strategic importance of the country's geographic position in order to send militants all over Europe and start undercover activities. The deterioration of the political, economic, religious, and social conditions in certain countries, and the extension of conflict in neighboring regions involve Italy not only because of the geographical closeness, but also because of the network of illicit traffic involving immigrants (including women for prostitution and slavery), arms, and drugs.

The actions of the new terrorist groups range from simple propaganda and proselytism activities to confessional claims or ethnic-separatist demands. Their strategy is not always uniform, underlying the different strategies among ethnic groups. From this point of view, Italy should be worried about the threat of renewed political terrorism and the support offered through criminal action or propaganda activity to those foreign groups with an Islamic fundamentalist matrix. It is not merely by chance that Italian security forces have verified in Italy and in other European countries a complex support network for terrorist groups, such as the more extreme Islamic radical groups like the one led by Osama bin Laden with his repeated calls for holy war.

Financial Support for the New Terrorism and the Struggle against Money Laundering

A basic problem for any terrorist movement is its financial support. Because of that problem, the most effective way of fighting terrorism is to interrupt the financial flows that the organization requires in order to pay for arms, explosives, and logistic bases.

The transnational vocation of the new terrorist groups presupposes that the financial support comes particularly from drugs and international arms trafficking, and from laundering dirty money all over the world. Criminals who immigrated illegally to Italy adopted the traditional instruments of financing terrorism: robberies and kidnapping.

The most disturbing phenomenon regarding the new subversive organizations is the possibility of synergy in action and the exchange of reciprocal favors among terrorist groups, international subversive organizations, and the traditional criminal organizations. The number of terrorist attacks has fallen, and with that fall, the propaganda and recruitment have declined. But the number and seriousness of illicit activities aimed at self-financing and calls for international support has increased. In actual fact, after twenty years of subversive activity between the 1960s and the 1980s, the new form of terrorism in Italy has taken on connotations that were once exclusive to international subversive movements. Inevitably, those links with organized crime, already identified at the end of the 1980s with active criminal groups in Bulgaria, Turkey, Greece, Spain, and the United States, have been strengthened.

Drugs and arms trafficking, therefore, represent serious threats to national security, especially if they are associated with destabilization plans originating in foreign countries. In fact, one of the largest producers of synthetic drugs in the world is the Russian Mafia: some analysts think that the production and distribution of such drugs, which represent some of the most conspicuous ways of getting rich, are also closely linked to plans to destabilize Western countries. Alongside drug trafficking, the sale of arms and explosives is another flourishing activity of Russian criminality in Europe.

As a consequence of the globalization process, one of the most disturbing phenomena of this form of criminal subversion is the opportunity to invest immediately and directly in all kinds of economic and financial activities. The new terrorism has adopted the operational techniques typical of the most organized criminal groups; and this fact is true also for the laundering activity of illicit profits. In the last decade, such behavior has enabled terrorist organizations to raise the level of their activity. Unlike the past terrorist experience, the subversion of the new millennium does business with banks, holding, and investment fund companies. Through very disparate operations in the various markets, illicit money becomes legal. Real market professionals, such as brokerage and investment firms, are contacted to transfer huge sums of money to other countries. The money is "cleaned" and then invested in commercial activities, phantom companies, or in the so-called tax havens, countries whose laws on bank secrecy prevent any form of transparency of economic and financial activities, thus favoring organized crime. In this way, the origins of illicit profits are hidden, their beneficiaries remain secret, and new international links are created that are difficult to identify.

Mafia terrorism, collusion between organized crime and subversive groups, drugs and arms trafficking, and money laundering through licit activities: these are the new terms that are used to describe the Italian subversive phenomenon. The authorities are now wondering how it is possible to face this global and uniform threat at a national and international level if the distinctive characteristics of the previous terrorist strategy have been changed so radically.

The history of subversion can certainly offer some clues as to how the activity can be fought, ignoring ideological, ethnic, and religious distinctions. However, the most dangerous terrorist threat comes from the Mafia's illicit sources of finance. Both the Mafia and terrorism are now expressions of highly developed criminality. Only the final targets, on a few occasions, separate subversive action from the pure and simple activities of the Mafia: the means, the forms, and sometimes even the men are the same.

How to Fight New Terrorist Threats

A first question is whether repentance, which worked so well against terrorism in the 1980s, can be proposed as a means to fight subversion today, when organized crime, as well as terrorism of all kinds, work together to destabilize established order. The perplexity that has accompanied the use of repentance at the beginning of the 1990s in the fight against the Italian Mafia is more evident when this measure is applied to the new subversive phenomenon linked to international organized crime. These criminals are the product of an economic and social context that reflects the history of a misguided culture. The culture of organized crime can be replaced, circumscribed, and also isolated: but it has produced a mentality, life style, and dependence on structures and values that do not belong to our civil and democratic society. For this reason, the repentance of members of organized crime is not totally credible and creates further problems when it is used to fight the new subversive threats. The repentant terrorists of the 1980s came from factory and university backgrounds. They had chosen to fight a system that they did not trust, and they fought for a final revolution inspired by ideologies. Hampered in these aims by the authority's response, terrorists could repent or dissociate, deciding to settle their own account with justice. Such action is not worthwhile for a member of the new foreign subversive groups operating from Italy to the rest of European and Mediterranean areas. This is more evident in the case of terrorists belonging to Muslim fundamentalism.

The repressive measures against this new terrorist phenomenon must include those structures and means that were used both at the national and international level to fight organized crime successfully. They must not depend on "good luck" or on the "good will" of questionable repentant terrorists, but on efficient organization, such as the cooperation of different police forces, and greater specialization and concentration in investigations. Although foreign organized crime in Italy operates alongside national criminals and sometimes their interests clash and their operative systems differ, their strategies are very difficult to understand if they are judged by traditional methods. So it has become indispensable to work in a context that has no frontiers, with support from international police authorities that enables the local authorities to be aware of and to value the different criminal phenomena. The rapidity and efficiency of repressive action against these subversive manifestations can be successful only if there is a high level of specialization by the appointed authorities and by the anticrime officers.

Specialized organizations are needed to fight crime and terrorism. These organizations already exist, thanks to collaboration among different security force agencies and through agreements between Italy and foreign countries regarding specific issues, for example, legal cooperation and information exchanges. These agencies are beginning to be able to match international criminal systems and uncover their dynamics and economic support. This fact is true for the complex mechanism of money laundering: in fact, only a part of the enormous profits that the new international subversive groups obtain from their illicit trade is used for self-financing. The rest of the money is invested in the world's financial markets through many and complex operations, using the usual channels with which the rest of the economic world works. Because of the normal relations that these subversive criminal organizations manage to establish with "clean" corporations, it is necessary to find new ways of fighting them. If it is correct that the financial and industrial community must be protected from attacks by "terrorist finance," it is also desirable that the same community acts to prevent the interference of illegal actions by terrorism and Mafia criminals.

However, given the transnational character of the phenomenon, it is indispensable that such structures are in force internationally. For example, it is necessary to have an international definition of a crime, such as "terrorism" and "Mafia criminal conspiracy," that considers all persons who do nothing to prevent crime as being responsible for it.

Terrorism in Italy must, therefore, be monitored and pursued by a counterterrorism authority that works in cooperation with the national anti-Mafia organization. There are also some people who propose that a single wide-ranging counterterrorist agency be created, to deal with both the activities of Mafia terrorism and those of terrorism. An efficient counterterrorist and anticrime system must pass the test of being legal, efficient, and transparent. It is necessary for the police and judiciary authorities to take action at an international level. Up to now, many initiatives have been taken to fight terrorism and crime by tightening financial control, which is proof that there is the political will to eliminate organized crime and terrorist groups.

The task appears to be very difficult also because there are states that today, just as during the Cold War, support people responsible for terrorist plans or those who advocate terrorist attacks in the name of a "holy war." These countries finance and sustain terrorist movements at different levels. Subversive groups also work in the drug and arms trades, protected by the complex political situations that still exist in different parts of the world, particularly in the Middle East. These states organize terrorism by allowing the training of armed groups or helping to form terrorist groups, ready to make supreme sacrifices. Possible ways to take action against these countries are through economic boycotts and embargos; even if, as in some cases, the results have been disappointing.

The danger of terrorist activities can be limited by guaranteeing stable economic growth, adequate employment for an increasing labor force, human rights, democracy, and the rule of law to those countries that are the sources of the most serious threats to international security.

PART II
by Sergio Marchisio

Terrorism after September 11

In its recent history Italy had to fight a very hard battle against domestic terrorism and highly aggressive forms of organized crime, which have progressively strengthened their international links and financing sources. The events of September 11, 2001, furnished dramatic impetus to the already detected need for strong intergovernmental cooperation in order to combat terrorism, giving top priority to the use of financial measures to cut off its illicit international financing circuits.

After the World Trade Center attack, terrorism threats in Italy have more clearly assumed two different features. On the one side, traditional domestic terrorism has continued to operate, mainly against the "symbols of capitalism." A direct link connecting extreme fringe groups was detected in the anti-globalization movement, especially between a group calling itself July 20th (the date of the killing by police of an anti-globalization protestor during the 2001 G8 Summit of Genoa),the separatists from the Sardinian Autonomy Movement (MAS), and other extremist groups such as the Revolutionary Front for Communism. Not to speak of the evergreen *Brigate Rosso*. In 2004 four members of the BR, who were arrested in connection with the March 19, 2002, slaying of Marco Biagi, were sentenced to life imprisonment.

Conversely, Italy has experienced the growing threat of Islamic fundamentalist terrorism. From a general point of view, it is to be noted that until March 11, 2004, there was a feeling that, notwithstanding threats coming from leaders of the main terrorist organizations of Islamic inspiration, Italy was not considered a direct target of the Islamic terrorism, but a sort of logistic background used for supporting activities: forging documents, recruiting fighters for war areas among illegal immigrants, and raising funds to support and finance Islamic terrorism. However, the massacre in Madrid of March 11, 2004, obliged all to a hard landing, thereby confirming the views of those who had always feared the worst. Therefore, public authorities, judges, and police forces were pushed to provide new tools of knowledge, analysis, and counterterrorism strategies.

These analyses led to the conclusion that an informal network of Islamic cells active in Italy linked from the operational point of view, but not rigidly structured in a hierarchical organization with al Qaeda at its summit. Islamic terrorists come mainly from North African countries and Pakistan. They have preserved their national identity, mainly Algerian groups of the Armed Islamic Group and Takfit w-al-Higra, Egyptians of al-Jihad and al-Gamà al-Islamia, Moroccans of Ansar al-Islam, and Tunisians. Thanks to covert activities, they live above suspicion in the suburbs of the big towns, raise resources to finance the fighters in war zones or in training sanctuaries, and maintain operational links with terrorists living in other countries. In 2004, an Egyptian citizen was arrested in Milan who was directly connected to the preparation of the Madrid attack of March 11, 2004, and was a central element of a European terrorist network.

Another major point was the evidence of growing links between terrorist cells and common criminality. It has been suggested that the collaboration might have begun when a Camorra member who converted to Islam met fellow Muslims jailed in Italy.

The conclusion was that Italy has become, for its geographical position, a privileged target for terrorist groups and single radicals who decide to realize individual acts of jihad, while Islamic mosques can play a central role not only from the religious point of view, but also for the spreading of hate messages.

In fact, the Italian government stepped up its counterterrorism efforts following the September 11 attacks and supported the United States diplomatically and politically and took a prominent role in the international Coalition against al Qaeda. It declared its support for the U.S.-led war and offered to contribute military forces, including naval, air, and ground units. Italian law-enforcement officials intensified their efforts to track and arrest individuals they suspected of having ties to al Qaeda and other extremist groups. In February 2002, a judge in Milan sentenced four members of the Tunisian Combatant Group to up to five years in jail for providing false documentation and planning to acquire and transport arms and other illegal goods. Italian authorities also suspected the group was planning a terrorist attack against the U.S. Embassy in Rome. This was the first time al Qaeda associates were convicted in Europe since September 11, 2001.

In October 2002, Italian authorities arrested four Tunisians for document forgery; they may have also been planning to conduct a terrorist attack in Europe, possibly in France. They also believed that the Vatican, where security was beefed up, had become a prime target for an attack because of its religious significance and because its open spaces were difficult to protect. Cells of Muslim militants—mainly Ansar al-Islam, the terrorist group from the al Qaeda network led by the Jordanian terrorist Abu Musab al-Zarqawi—were suspected of willingness to carry out suicide bombings. They were also detected in several areas of Italy planning large-scale attacks in the country. The Italian government intensified its antiterrorist campaign following the March 11 bombings in Madrid, fearing that the terrorists were planning to attack targets in Italy.

The first response to cope with the new threats has been to strengthen the antiterrorism legislation. Since September 11, 2001, several international obligations have been imposed by treaties and resolutions of the UN Security Council concerning the adoption of legislative and operational measures to counter international terrorism. In order to fulfill such obligations, and those stemming from its participation in the European Union, Italy has amended its penal code, extending antiterrorist laws and powers against organized crime and the Mafia to offenses connected with international terrorism, and has put in place new mechanisms to combat the illegal funding of terrorist associations.

Criminal Law

Decree-Law 374/2001 "Urgent measures to prevent and suppress crimes committed for the purposes of international terrorism," approved by the Italian government on October 18, 2001, and converted into Law No. 438/2001 on December 15, 2001, amended the criminal code (art. 270 *bis* and article 270 *ter*) to introduce the crime of conspiracy to commit acts of international terrorism or to provide assistance to criminal conspirators. These amendments make it possible to punish anyone promoting, creating, organizing, managing, or financing an organization intending to commit acts of violence for the purposes of international terrorism, as well as any conduct by persons aiding and abetting members of any such terrorist organizations (by providing them safe harbor, board, lodging, means of transport or communication). The punishment for the foregoing offenses ranges from seven to fifteen years, whereas five- to ten-year sentences are applicable for participation in such an association. Offering refuge, hospitality, means of transport, or instruments for communication to persons participating in such associations are offenses carrying sentences of up to four years in prison.

The same Decree-Law No. 374 of October 18, 2001, expressly provided that for the purposes of criminal law, acts of violence against a foreign state, institution, or international organization are considered to be an act of terrorism.

Decree-Law No. 374 of October 18, 2001, lastly, increased the powers of the judicial police, extending preemptive and court-authorized wire-tapping and interception of communications to investigate crimes committed in the pursuit of international terrorism, together with other existing statutory provisions which already make it possible in certain cases (to combat drug trafficking, money laundering, and illegal immigration) to delay the issue of arrest warrants, carry out arrests and sequestration orders, search buildings, and conduct undercover operations. A similar extension is also possible for preventive action and the monitoring of assets under current legislation to combat the Mafia and other serious crimes.

Financial Measures

As regards the use of financial measures to combat terrorism, Italy took action designed to strike efficiently and globally at financial assets, adopting legislation to freeze the property of individual terrorists and terrorist organizations, fully implementing its obligations undertaken with the United Nations to deal with the Taliban and al Qaeda, and to apply the autonomous system of penalties laid down by the European Union.

Under Decree-Law 353/01, enacted as law No. 415 on November 17, 2001, (Penalties for Violations of the Measures Adopted against the Afghan Taliban faction), Italian legislation put in place administrative penalties for offenses in violation of Commission Regulation (EC) 467/2001 implementing UN Security Council Resolutions 1267/1999 and 1333/2000. This regulation provides for the freezing of all capital and all financial resources belonging to any natural or legal person, entity or organization named by the Sanctions Committee established by the UN Security Council Resolution 1267/1999.

Section 2 of Decree-Law No. 369/01, enacted as law No. 431 on December 14, 2001, provides that any acts performed in violation of the provisions prohibiting the export of goods and services, involving the freezing of capital or other financial resources set out in regulations adopted by the European Union Council, also in implementation of UN Security Council resolutions, are null and void. Italy has thus fulfilled its obligations under Commission Regulation (EC) 2580/2001, implementing UN Security Council Resolution 1373/2001, and providing for the freezing of capital and other financial assets or economic resources of persons committing or attempting to commit, participating in or facilitating the commission of any act of terrorism.

Under Italian legislation, economic assets and financial resources linked to terrorist organizations can be seized through a criminal sequestration order. In this case, the sequestration order is issued by the courts (the public prosecutor or the judge) as part of a criminal proceeding for crimes linked to international terrorism.

Structures and Responsibilities

The Italian government's action to combat terrorism involves a coordinated effort among the main governmental departments, Foreign Affairs, Home Affairs, Defense, Economy, Infrastructure, Health, as well as the Bank of Italy, the Police, the Carabinieri (one of the Italian Armed Forces with responsibility for territorial police), the Guardia di Finanza (Customs and Excise Police), and the intelligence services. Specific interdepartmental coordination bodies and ad hoc units have been created, to deal with operational issues, and other existing government organizations have been greatly enhanced, in order to provide a coherent framework to combat terrorism with the required instruments in all its various manifestations.

The role, powers, and responsibilities of the Political-Military Unit (NPM), set up within the Office of the Prime Minister, have been strengthened since the state of emergency following the September 11 events. The members of this unit are senior representatives of all the government departments and agencies responsible for combating terrorism and protecting the population throughout Italy. The NPM is, therefore, the body with the most wide-ranging and comprehensive functions. The NPM has also coordinated action plans and operations relating to transport safety, bioterrorism, the strengthening of preventive operations, the suppression of terrorist crime by the police forces, and the enhancement of preemptive measures, civil and military. Equally important in this connection is the role of the Committee for Security and Public Order, chaired by the Minister of Home Affairs. It has a long-established coordination responsibility and has been further extended.

The Financial Security Committee (CSF), comprising senior officials of various ministries, including Finance, Foreign Affairs, and Justice, and representatives from law-enforcement agencies, was created in October 2001 to identify and block the funding of terrorist activity. The chairman of this committee is empowered to submit data and information to the Executive Committee of the Intelligence and Security Services (CESIS) and to the directors of the Intelligence and Security Services so as to enable the prime minister to carry out the coordination function for which he is responsible under Law 801/1977. The CSF is also responsible for cooperating with the agencies performing similar functions in other countries, in order to improve international coordination also in light of the relevant decisions made by the Financial Action Task Force (FATF).

Italy also concentrated on dismantling not only indigenous terrorist groups that in the past attacked Italian and U.S. interests, but also groups suspected of international terrorist affiliations operating within and outside Italy's borders. Italy supported U.S. prevention of terrorism and pushed to alleviate terrorism. Italian commitment to a campaign to freeze terrorist funds was also strengthened by establishing the Financial Intelligence Unit, consisting of the Treasury Department, the Bank of Italy, and the financial police, coordinated closely with other G7 governments and Italy's intelligence services. In August 2002, working with the U.S. Treasury Department, Italian authorities froze the assets of twenty-five individuals and organizations designated by the United States under Executive Order 13224. Eleven were individuals connected to the Salafist Group for Call and Combat. Fourteen were organizations linked to two known al Qaeda-linked financiers.

Finally, a Coordinating Structure for International Counterterrorism Cooperation has been instituted at the Ministry of Foreign Affairs as a means of stepping up the response to the emergency caused by the events of September 11. Its purpose is to coordinate and facilitate a consistent effort by Italy in the international fora responsible for combating terrorism in all its forms. This applies to actions undertaken within the UN, G7 and G8, EU, Council of Europe, Organization for Security and Cooperation in Europe, as well as bilaterally, through appropriate coordination both within the Ministry of Foreign Affairs and in liaison with the other government departments concerned. This body has been specifically designated as the National Contact Point of the Counter-Terrorism Committee (CTC), established by the Security Council.

Operational Measures

At the operational level, the Italian government approved a "Program for the Use of Military Contingents for the Surveillance and Control of Sensitive Targets." Over four thousand servicemen are being used to guard more than one hundred fifty military and civilian facilities and infrastructure sites considered to be at risk.

Numerous precautionary measures have also been implemented to guarantee the safety of transport, by increasing the number of armed guards on duty in aircraft parking areas; making more stringent checks on passengers, crew members, and personnel; and strengthening boarding gate controls and checks on baggage and post. With regard to biological terrorism, the Ministry of Health has adopted an action plan setting out instructions for dealing with risks to the general public.

Recent Antiterrorism Strategies

More recently, the World Summit Outcome, adopted by heads of state and government gathered at the United Nations from September 14 to 16, 2005, summarized the general principles applicable in the fight against terrorism. On the one hand, the report condemned terrorism in all its forms and manifestations, committed by whoever, wherever, and for whatever purposes, as it constitutes one of the most serious threats to international peace and security and, on the other hand, the report confirmed the necessity that international cooperation to fight terrorism be conducted in conformity with international law, including the Charter of the United Nations, relevant international conventions and protocols, in particular human rights law, refugee law, and international humanitarian law. Finally, it stressed the importance of assisting victims of terrorism and of providing them and their families with support in coping with their loss and grief. International law has indeed established a clear set of obligations incumbent on all states to prevent, detect, prosecute, and punish terrorist offenses and to ensure that they are punishable by penalties which take into account their grave nature.

Therefore, Italy has taken supplementary measures to ensure that acts of terrorism are defined as offenses under national law and are punishable by effective, proportionate, and dissuasive criminal penalties. It has also adopted domestic legislation to ensure that persons who are perpetrators, instigators, or accessories in acts of terrorism can be held liable under criminal law. At the same time, Italy has tried to understand the real scope of the threat, in order to develop proportional responses through adjustment of legislation or other instruments in its counterterrorist toolbox. The London bombings have shown the asymmetric threat of terrorism, which is likely to be enduring in nature and, potentially, the United Kingdom's civil liberties debate as deeply divisive within our democratic societies.

These actions are in line with the general objective of the new Convention of the Council of Europe on the Prevention of Terrorism opened to signature on May 16, 2005, in Warsaw, and Resolution 1624 (2005), adopted by the Security Council on September 14, 2005.

This new generation of legal texts is integrating previously existing legal instruments dealing with counterterrorism. They make express reference to incitement of terrorist acts and attempts at the justification or glorification (*apologie*) of terrorist acts that may incite further terrorist acts, condemning such behaviors. They recognize that incitement of terrorist acts motivated by extremism and intolerance poses a serious and growing danger to the enjoyment of human rights, threatens social and economic development, undermines global stability and prosperity, and must be addressed urgently and proactively.

The New Criminal Offenses

The new Italian legislation passed in July 2005, law No. 144 on Urgent Measures to Counter International Terrorism, provides that individuals can be kept in custody for up to twenty-four hours without charge, compared to twelve hours before the enactment of the law. It allows law enforcement authorities to interrogate suspects without the suspect having a lawyer present and reinforces the rules concerning criminal offenses such as "public provocation to commit terrorist offenses," "recruitment for terrorism," and "training for terrorism," coupled with a series of accessory crimes. These offenses are considered terrorist offenses of a serious nature as they could lead to the commission of terrorist acts. However, they do not require that a terrorist offense be committed.

Public provocation to commit a terrorist offense includes the instigation of ethnic and religious tensions, which may provide a basis for terrorism; the dissemination of "hate speech," and the promotion of ideologies favorable to terrorism. It implies the distribution, or otherwise making available, of a message to the public, with intent to incite the commission of a terrorist offense, where such conduct, whether or not directly advocating terrorist offenses, causes a danger that one or more such offenses may be committed.

Distribution refers to the active dissemination of a message advocating terrorism and making it easily accessible to the public, for instance, by placing it on the internet or by creating or compiling hyperlinks in order to facilitate access to it.

It is been discussed whether this offense is consistent with the freedom of expression, one of the essential foundations of a democratic society, which applies not only to ideas and information that are favorably received or regarded as inoffensive but also to those that offend, shock, or disturb. Without denying that the question where the boundary lies between indirect incitement to commit terrorist offenses and the legitimate voicing of criticism is a difficult one, one has to note that, in contrast to certain fundamental rights which admit no restrictions, interference with freedom of expression may be allowed in highly specific circumstances. In any case, the European Convention on Human Rights (ECHR) lays down the conditions under which restrictions on the exercise of freedom of expression are admissible,[8] while it provides for possible derogations in time of emergency.[9] The European Court has already held that certain restrictions on messages that might constitute an indirect incitement to violent terrorist offenses are in keeping with the Convention.

As far as recruitment of possible future terrorists is concerned, this crime is to be understood as solicitation to carry out terrorist offenses whether individually or collectively, and whether directly committing, participating in, or contributing to the commission of such offenses. For the crime to be committed, it is necessary that the recruiter successfully approach the addressee. It is known that active recruitment occurs across Europe principally in certain radical environments, such as prisons, mainly in France and Italy, and on websites used to disseminate terrorist ideology.

Another key development regards criminalization of training for terrorism, namely the supplying of know-how for the purpose of carrying out or contributing to the commission of a terrorist offense. This means providing instruction in methods or techniques that are suitable for terrorist purposes, including the making or use of explosives, firearms, and noxious or hazardous substances. For such conduct to be criminally liable, it is necessary that the trainer knows that the skills provided are intended to be used in the commission of or to contribute to committing a terrorist offense.

Furthermore, we must consider ancillary offenses as attempts at, or complicity in the commission of, other crimes, such as participation as an accomplice in the commission of any crimes related to terrorism. Liability for such complicity arises when the person who commits a crime is aided by another person who also intends that the crime be committed.

Investment in Intelligence and Judicial Cooperation

Another main feature of the developments occurring in Italian antiterrorist strategy concerns the new preventive measures which call on exchange of information, training, and formation of joint teams for analysis and investigation with other states. It is now commonly understood that investment in intelligence is the first line of defense against terrorism. Toward this end there is further room for each state to improve intelligence-gathering, analysis, and intelligence-sharing.

Concerning judicial cooperation, recent trends in Italy are illustrated by the introduction of the European arrest warrant, which came into effect in 2004 and noticeably streamlined traditional extradition procedures. The European warrant procedure has recently applied between Italy and the United Kingdom for the surrender of one of the alleged offenders in planning new terrorist activities in London (case of Hamdi Isaac). The most positive aspect of this procedure is that it departs from the traditional extradition system, under which the Italian judicial authority (*Corte d'appello*) is asked to rule on the legality of the surrender, and can postpone it arguing the priority of Italian jurisdiction.

However, safeguards are provided with regard to extradition and mutual legal assistance which make clear that these procedures cannot derogate important traditional grounds to refuse cooperation under applicable treaties and laws. Examples of such deviation include refusal of extradition where the person will be subjected to torture or to inhuman or degrading treatment or punishment by the death penalty. When the person is not extradited for these or other reasons, it is provided that he or she will be prosecuted domestically.

Terrorism and Human Rights

Italy is committed that all measures taken in the fight against terrorism must respect the rule of law, democratic values, human rights, and fundamental freedoms as well as other provisions of international law, including, where applicable, international humanitarian law.

In this vein, antiterrorist strategy is beginning to recognize in a more complete way the relationship between terrorism and basic human rights. There is a growing focus on the rights to life and security. The right to life is the supreme right of the human being. It is basic to all human rights and without it all other rights are meaningless.

In this respect, it is true that there has been, until now, a greater emphasis on national security rather than on individual security as a human right, and that it is the duty of the state to protect human life against terrorist violence by making effective provisions in criminal law to deter the commission of acts of terrorism, and the establishment of law enforcement machinery for the prevention, suppression, investigation, and penalization of acts of terrorism.

However, the human rights that must be respected are not only the rights of those accused or convicted of terrorist offenses, but also the rights of the victims, or potential victims of those offenses. From this perspective, a number of provisions regarding the protection, compensation, and support of victims of terrorism are consistent with recent developments in counterterrorism strategies.

The protection afforded to victims might also include many other aspects, such as emergency and long-term assistance, psychological support, effective access to the law and the courts (in particular access to criminal procedures), access to information, and the protection of victims' private and family lives, dignity, and security, particularly when they cooperate with the courts. A good example in this direction is law No. 206 of August 3, 2004.

Yet, another issue of major concern regards the *practice toward asylum-seekers, including expulsions and removal of the immigration risk offshore.* There is in fact a tendency to increase the number of aliens who may be removed. This is the case under the abovementioned law No. 144 on Urgent Measures to Counter International Terrorism according to which the Minister of the Interior can expel an alien in derogation to the normal procedures provided for by immigration laws, if there is reason to believe that his or her presence within the Italian territory might help support terrorist activity or poses a security threat to Italy. It will then be possible to appeal against the expulsion order to an administrative court.

In the end, we can pose the question whether an effective fight against terrorism that fully respects human rights is possible. It depends, of course, on what we mean by fully respects. There is no doubt that a certain degree of restriction is inevitable, not only for the rights of suspect terrorists but of everyone. Now, certain rights may not be derogated from under any circumstances. They include the right to life, the freedom of thought, conscience and religion, freedom from torture or cruel, inhuman or degrading treatment, and the principle of precision and non-retroactivity of criminal law except where a later law imposes a higher penalty.

As regards other rights, derogation must be permitted in the special circumstances defined in international human rights law. It must be of exceptional character and legally weighted, and any such measures must be strictly limited in time and substance by the exigencies of the situation. Finally, it must be subject to regular judicial review.

Since many legal democratic systems are under pressure, it should be ensured that the balance is constantly readjusted as circumstances change, in accordance with law.

Defining Terrorism

It is important to note that the fight against terrorism would be better achieved if an international convention helped to fill normative gaps at the national level, occasioned in part by the less-than-comprehensive ratification of the separate, existing treaties. Judges have often thrown out terrorist charges, finding insufficient evidence to link suspects with nebulous Islamic militant networks, and thus sentencing those suspects to lesser offenses such as forging documents. In early 2005, a judge in Milan set off a storm of controversy by ruling that some Islamic militant activists were not terrorists but supporters of insurgents in Iraq and for this reason could not be found guilty of the crime of international terrorism provided for by Article 270 *bis* of the Italian Criminal Code. The first time prosecutors managed to secure convictions using tough international terrorism legislation introduced by Italy in the wake of September 11 was later in 2005 in the Tribunal of Brescia. The suspected terrorists were convicted because they were part of a cell that had planned to attack a subway station in Milan.

Currently, Italian legal texts do not define terrorist offenses in addition to those included in the existing international conventions against terrorism, but usually refer to the treaties in force. Many are international conventions relating to various aspects of the problem of international terrorism which condemn certain specifically defined criminal offenses as *acts of terrorism*. These acts of terrorism are all the acts, methods, and practices, criminal and unjustifiable, wherever and by whoever that are committed and/or supported directly or indirectly (including by states). Such offenses always endanger or take innocent lives, jeopardize fundamental freedoms, seriously impair the dignity of human beings, and undermine the democratic basis of society.

There is a case, accordingly, for saying that key rules should be gathered together under a new umbrella convention, which does clearly and unequivocally articulate the basic norms which should drive all law and policy. Such a universal convention already exists in draft form in the United Nations but the essential obstacle that prevents its adoption is the problem of definition.

Different views were expressed with respect to how a definition should be formulated. The working group recognized the significant progress made in identifying the key elements of a definition of terrorism in Security Council resolution 1566 (2004) and paragraph 164 of the report of the UN High-Level Panel on Threats, Challenges, and Change, which would facilitate international consensus on the issue. Against this background, they decided not to propose a definition of their own or to endorse any existing proposal. However, the members of the group agreed that, irrespective of how a definition is formulated in legal technical terms, it should be clear that terrorist acts can never be justifiable by considerations of a political, philosophical, ideological, racial, ethnic, religious or similar nature. In essence, this means that acts specifically targeting civilians or non-combatants, whatever the context and whatever the motive, must be outlawed.

A clear-cut and universally endorsed definition of terrorism that would trigger remedial measures by states and international organizations would further the process of de-legitimating terrorism in part by detailing those acts deemed "terrorist."

However, the commonsense definition of terrorism is not enough to forge a universally accepted legal definition. There are those who argue that the definition of terrorism should be narrower, in the sense of excluding so-called freedom fighters, or wider, in the sense of including those who target individuals in some official capacities. Therefore, it is critical to articulate the central core of the prohibition on which there should be no disagreement. Even though they do not define the crime of terrorism, the most recent treaties and antiterrorism legislation recognize that terrorist offenses are characterised by so-called terrorist motivation. In fact, acts of terrorism have the purpose, by their nature or context, of seriously intimidating a population or unduly compelling a government to perform or abstain from performing any act, or of seriously destabilizing or destroying the fundamental political, constitutional, economic, or social structures of a country.

In this vein, it seems that the specific aim of a comprehensive convention should be to outlaw once and for all those acts specifically motivated by their terrorist purpose and targeted against civilians or noncombatants. Nor should these terrorist acts ever be justifiable by considerations of a political, philosophical, ideological, racial, ethnic, religious or similar nature.

5
EGYPT

Ahmed Abou-el-Wafa

A cts of terrorism have existed for thousands of years. They have developed to the extent of constituting a severe menace to the life and safety of persons as well as the security of property. Such acts are increasing at an alarming rate.

It is worth noting that the case study of a state, such as Egypt, and its efforts regarding problems of terrorism have a threefold objective, namely to:

- know how a state behaves *in concreto* in this field;
- keep in mind its experience in this context; and
- try to benefit from the positive results and, at the same time, to evade negative effects resulting therefrom, in order to improve the machinery used for dealing with the phenomenon in question.

This report cannot exhaust the subject. No single report is likely to do that. Accordingly, this study does not attempt to put forward *in extenso* the entire experience of Egypt in the field of combating terrorism, be it domestic or international. Rather, it seeks to discuss the most important actions and methods used in this field.

Additionally, this work touches only on what has been applied by Egypt with regard to the terrorist phenomenon. Its main focus is, therefore, to analyze the content, methods of operation, and acts taken to confront that phenomenon.

Finally, the primary purpose of this report is to help identify and define an agenda for establishing policies to deal with the terrorist phenomenon. Therefore, in order to understand the legal and practical questions relating to Egypt and the terrorist phenomenon, this report is divided into two main parts: the terrorist phenomenon in Egypt;[1] and the attitude of Egypt with respect to the terrorist phenomenon.

The Terrorist Phenomenon in Egypt

It is well established that terrorism is as old as history. Since immemorial times, Egypt has been a calm and tolerant country.[2] In recent years, it has been in the grip of violent events. The latter followed in quick succession; and soon the list became long.

For these reasons, and in addition to the importance of the subject itself, it is necessary and appropriate to review the terrorist phenomenon in Egypt.

Background

The historical dimension of violent activities started in Egypt with the appearance in 1979 of the jihad organization and the Islamic group (Gama'at Islamia). After the assassination of Egypt president Anwar el-Sadat in 1981, violent acts enormously increased. This phase of the terrorist phenomenon culminated in 1992–1993.[3] Violent acts decreased from 1994–1995 to the present.[4] Nevertheless, some deadly strikes were committed, as mentioned below, in 1997, 2004, 2005, and 2006.

Violent acts committed in Egypt are initiated by some elements abroad, particularly in the United States, Western Europe, Pakistan, Afghanistan, and some Arab countries. Additionally, a central leadership inside Egypt organizes and plans terrorist acts. It works in coordination with leaders residing abroad.[5]

Violent acts have been directed against tourists, economic establishments (e.g., Egyptian and foreign banks, hotels, tourist buses, shops and boats, cinemas, video clubs, trains, police forces, and political personalities).[6]

The most important objectives of violent acts committed in Egypt are the following:[7] to destabilize society through the use of violence and the killing of innocent people with a view to creating general chaos; to affect the political status in the society; and to combat the Egyptian national economy by damaging a fundamental economic sector, for example, tourism; and affecting some other sectors, such as investment.

Reasons for Terrorism in Egypt

Violent terrorist acts have been committed and carried out worldwide for a variety of reasons. As for Egypt, these reasons may be divided into two essential categories: internal and external.[8]

The most important internal causes of the escalation of acts of terrorism in Egypt before 1995 may be outlined as follows:

● economic and social causes: e.g., poverty,[9] collapse of economic and social services in some regions, unemployment,

and vastness of the gap between social classes;
- political and institutional causes: e.g., violations of some rights and liberties, the absence of state institutions in some regions, and weakness and ineffectiveness of political parties, as well as professional and youth organizations;
- cultural and religious causes: e.g., lack of cultural and religious tolerance;

External causes may be classified into general and specific:

- general external factors: especially the occurrence of real attacks on Muslims in some regions of the world, without any intervention from states or the international community, which applies, in this regard, a double standard (*deux poids et deux mesures*) policy;
- specific external factors: the desire to weaken the Egyptian economy with a view to placing Egypt under the control of some foreign states, the desire of some elements of Egyptian society that the "ruling Authority" in Egypt devote its energies to internal security and internal problems with the result that it will not pay due account to its role in the region, and the return of the "Arab Afghans" or "Egyptian Afghans" to Egypt.[10]

Financing, Training, and Armament

Financing, training, and armament of terrorists employ both internal and external resources. Internal resources include donations, theft of gold, management of small enterprises, and taking of arms by assassinating policemen. External resources include relationships and links with terrorist leaders in Afghanistan, Pakistan, and Western Europe.[11]

Methods of Terrorism

The main methods used by terrorists are assassination, religious violence, targeting the economy, social violence, and incitement against the ruling system.[12] Assassinations of political, security, and public personalities, include assassination of policemen, of President Anwar el-Sadat in 1981, and of the speaker of the People's Assembly in 1990. Religious violence has occurred in the form of attacks against Christians and churches, or against mosques. Examples of violence directed at an economic sector are attacks against tourist establishments, services, means of transport, foreign and Egyptian banks, cinemas, and video clubs;[13] methods of largely organized social violence occurs in villages or cities in order to weaken the state's authority and control a certain region.

Finally, wide incitement against the ruling system happens through disbursement of pamphlets, religious speeches, and private colloquia.

Confronting Terrorist Acts

In Egypt, the confrontation of terrorism occurs at various levels, by the police, religious groups, the legislature, media, international entities, and domestic political sources:

- police confrontation, e.g., using technical vulnerabilities and devices, the police pursue terrorists and organized crime and gather intelligence resources;
- religious confrontation, e.g., by propagating sound religious doctrine, as well as by insisting on the fact that Islam does not admit violence or terrorism against innocent human beings and property;
- legislative confrontation, especially the adoption of law No. 97 of 1992, which defines terrorism for the first time and determines terrorist acts as well as applicable penalties;
- media confrontation, particularly by focusing on the negative aspects of terrorist attacks, media objectivity, credibility of information published about terrorism, and appropriate technological planning;
- external confrontation through direct diplomatic and police contacts with the states concerned as well as through regional and international cooperation;
- internal confrontation, e.g., the adoption of social and economic measures such as the supply of transportation, education, water, electricity, education, and health services, with a view to improving conditions of life of regions and citizens.[14]

Tables Concerning Terrorist Acts in Egypt

It appears from Tables 1 through 6 that:

- terrorist acts against Egypt have been committed inside and outside Egypt; however, the overwhelming majority of those acts have occurred inside the country;
- terrorist acts have been directed against policemen and civilians (be they nationals or foreigners);
- cases committed by unknown persons are few in number (only 5 in 1993–1995), compared with those discovered during the same period (about 464);
- terrorist acts have been directed against many targets (e.g., public services, cinemas, video clubs, and jewelry stores).

Table 1: Terrorist Incidents Against Public Egyptian Personalities, 1992–1995

Year	Inside Egypt	Outside Egypt
1992	1	-
1993	4	-
1994	1	-
1995	-	1
Total	6	1

* Source: Report No. 18, p. 47

Table 2: Terrorist Attacks Against Egyptians Inside and Outside Egypt, 1992–1995

Year	Inside Egypt	Outside Egypt
1992	112	-
1993	158	-
1994	86	-
1995	85	2
Total	441	2

* Source: Report No. 18, p. 45

Table 3: Number of Victims of Terrorism in Egypt, 1992–1995

Year	Officers Killed/Injured		Soldiers Killed/Injured		Civilians Killed/Injured	
1992	2	10	12	24	32	91
1993	22	28	57	58	57	202
1994	11	21	76	83	28	79
1995	7	15	75	68	49	66

* Source: Report No. 18, p. 48

The Attitude of Egypt with Respect to the Terrorist Phenomenon

In accordance with norms and rules of customary international law, a state has the primary responsibility to apprehend, prosecute, and punish terrorists. Accordingly, Egypt follows a policy of condemning, overcoming,

Table 4: Number of Cases of Terrorism, 1993–1995

Year	Cases Discovered In statu nascendi (*before committing the acts*)	Cases Committed by Unknown Persons	Total
1993	244	-	244
1994	140	5	145
1995	80	-	80

* *Source: Report No. 18, p. 48*

Table 5: Number of Cases of Terrorism Committed Against Persons and Economic Sectors, 1993–1995

The Case	No. of Incidents	Killed	Injured
Against tourist sector	17	5*	48**
Against policemen	38	24	33
Against public services	2	4	9
Against video clubs	9	-	1
Against cinemas	2	-	-
Against jewelry stores	6	2	5
Against public personalities	3	1	2

Source: Report No. 14, pp. 99-103

* *3 foreigners and 2 Egyptians*
** *27 foreigners and 21 Egyptians*

combating, and preventing the spread of terrorism in all its forms and manifestations. This is true on the international and domestic levels.

On the International Level

Terrorism is a comprehensive threat to states; therefore it inevitably requires an equally broad-gauged response. Nevertheless, international co-operation with respect to combating international terrorism has been almost entirely lacking until recent years.[15] Egypt has participated in all actions and fora sponsored by the United Nations (UN), the League of Arab States (LAS), and other regional and international fora to combat and prevent terrorist crimes.[16] In addition, Egypt has concluded bilateral treaties with other states. This means that Egypt has taken part in efforts to combat international terrorism on the global, regional, and bilateral levels. All these aspects will be examined as follows:

Table 6: Recent Cases (1997–2006)

Place	Killed	Injured
Luxor*	62	-
Taba**	34	more than 100
Sharm el Sheikh***	64	124
Dahab****	18	90

Source: Al-Ahram, July 25, 2005, p. 1 (in Arabic), International Herald Tribune, July 25, 2005, pp. 1–4, Al-Ahram, April 25, 2006, p. 1 (in Arabic), Al-Ahram, April 30, 2006, p. 22 (in Arabic).

* *In 1997, a machine-gun attack on European tourists at Luxor left 62 dead.*
** *On October 6, 2004, in a deadly terror strike consisting of three synchronized blasts in and near Taba, in the northeast corner of the Sinai peninsula, 34 people were killed and more than 100 were wounded.*
*** *On July 23, 2005, Egypt suffered from one of the country's deadliest attacks when three nearly simultaneous bombings after 1 a.m. rocked the Red Sea resort of Sharm el Sheikh: A car bomb exploded in the front driveway of Ghazalah Garden Hotel, another bomb exploded in a parking lot, and a third one in the old market. The death toll was 64 persons: 7 westerners, 26 Egyptians, and 31 people who were unidentified. Moreover, 124 people were injured: 19 foreigners and 105 Egyptians. More than 80 cars and 50 shops were destroyed.*
**** *On April 24, 2006, three explosions occurred in Dahab (Sinai): 18 were killed (among them were 14 Egyptians and 4 foreigners) and 90 were injured (among them were 58 Egyptians and 32 foreigners).*

On the Global Level

On the international level, Egypt has participated in all global efforts concerning international terrorism, be they conventional, institutional, or international.

It is well known that there are various international conventions concluded or adopted on the global level concerning the terrorist phenomenon, the most important of which are the following:

- Geneva Convention for the Prevention and Suppression of Terrorism (1937);
- Convention on the Offenses and Certain Other Acts Committed on Board Aircraft (Tokyo 1963);
- Convention for the Suppression of Unlawful Seizure of Aircraft (The Hague 1970);

● Convention for the Suppression of Unlawful Acts Against the Safety of Civil Aviation (Montreal 1971);
● Convention on the Prevention and Punishment of Crimes Against Internationally Protected Persons, Including Diplomatic Agents (New York 1973);
● International Convention Against the Taking of Hostages (New York 1979);
● Convention on the Physical Protection of Nuclear Material (Vienna 1980);
● Protocol for the Suppression of Unlawful Acts of Violence at Airports Serving International Civil Aviation (Montreal 1988), Supplementary to the Convention for the Suppression of Unlawful Acts Against the Safety of Civil Aviation (Montreal 1971);
● Convention for the Suppression of Unlawful Acts Against the Safety of Maritime Navigation (Rome 1988);
● Protocol for the Suppression of Unlawful Acts Against the Safety of Maritime Navigation (Rome 1988);
● Convention on the Marking of Plastic Explosives for the Purpose of Detection (Montreal 1991);
● Convention on the Safety of United Nations and Associated Personnel (A/49/59);
● International Convention for the Suppression of Terrorist Bombings (A/52/164).
● International Convention for the Suppression of Acts of Nuclear Terrorism (New York, April 18, 2005).

Egypt has signed or ratified the overwhelming majority of the above-mentioned conventions as well as other conventions, specifically the Convention for the Prevention and Punishment of Terrorism, to which only a few states have acceded (twenty-four states) and the Convention Against Transnational Organized Crime (Palermo, December 2000).[17] Moreover, the International Convention for the Suppression of the Financing of Terrorism, signed in New York on January 10, 2000, has been ratified by the decision No. 426 of 2004 of the President of the Republic and that of the People's Assembly of February 1, 2005.[18] Thus, Egypt exhibits substantial willingness to negotiate and conclude international antiterrorist treaties in order to react to terrorist activities.[19]

Under Article 151 of the Egyptian constitution, international treaties, which have been signed, ratified, and published, shall have the force of law and so become an integral part of the Egyptian legal order. Accordingly, no additional or supplementary measure is required for them to be incorporated into that order.[20] However, to be applied, some conventions, such as those necessitating the determination of applicable penalties, need the adoption of supplementary or additional legislation. This is a mere application of the principle *nullum crimen nulla poena sine lege* ("no crime nor penalty without law").

Moreover, Egypt always seeks to ensure compliance of its laws with the provisions of international conventions. One can mention Article 1 of law No. 80 of 2002 on combating money-laundering, which matches with the definition of the acts referred to in the International Convention for the Suppression of the Financing of Terrorism; Articles 86 and 86 bis of law No. 97 of 1992 agrees with Article 2 of the same convention.

Egypt evidences also a great support for decisions adopted by international organizations concerning the terrorist phenomenon. Thus, Egypt has supported and voted in favor of the following decisions:

- Declaration on Measures to Eliminate International Terrorism, adopted by the General Assembly of the UN (Resolution 49/60 of December 9, 1994);[21]
- Consideration of Effective Measures to Enhance the Protection, Security, and Safety of Diplomatic and Consular Missions and Representatives (Resolution 53/97 of 1998).

Moreover, in October 1995, Egypt submitted a draft resolution to the General Assembly of the UN, providing:

- the study of the topic concerning terrorism every year, instead of once every two years, as has been decided;
- the presentation by the Secretary General of an annual report on terrorist accidents that occurred during the previous year;
- the enhancement of cooperation among states for combating terrorism;
- the increasing of cooperation between the UN and specialized agencies in the field of combating terrorism.[22]

It is well known that various conferences have been convened with a view to combating international terrorism. One can mention, for example, the following: (1) the International Conference for Combating Terrorism (held at Alexandria in September 1994, in which one hundred fifty states participated); (2) the Ninth UN Congress on the Prevention of Crime and the Treatment of Offenders (Cairo 1995); (3) the Preparatory African Regional Meeting (Kampala 1994); (4) the Preparatory Regional Meeting for the Western Asian States (Amman 1994); (5) the International Ministerial Conference Concerning Transboundary Organized Crime (Italy 1994); (6) the International Conference for Combating Terrorism (the Philippines 1996).[23]

Egypt has taken part in nearly all international conferences [24] held for the purpose of preventing, studying, and combating international terrorism. In those conferences, Egypt has played an important role and exerted the utmost efforts in order to achieve a positive result.

Egypt keeps strict relations and a liaison with the International Criminal Police Organization (INTERPOL) in order to exchange information and data on the terrorist acts and organizations in member states.[25] After the events that occurred in the United States on September 11, 2001, the Security Council adopted Resolution 1373. The resolution established the Counter-Terrorism Committee (CTC) composed of all the fifteen members of the Security Council. The CTC monitors the implementation of Resolution 1373 by all states and tries to increase the capability of states to fight terrorism.

Pursuant to the aforementioned resolution, Egypt submitted to the Security Council five reports and responded to comments and questions requested by the CTC, respectively in 2001, 2002, 2003, 2004, and 2005.[26]

On the Regional Level

Egypt has also exerted various actions on the regional level in order to combat, prevent, and eliminate terrorism. Egypt has ratified, and consequently has become a party to, treaties and conventions concluded under the auspices or within the LAS,[27] which are applicable, in one way or another, to terrorist acts.

In this regard, the most important conventions are the following:

● Convention on Extradition of Criminals, adopted by the Council of the LAS, on September 14, 1952, and ratified by Egypt on March 8, 1954;[28]
● Convention on Declarations and Judicial Delegations, adopted by the Council of the LAS, on September 14, 1952, and ratified by Egypt on March 15, 1954;[29]
● Convention on the Execution of Judgments, adopted by the Council of the LAS, on September 14, 1952, and ratified by Egypt on July 25, 1954;[30]
● The Arab Antiterrorism Agreement, adopted by all the Arab state members of the LAS (twenty-two states) during a joint meeting of the Councils of Arab Interior and Justice ministers on April 22, 1998, and ratified by Egypt on December 14, 1998.[31] The convention entered into force in May 1999.

Article 1, paragraph 2, of the agreement defines terrorism as:

any act of violence or threatening with violence, regardless of its motives or purposes, that takes place in execution of a criminal undertaking, individual or collective, which aims at horrifying people, horrifying them through inflicting harm upon them, endangering the lives, freedom or security, harming

the environment or any of public or private utilities and properties, occupying them, seizing them or endangering any of the
national resources.

To define the crimes of terrorism, the agreement as well refers to
some international conventions and protocols, the provisions of which
are considered as an integral part of the antiterrorism agreement.[32] Moreover, the agreement stipulates the measures of Arab cooperation for combating terrorism.[33]

Additionally, in the African and Islamic context, Egypt signed and
ratified the Convention on the Prevention and Combating of Terrorism
adopted by the Organization of African Unity (1999) and the Convention
of the Organization of Islamic Conference on Combating Terrorism (1999).

Egypt always votes in favor of decisions concerning regional prevention and combating of terrorism. It suffices to refer to the following
examples:

● Egypt supported the Baghdad Declaration to Combat Illegal
Acts Against the Safety of Civil Aviation, adopted by the League
Council in its Resolution No. 5303 (1993), and by the Council
of Arab Transport Ministers in its Resolution No. 115 (1992);[34]
● Egypt voted in favor of Resolutions No. 5862 (adopted on
March 18, 1999) and 5908 (adopted on September 13, 1999),
titled "Request from States which Harbor Terrorists to Extra-
dite Them and to Stop Adopting and Supporting Terrorism."

In those two resolutions, the Council of the LAS decided:

● to refuse and condemn terrorism in all its forms and manifestations;
● to distinguish terrorism from the right of peoples to resist foreign occupation in order to achieve national liberation;
● to request states that harbor terrorists to extradite them to
the states to which they appertain as persons wanted by justice;
● to discuss with the European states the facilities offered to
terrorists under the cover of political asylum.[35]

Egypt voted in favor of Resolution 6345 (of September 9, 2003)
adopted by the Council of the LAS. The resolution confirmed two essential points, namely the necessity to distinguish terrorism from the right
of peoples to resist occupation and foreign aggression and the refusal to
accuse Islam and Muslims of terrorism; and the consultations and cooperation between Arab states as regards the sound implementation of
Security Council Resolution 1373 (2001) with a view to enhancing Arab
coordination in this regard.[36]

Within the LAS, Arab cooperation to combat terrorism takes three essential forms. First, cooperation within the Council of Arab Interior Ministers: The Council was set up by a decision of the League Council (in September 1982). It includes various organs, for example, the Secretariat General, the Arab Office for Combating Crime, the Arab Office for Criminal Police, and the Arab Center for Security Studies. In 1992, at the initiative of Egypt, the council focused its attention on the terrorist problem. Moreover, in 1993 and 1994 Egypt failed to pass a strategy and a plan to combat terrorism, owing to refusal of some Arab states. In January 1995, efforts made by Egypt, Algeria, and Tunisia succeeded in including terrorism on the agenda of the council. In that meeting, Egypt proposed, inter alia: the composition of a governmental working team to draft a code of conduct for member states to combat terrorism; the condemnation of all acts, methods, and practices of terrorism, whatever their source, reasons, and ends; the enhancement of cooperation between Arab states; and the consolidation of bilateral or multilateral cooperation.[37] In January 1996, the Egyptian proposal was adopted. Second, cooperation within the Council of Arab Ministers of Information: In its twenty-sixth session (held in Cairo in 1993), the council discussed, for the first time, a plan to confront terrorism. In 1995, the council adopted a "code of conduct for member states in the Council of Arab Ministers of Information to combat terrorism."[38] Third, cooperation within the Council of Arab Ministers of Justice: In 1994, the council called for the drafting of an Arab convention to prevent terrorism. The draft articles of the convention were sent to member states, and the convention was adopted, as mentioned above, in April 1998.[39]

Egypt has also exerted efforts within the Organization of Islamic Conference (OIC), which resulted in the drafting and adoption of a "code of conduct for member states of the OIC"[40] as well as the convention of 1999 concerning combating terrorism.

On the Bilateral Level

Egypt has entered into negotiations with some states with a view to concluding bilateral[41] agreements relating, in one way or another, to terrorism. We shall first review some of those agreements, and then we shall provide an analysis. Especially in recent years, Egypt concluded a multitude of bilateral agreements concerning criminal matters and the question of terrorism.[42] The bilateral conventions concluded by Egypt, nearly and *mutatis mutandis* ("upon changing that to be changed"), follow a standard pattern with regard to their subject matter and their field of application.

The overwhelming majority of agreements have been concluded with a view to:

- encouraging other states to take immediate steps to prevent the use of their territories or resources to aid, give refuge, or provide sanctuary to individuals committing acts of terrorism;
- trying to isolate perpetrators of terrorist acts;
- preventing and suppressing acts of terrorism;
- extraditing criminals and perpetrators of terrorist acts.

Some of the agreements (e.g., Agreement Between Egypt and Hungary Relating to Organized Crime) refer to other multilateral agreements, for example, Tokyo Convention (1963), Montreal Convention (1971), and the International Convention Against the Taking of Hostages (1979).

Some agreements provide that in certain circumstances, they may not be applied. Thus, Article 8 of the Agreement Relating to Security Matters Between Egypt and Poland provides that each contracting party may refuse, wholly or in part, the application for aid or cooperation, if the application:

- is in conflict with the national sovereignty of the state;
- threatens its security or basic interests; and
- violates its national system and legislation.[43]

Some of the agreements (e.g., the Agreement Relating to Security Cooperation between Egypt and Pakistan, the Understanding Concerning Security Cooperation between Egypt and Sri Lanka) enumerate the obligations incumbent on the parties, as follows:

- exchange of information about activities and crimes of terrorist groups and organizations, as well as those related to organized and transboundary crimes;
- exchange of information about the development of, and new methods concerning the suppression of, terrorism, organized crime, and transboundary crime;
- adoption of measures concerning the detection, search, and arrest of perpetrators of the aforementioned crimes;
- adoption of effective and decisive measures to prevent criminal acts, organized crime, and transboundary crime, especially measures to prevent:
- the use of territories of the contracting parties to plan, organize, or carry out those crimes;
- the infiltration of terrorists and their residence inside the territories of the contracting parties;
- the acquisition by terrorists of funds or training; and

• the conservation of the secrecy of the information in possession of each party.

As for the political defense exception, it is well established that it constitutes a major impediment to the effective apprehension and prosecution of perpetrators of terrorist crimes. In recent times, the defense of the political offense exception is not accepted with respect to those crimes. This constitutes, prima facie, an exception to the exception.

It should be noted that Egypt is inclined to exclude from extradition agreements the political defense exception with regard to terrorist crimes.[44]

The overwhelming majority of agreements provide that they are concluded for an indefinite period, with the possibility for each party, by a written notification, to terminate the operation of the agreement. This termination takes effect either immediately (e.g., Article 9 of the agreement relating to cooperation between Egypt and Yemen) or with the lapse of a certain time, for example, three months (Article 11 of the agreement relating to security cooperation between Egypt and Pakistan), or six months (Article 6 of the agreement relating to security cooperation between Egypt and Cyprus).

Some of the agreements (e.g., Article 9 of the agreement concluded between Egypt and Sri Lanka) expressly provide that their application is ensured either individually by each contracting party, or through diplomatic channels.

Egypt's experience argues for bilateral agreements to be concluded with regard to judicial assistance. In fact, measures of mutual assistance among states in apprehending and prosecuting persons accused of terrorist crimes constitute a *sine qua non instrumentum* ("the instrument without which it could not be") to combat terrorism. Judicial assistance in criminal matters is a term commonly used to refer to some arrangements between states, such as the exchange of information regarding criminal investigations, interrogation of witnesses, transfer of criminal proceedings, enforcement of criminal judgments, and transfer of criminals convicted in the other country. The need for widespread methods of judicial assistance in criminal matters through bilateral and/or multilateral conventions is indispensable for combating international terrorism. Such assistance may be considered as an inducement to lawful rendition of terrorists.

With regard to extradition, it is also important for the development of friendly relations and good neighborliness among states. It constitutes a means of international rendition of offenders to states where they are wanted for prosecution (whereas expulsion or deportation does not necessarily imply that effect).

Nevertheless, some states may have sympathy for the terrorist cause. They may harbor terrorists who have committed crimes in another state, give them a safe haven, and even support them *expressis verbis* or *sub silentio* (expressly and in silence). However, it is well known that if a state does not agree to extradite a terrorist, it should prosecute him. This is a mere application of the formula *aut dedere aut judicare* ("extradite or submit to prosecution"). Recently, Egypt concluded a number of extradition agreements with several states,[45] with a view to confronting the terrorist phenomenon.[46]

On the Domestic Level

Clearly, legislation is one of the most effective and efficient weapons to combat terrorism. As is the case in many states, such as France, Italy, Spain, Germany, the United States, and the United Kingdom, Egypt has adopted laws concerning the terrorist phenomenon, the most important of which is law No. 277 of 1992. This constitutes the central response in Egyptian law to terrorism.[47] It is not an independent law or an omnibus legislation for combating terrorism. Rather, it is incorporated in the penal code. It has also, as will be indicated below, introduced some amendments to other laws relating to terrorist activities. Egypt has also adopted other measures and policies to combat terrorism and terrorist acts.

Definition of Terrorism under Egyptian Law

Law No. 277 of 1992 was adopted in order to address the phenomenon of terrorism.[48] It amended the provisions of the penal code, the criminal proceedings code, the law setting up national security courts, the law on the secrecy of bank accounts, and laws regulating the possession of weapons. Article 86 of the penal code, as amended by law No. 97 of 1992, states:

> For purposes of the application of the provisions of the present law, "terrorism" means any use or threat of the use of force, violence, threat or intimidation by a criminal in order to carry out a criminal project, collective or individual, with a view to disrupting public order or endangering the safety and security of the society, if it involves hurting or intimidating its members, endangering their lives, freedoms or security, damaging the environment, public telecommunications, means of public transportation, public funds, buildings, public or private property, or the occupation or seizure (taking possession) of such property, or preventing or impeding public authorities, places of worship and institutions of learning of their functions, or undermining the application of the constitution, laws and regulations in force.

The law also contains a list of terrorist offenses, such as (1) establishing or subscribing to organizations threatening the state; (2) compelling other persons to join illicit organizations; (3) communicating with a foreign state or organization for the purpose of committing terrorist acts against the state; (4) joining the armed forces of a foreign state or joining foreign terrorist bands; (5) seizing public means of transportation; (6) engaging in conflict with law enforcement authorities controlling terrorism; (7) inviting another person to join an agreement aimed at the commission of a crime in connection with terrorist activity, even if this invitation has not been accepted, or having knowledge of the existence of a plan to commit such crimes and failing to inform the authorities thereof.

With regard to the aforementioned law, the following two remarks are to be put forward. The first concerns the wide nature and scope of the definition set forth by the law. In fact, it contains a broad list of acts and offenses punishable there under; and the second relates to the fact that the law concerns any act that appears to have been done in the commission, preparation, and instigation of acts of terrorism as well as any act that appears to have been done in furtherance of, or in connection with, such acts.

Egypt's "No Concessions" Policy

The adoption of a hardline position or a softline (flexible) one constitutes, with respect to terrorist acts, a difficult decision. Egypt adopts a hard, firm, and uncompromising line. This means that the principle of no negotiations with and no concessions to, perpetrators of terrorist acts is the *rule* applied by Egypt. Accordingly, Report No. 14 states that it is impossible to have a dialog with terrorists who have used guns and consider them as the sole language of understanding, because they are thus outside the law and legitimacy.[49]

Media Coverage and Terrorist Activities in Egypt

Undoubtedly, mass media and other means involved in providing information services have an important role with regard to the manner in which a state combats terrorism. Egypt has affirmed, in this respect, that, "The media has a considerable effect in crime prevention both in urban and rural areas. Media material, films and programs should refrain from depicting crime, violence, sex which would have crimogenic effects on the young generation. Instead, positive attitudes should be emphasized by focusing on religious values and ethical teaching to safeguard youngsters against crime and violence."

Moreover, the Ministry of Interior has adopted the following:

- a strategy was formulated to address violence, terrorism, and crime through the media;
- a modern information center was established that is well

equipped with facilities for communication with the media at the domestic and international levels with a view to building an effective communication system for the rapid exchange of data;

- television material for raising public awareness was produced;
- scientific studies and public opinion surveys were undertaken on various social strata in order to produce inputs for the formulation of a media plan to combat crime.[50]

Pursuit and Sentencing of Perpetrators of Terrorist Acts

In Egypt, perpetrators of terrorist acts are tried either before the Supreme Court for the Security of State, in other words, Emergency Courts,[51] or before military courts, in accordance with a decision of the president of the Republic.[52] It is worth recalling that law 97 of 1992 on counterterrorism provides that the investigation of the offenses is the responsibility of the Supreme Public Prosecutor for State Security which is directly under the Attorney General's office. Additionally, penalties to be applied include some preventive measures, imprisonment, reinforced life imprisonment, and capital punishment.

Jurisdiction of Egyptian Law with Regard to the Pursuit of Offenders in Transboundary Terrorist Acts

Under the principle of territoriality, the state on whose territory the crime or a part of the crime takes place has jurisdiction to pursue the offender, regardless of the nationality of the offender or that of the victim. This is provided by Article 1 of the Egyptian penal code.

Moreover, in accordance with the principles of personal active jurisdiction and dual criminalization, if an Egyptian commits, in another state, an offense constituting a crime or misdemeanor under Egyptian law and provided that the offense is punishable by the law of that state, he is to be tried before Egyptian courts, provided that he has not been exonerated by a competent foreign court or, in case of a final judgment issued against him, fully served the sentence there.

Additionally, under Article 40 of the Egyptian penal code, the various forms of complicity in an offense (e.g., incitement, conspiracy, or assistance) are penalized. Article 45 penalizes, as well, the attempt to commit a crime when the commission of the latter is halted or aborted for reasons independent of the perpetrator's will.

Finally, Egyptian law and courts have jurisdiction under the *in rem* ("against the matter") principle for crimes committed outside Egyptian territory by an Egyptian or an alien, provided that such crimes affect Egyptian security or interests. This includes terrorism and terrorist offenses. Act No. 97 of 1992, the provisions of which are embodied in the penal code (Articles 86 to 102), deals with acts of terrorism, whether committed or attempted in Egypt or abroad. If the crime was committed outside Egypt and against another state or one of its nationals, the decision to extradite the criminal is governed by international conventions in force; otherwise, extradition is within the discretionary power of Egyptian authorities.

Egypt has prepared a draft law on international judicial cooperation in criminal matters. The main two characteristics of the draft are: it is of a general nature, in other words includes extradition, letters rogatory, transfer of criminal proceedings, recognition and enforcement of criminal judgments, transfer of convicted persons; it provides that cooperation with international criminal courts is permissible.[53]

Egyptian Law and the Control of Funds Sent for Purposes of Terrorist Acts

The prevention of terrorist financing and money-laundering offenses are among the priorities of each legal system, be it national or international. In this context, Egypt maintains that control systems in national banks should be tightened to enable the monitoring of dirty money and facilitate the early detection without violating the rules of secrecy of bank accounts and bank transactions. This requires the establishment of committees or units within the bank itself, to ensure the transparency of capital movement on the one hand, and secrecy of transactions on the other. Financial institutions should also be empowered to check on the legality of the money deposited, if there be circumstantial reasons for doubt.

Egyptian law No. 205 of 1990, as amended by law No. 97 of 1992, concerning the secrecy of accounts, is cognizant of such aspects. The law provides for the exchange of information between the Central Bank and other banks, and the right of control authorities possess to access information about accounts.[54]

Additionally, in accordance with Article 3 of the same law, the Attorney General or any public prosecutor may request the Cairo Court of Appeal to permit him to take data or information relating to accounts, deposits, trusts, safes, or safety deposits, if this is necessary to provide evidence of a crime.[55] The same law empowers the Attorney General to order the examination of bank accounts of accused persons.

Moreover, Article 17 of law No. 84 of 2002, concerning nongovernmental societies and associations (private institutions), provides that the acceptance by the association of donations from outside Egypt is only possible with the permission of the Minister of Insurance and Social Affairs, who first establishes their provenance and purposes.[56]

Finally, Article 98 (e) Egyptian penal code provides that assets which have been considered to be earmarked for expenditure on terrorist organizations should be confiscated.

Undoubtedly, money laundering is a dangerous means usually used by perpetrators of terrorist crimes. It consists of concealing or misrepresenting the source of money, changing facts relating to it, or preventing access to the persons who committed the crime from which the money has been derived. Combating it is, accordingly, a *sine qua non conditio* ("without which it could not be") for fighting terrorism. This should include[57] confiscation, tracing, freezing, or provisional seizure of assets or proceeds resulting from money laundering.

Law No. 80 concerning combating money laundering was adopted in 2002; the law has been amended by law No. 78 of 2003.[58] The law prohibits any money laundering resulting from crimes of terrorism (Article 2). It also provides for the possibility of the seizure of the assets of the accused, including a ban on his disposition or administration of them (Article 5). Under Articles 15 and 16, imprisonment and a heavy fine may be imposed upon the accused.

A unit for combating money laundering (the Anti-Money-Laundering Unit) was established within the Central Bank of Egypt in 2002.[59] The formation of the unit and the rules governing its management, operation, and personnel have been determined by the presidential decree No. 164 of 2002 and by the decrees of the Prime Minister No. 1599 of 2002 and No. 951 of 2003.

Since June 2001, Egypt has been subject to "assessment by the Financial Action Task Force (FATF) aimed at monitoring the extent of Egypt's commitment to implementing the FATF recommendations on terrorist financing and money laundering. Egypt had been included on the list of noncooperative countries and territories (NCCTS), but was removed from the list in February 2004 in view of the institutional and practical changes it had introduced in that area."[60]

Egyptian Law and Compensation of Diplomatic Agents Who Are Victims of Terrorist Attacks

Because Egyptian diplomatic agents may become victims of terrorist acts, the law No. 45 of 1982 concerning diplomatic and consular function provides that they have a right to compensation, for example, for any damage resulting from being taken hostage by terrorists.[61]

Measures Taken by Egypt to Stand Against Terrorist Crimes

It is well established that state responsibility for injuries to aliens, particularly occasioned by terrorist acts, may arise if the state fails to provide the necessary measures for protection of such individuals (the "due diligence" doctrine), fails to apprehend or punish perpetrators of terrorist attacks, or actively supports terrorist activities by providing arms, funds, or training facilities.

Increased supervision of the efficacy, practicality, and efficiency of security measures and law enforcement is necessitated by the above-mentioned responsibility. This is applied, *grosso modo,* in Egypt.[62]

The Adoption of Preventive Measures to Counteract Terrorist Acts

It goes without saying that "to prevent is better than to cure." It is preferable to prevent terrorism than to combat attacks already sustained. To secure frontiers as well as points of entry and exit by land, air, and sea is indispensable in this regard. For that purpose, some measures have been enacted by Egypt in order to prevent terrorist acts or infiltrations. One can mention, for example, the following:

(1) Decision of the president of the Republic No. 298 of 1995 relating to "securing eastern borders of Arab Republic of Egypt." The decision prohibits and punishes:

● any illegal infiltration therefrom;
● any person who digs an underground road or tunnel in the aforementioned area, especially for purposes of entry or exit of arms, ammunition, or explosives inside or outside the Republic.[63]

(2) Order of the prime minister and the deputy general military governor, No. 6 of 1996, prohibiting and punishing:

● photocopying of identity cards of armed forces and policemen;
● manufacturing, production, and selling of the official uniform of armed forces and policemen.[64]

(3) Order of the prime minister and the deputy general military governor, No. 3 of 1998. The order:

● prohibits the import, manufacturing, or possession of bugging devices in any cases not authorized by law;
● punishes any breach thereto, by imprisonment for a period not less than one year; and provides that the penalty is imprisonment if the crime is committed to carry out a "terrorist purpose."[65]

(4) Unauthorized possession of arms is prohibited by Egyptian law.[66] The penalty is aggravated if those arms are used or intended to be used in an activity that constitutes a disturbance of the peace and public safety in the country.[67]

(5) The supplying of terrorist gangs or groups with weapons, ex-

plosives, funds, materials, or instruments is penalized by the penal code (Article 86/a).

(6) Article 11 of law No. 48 (2002) concerning nongovernmental associations prohibits any nongovernmental association from establishing any "military or para-military groups."[68]

(7) Providing all national land, sea, and air points of exit and entry with modern equipments for detecting falsified documents as well as explosives, weapons, bombs, etc.

(8) Surveillance or interception of modes of communications (e.g., on the internet, letters, parcels, telegrams, messages, and conversations on wired or wireless networks) is possible. This requires a special authorization from an investigating judge. However, in case of terrorist acts, the public prosecutor's office issues such an authorization.

(9) Egyptian authorities check the identity of passengers of international flights before their departure or after their arrival. Various lists, e.g., travel-ban lists, pre-arrival screening lists, and checklists, are kept at all points of entry to the country (ports, airports, and land accesses).[69]

The Policy of Repentance

The acceptance of repentance of persons who have committed violent acts is a policy followed by Egypt. This aims at achieving four objectives, namely:

- to create a friction, tension, and conflict inside terrorist organizations;
- to obtain information from repentants which may benefit police authority;[70]
- to give the repenter a chance to come back to the right path;
- to encourage others to reject violence, by showing them that terrorism, violence, and organized crime do not pay.

The Application of Severe Penalties and Exclusion of Amnesty

Law No. 97 of 1992 illustrates that penalties to terrorist crimes as well as the illegal possession of weapons and ammunitions have been stiffened (Articles 2 and 7). The penalties include: death penalty and lifelong imprisonment for perpetrators of terrorist crimes as well as persons cooperating with them. Moreover, Article 4 of the same law provides that terrorist offenses may not lapse, meaning statutory limitations are not applicable to those crimes.[71] This is mainly because terrorist offenses are crimes affecting freedoms of individuals.[72] The practice followed by Egypt is that decisions of amnesty, issued by the president of the Republic, do not apply to terrorist offences set forth in law No. 97 of 1992.[73]

No Safe Haven for Perpetrators of Terrorist Crimes

Egypt follows a policy of denial of safe haven to those who commit terrorist offenses.[74] Moreover, decision No. 331 (1980) of the president of Egypt was adopted in conformity with the UN convention relating to the status of refugees (1951).[75] The convention does not apply to any person with respect to whom there are serious reasons that he has committed a serious nonpolitical crime outside the state of refuge prior to his admission to that state as a refugee.

The National Committee for International Cooperation in Combating Terrorism

The prime minister's decision No. 847 of 1998 set up a national committee for international cooperation in combating terrorism. The committee is chaired by the Minister of Justice and has members representing the Ministry of Justice, the Ministry of the Interior, the Ministry of Foreign Affairs, and the Intelligence Service. The committee is responsible for: preparing, within the legal rules defined by the laws of the countries concerned, the documentation needed to request the handing over to the Egyptian authorities of terrorists who have fled abroad, or at least to thwart their criminal activities in the countries where they are located and to consider the legal, political, and other measures that can be taken to neutralize those activities; proposing the desired agreements and participating in their preparation with the other parties concerned; and taking measures to ensure that terrorists who have fled are prosecuted in accordance with the rules of international law and the treaties and legislation in force, and coordinating counterterrorism efforts.

Conclusion

It goes without saying that terrorism is in conflict with the principle of the "bodily integrity of persons" and the rule according to which "each people has an inherent right to the integrity of its members and their belongings."[76]

Egypt is not an exception in this regard. It has suffered from many terrorist acts and has been affected by various forms of terrorist activities, be they domestic or international.

Once the phenomenon of terrorism emerged, the Egyptian legislature included terrorist offenses in the penal code among the serious crimes. Steps taken by Egypt (be they of a legislative, executive, or administrative nature) as well as those under consideration, in other words those that may be taken, are envisioned to be taken, or are currently being implemented, prove that Egypt has applied necessary measures for fighting terrorism. These actions are owing to the fact that terrorism has always been devastating and has had an extremely serious impact on the country's social, economic, cultural, and political interests.

An Outline of Egypt's Attitude Vis-à-vis the Terrorist Phenomenon

The most important remedies adopted by Egypt in order to combat the terrorist phenomenon are the following:[77]

(1) adoption of legislative amendments (e.g., law No. 97 of 1992);[78]

(2) acceptance of repentance of persons who have committed terrorist acts;

(3) adoption of a comprehensive strategy for confronting terrorism on the security, economic, political, cultural, mass media, educational, religious, and other levels, which has treated the roots of the problem as well as its manifestations;[79]

(4) encouragement of international cooperation on global, regional, and bilateral levels;

(5) adoption of other measures, such as:

● improvement of public services and the presentation of services to citizens;
● control and supervision of mosques by the Ministry of Waqf;
● prevention of many terrorist projects before their achievement as well as the arrest and pursuit of a great number of terrorist leaders and elements;
● building of a database concerning terrorist organizations;
● improvement of police force efficiency;
● control of Egyptian borders, by taking all necessary measures to prevent the infiltration of terrorist elements, weapons, and

funds through frontiers (about one hundred persons who attempted to cross borders from neighboring states were arrested
in 1994–1995);[80]

(6) the application of severe penalties.

In summary, Egypt has effectively acted against all forms of terrorism as well as any act to encourage, instigate, or organize the
commission or preparation of terrorist acts.[81] Nevertheless, a completely
comprehensive set of measures for combating and eliminating terrorism
is an impossible task. These measures should ensure a decisive balance
between three requirements, namely:

● protection of national security;
● preservation of lives and properties of innocent persons; and
● respect for, and observance of, rights and fundamental freedoms of the accused and suspected persons.[82]

What Works and What Does Not Work in Fighting Terrorism in Egypt?

From the foregoing analysis, one can affirm that domestic measures taken by Egypt (e.g., the adoption of legislation for the sake of
combating terrorism, Egypt's no concessions policy, media coverage,
sentencing and pursuit of criminals, the control of funds, frontiers,
and money laundering) have achieved their purposes.

However, with respect to international agreements, especially
bilateral ones, their success is not entirely satisfactory. This is owing
to two major reasons. First, states are still reluctant to conclude such
agreements with Egypt. Second, in some of the agreements that have
been concluded, there are some texts permitting each party, as mentioned above, to refuse to carry out its obligations for reasons of national security and/or sovereignty.

Islam Has No Linkage with Terrorist Acts Committed in Egypt

It is well established that Islam is a tolerant religion that prohibits
illegitimate violence, intimidation, and terror.[83] However, in the Western
world (particularly in the United States and in Europe), some writers do
not make a clear distinction between Islam and terrorist acts that occur
in or outside Egypt. They think that Islam is responsible for those acts.[84]
This notion is gaining currency now, but is untenable and ill founded. In

fact, Islam prohibits any unjustified or illegitimate violence. Terrorism is strange to Islam, because the final end of Islam is to preserve the life of man, the reproduction of human beings as well as their properties and belongings.[85] If some Muslims practice terrorism, this does not mean that Islam welcomes their acts.[86]

Islam is even considered as a *sine qua non instrumentum* to combat terrorism.[87] In this connection, the concept of Islam is clear. It is forbidden to attack the life of others. As the Holy Qur'an says: "Take not life which God Hath made sacred, except by way of justice and law" (6/ 151). According to the Holy Qur'an, the protection of the lives of others is a matter that belongs to humanity in its entirety. Thus, the Qur'an says: "That if anyone slew a person—unless it be for murder or for spreading mischief in the land—it would be as if he slew the whole people; and if anyone saved a life, it would be as if he saved the life of the whole people."

The above-mentioned verse of the Qur'an connotes three consequences. First, terrorists are to be considered as *hostis humane generis* (enemies of humanity). They must be reckoned as outside the pale of humanity. Their existence is considered injurious to all mankind. Second, this inevitably means that respect of human life, in Islam, is a duty owed to all the world (i.e., *erga omnes*), not only toward a certain person (i.e., *si omnes*).[88] Third, the Holy Qur'an considers homicide as an attack against all mankind and saving a man's life as saving the lives of all mankind (i.e., it is *delicta juris gentium*).

6

SRI LANKA

Vernon L. B. Mendis

Sri Lanka, formerly Ceylon, is a pearl-shaped island the size of West Virginia, suspended off the Indian subcontinent, in the Indian Ocean. The majority community of indigenous Sinhalese, mostly Buddhist, today consists of 73 percent of the population. The minority community of indigenous Tamils, mostly Hindus, accounts for 12.6 percent of the population.

The Sinhalese had for centuries lived in comparative harmony with the indigenous Tamils. However, with the imposition of British colonial rule in the late eighteenth century, the "divide and rule" policy was followed with impunity, with preferential treatment to the Tamil community over the majority Sinhalese. The onus was on the Sri Lankan leaders who took over the reins of power from the British, following independence on February 4, 1948, to rectify this situation and correct the imbalance created in the system.

However, in the move to satisfy the Sinhalese, there was inevitable displeasure incurred among the Tamils, who felt they were being discriminated against unfairly. The first communal riots of any magnitude occurred in 1956 and 1958, with aggression from the Sinhalese directed at the Tamils. The Sinhalese Only policy ushered in by former Prime Minister S. W. R. D. Bandaranaike, who broke away from the ruling United National Party (UNP) and formed his own party, the Sri Lanka Freedom Party (SLFP), in 1956, added fuel to the fire of ethnic tension, with Tamils forced to learn Sinhalese in order to communicate with the government. There were restrictions placed on higher education and the civil service with the installation of a quota system proportionate to the percentage of population. The Tamils, again, perceived this treatment as discrimination, for quotas as opposed to merit naturally gave more opportunity for the Sinhalese at the expense of the Tamils, as the Sinhalese were the majority community.

Within this unhappy setup, the indigenous Tamil community, who had, over the years, covertly indulged in ethnic cleansing in the North, chasing away the Sinhalese who had lived there among them for generations, became decisively violent beginning in the early 1970s. This was mani-

fest in the several acts of terrorism that took place in the Jaffna peninsula at the time. Alfred Duraiappah, a very moderate Tamil mayor in
Jaffna, became the first victim of Velupillai Prabhakaran, who at the
time was the leader of the Liberation Tigers of Tamil Eelam (LTTE), a
rebel group that sought a separate nation for the Tamil minority. In February 1971, bombs were thrown at the mayor's residence. On March 11,
1971, a bomb was placed in the mayor's car but did not injure him. On
August 27, 1972, Prabhakaran, then just an eighteen-year-old youth, exploded bombs in a carnival organized by the mayor at the Jaffna Sta-
dium. He repeated the performance at the same venue on September 17,
1972, as he had been unsuccessful in hitting his target. He failed again.
On December 19, 1972, he targeted the mayor's residence, but to no
avail. However, on July 27, 1975, Prabhakaran and two others assassinated Mayor Duraiappah, when the mayor drove to Krishnan Temple in
Ponnalai. The mayor was a representative of the central government in
Colombo. His murder was symbolic of the contempt that the rising Tamil
rebels had for representatives from Colombo governing the North. This
was Prabhakaran's initiation into bloodshed and murder.

The LTTE had its origins as the Tamil New Tigers (TNT), which
Prabhakaran later converted into the LTTE and which was covertly supported by the Tamil United Liberation Front (TULF), the political party representing the Tamil community in Colombo's political setup. The Tamil community gave the TULF consent only in 1977 to agitate for a separate state.
Appapillai Amirthalingam, TULF leader and opposition leader in parliament
from 1977 until July 5, 1989, when he was assassinated by the LTTE in
Colombo, used government stationery to write letters of reference for fund-
raising for the LTTE and helped it to become a significant force. Two prominent TULF youth members joined the LTTE—Uma Maheshwaran as chairman and Urmila Kandiah as its first female member. Amirthalingam introduced N. S. Krishnan to Prabhakaran; and Krishnan, in turn, introduced to
the LTTE its present high-profile theoretician and ideologue, Anton
Balasingham. The time had still not come for internecine warfare among
the Tamil insurgency groups, where LTTE would emerge victorious.

LTTE's Battle for a Separate State and the Ensuing Negotiation Attempts Since 1984

The LTTE's battle for a separate state has been relentless since the
violent communal riots of July 1983, except for a brief respite during the
ceasefires of 1989–1990, 1994–1995, and since 2001. However, no legitimate Sri Lankan government could ever accede to this demand for a separate state—the demand for one-third of the land and two-thirds of the coast
of Sri Lanka for 12.6 percent of the population.

However, it was always a tightrope walk for Sri Lanka to fight terrorism since this kind of fighting was, for so long, internationally relegated to "an internal conflict," with the international community more sympathetic to the LTTE than to the Sri Lankan government. Hardliners and nationalists in the Sinhalese community favored an all-out war on terrorism, but the government had the unenviable task of allocating money for war and also maintaining a positive image internationally in the face of intensive false propaganda globally by the LTTE.

The All Party Conference (APC) in Colombo, Sri Lanka

The government of President J. R. Jayewardene convened an APC in January 1984 to try to solve the ethnic conflict that was gathering momentum and escalating into a major wave of terrorism. The participants included the ruling UNP, the SLFP, the then opposition, the TULF, and five smaller Tamil political groups. G. Parthasarthy, then Indian Prime Minister Indira Gandhi's special envoy to Sri Lanka for mediatory efforts between the Sri Lankan government and the TULF, had extensive discussions with both sides to formulate a set of proposals. The Sri Lankan government agreed to convene an All Party Conference to consider these proposals (which came to be known as Annexure C). The proposals in Annexure C were centered on the creation of separate regional councils in the northern and eastern provinces of Sri Lanka. The main issue discussed at the APC was devolution, with the government proposing the granting of autonomy to the country's districts through the creation of district councils and other changes in local government. The government also proposed establishing a second house of parliament, a council of state, whose members would include the chairmen and vice chairs of the district councils, which would have both legislative and advisory roles. Tamil spokesmen rejected the proposals, as they did not offer special links between northern and eastern provinces.

The APC wound up on December 21, 1984. Although the plan had been to resume talks in 1985, they never materialized. Even if there had been an agreement on devolution, its implementation would have been difficult, with the SLFP and a smaller Sinhalese party, the Mahajana Eksath Peramuna, having withdrawn from the negotiations. Added to this, the proposals were denounced by militant Sinhalese groups like politically active Buddhist monks, who viewed the talks as a sellout to the Tamils.

APC Fails. Violence Intensifies

Even while the APC was considering alternatives to end ethnic strife in the country, the Tigers went on a massive ethnic-cleansing rampage, wiping out two entire Sinhalese farming villages on November 30, 1984: the Dollar and Kent farms. This massacre of more than one hundred civilians—men, women, children, and babies, while they slept—was the first of regular attacks on Sinhalese communities living in the areas demarcated by the LTTE for separation. As the Sinhalese suffered under wave upon relentlessly bloody wave of terrorism, the Sri Lankan government escalated its military operations against the LTTE, taking the stand that it would tackle "terrorism" before trying to reach a political solution. In tit-for-tat attacks, the LTTE committed sacrilege on May 14, 1985, storming the sacred precincts of the Sri Maha Bodhi, in Anuradhapura, shooting and killing one hundred twenty Sinhalese Buddhist pilgrims, and injuring eighty-five others.

Meanwhile, Sri Lanka's foreign policy veered sharply pro-Western and pro-American, with closer cooperation with Singapore, South Korea, and Southeast Asia. Particularly with Sri Lanka's own economic liberalization since 1978, the Jayewardene regime tried to reestablish diplomatic and military links with Israel to strengthen Sri Lanka's capacity to wage counterterrorism war against Tamil secession. Israel provided military training and military hardware for the government. This series of events displeased India, which perceived threats to its vision of regional security that disallowed the entrance of outside forces making use of its smaller neighbors. This inevitably led to tension in Indo-Sri Lanka relations.

Talks in Thimpu, Bhutan

The next attempt at peace talks with the LTTE was with Indian mediation, which was held in Thimpu, Bhutan. Two rounds of direct negotiations were conducted in Thimpu in July 1985 and August 1985. These talks were adjourned in mid-August without agreement, and there was still a very wide gap between the positions of the two sides. In fact, the second round of peace talks in August ended abruptly and unexpectedly in failure, when the Tigers and TULF leaders walked out.

The Sri Lankan side was prepared to concede the formation of separate provincial councils, albeit with limited powers. The Tigers repeated their unchanged demands for recognition of nationality with the right to self-determination and the right to an identified homeland—the merger of northern and eastern provinces. The moderate TULF also insisted on the need for a merger of the northern and eastern provinces and the granting of substantial powers to this Tamil linguistic province. (For the Tamils, the difficulty in accepting a separate Eastern Provincial Council lay in their fear that being only 40 percent of that province, they might not be able to form or control the provincial government when it emerged, and would not be able to stop the erosion of their demographic position in the area, or retain control over lands being colonized and over the law-and-order machinery.)

Sri Lanka's representative at the talks, H. W. Jayewardene, spent a week in New Delhi following the collapse of the Thimpu talks, speaking with Prime Minister Rajiv Gandhi and other senior Indian officials. The result of these talks was a fresh set of proposals presented in a working paper that served as the basis for further negotiations. The paper, carrying some specific commitments, was not a breakthrough in any sense. It did not provide for a merger of the North and East, but proposed for powers to be devolved to provincial councils by parliament with a simple majority vote. Though law and order were among the subjects to be devolved, the police would be drawn from the national police service. The most contentious issue, land allotment and settlement, was not clearly interpreted. The paper failed to define many important issues, but the power to determine national policies and the power to provide guidelines were retained by the center.

When the Sri Lankan government approved the paper, India was supposed to negotiate it with Tamils in its role as mediator of the conflict. On September 4, 1985, Sri Lanka's Foreign Minister, A. C. S. Hameed, informed the Indian High Commissioner in Colombo, J. N. Dixit, that the Sri Lankan cabinet and parliament were not ready to approve New Delhi's document. Specific objection to the basic proposals prepared by India included some constitutional and legal elements that could alter the unitary character of the Sri Lankan state, which could be the first step toward Tamil areas seceding from Sri Lanka.

TULF representatives met in Delhi later to discuss the working paper and matters relating to the maintenance of the cease-fire beyond the three-month period. The cease-fire, which was to expire on 18 September 1985, was unilaterally extended by Sri Lanka, with a committee set up by the government to monitor the workings of the cease-fire. For all practical purposes, the war raged on.

TULF leader Amirthalingam disagreed with the Indian draft and wrote to Rajiv Gandhi that there were three issues on which the Tamil delegation would never compromise. They were the Tamil homeland, the devolution of power in regard to land and land settlement, and law and order. India was concerned about reports that Sri Lanka was pursuing a military solution to the crisis, and about information that Israeli intelligence organizations and British security experts were involved with Sri Lanka.

New Sri Lanka Proposals

On January 30, 1986, the Sri Lankan government rejected a set of proposals put forward by the TULF, dismissed the federal form of government envisaged in the TULF's proposal, and insisted on the unitary character of the constitution. It also rejected the merger of the North and East to form a single unit. Subsequent to Rajiv Gandhi's comment of dissatisfaction, the Sri Lankan government revised its response about the granting of political rights to the northern and eastern provinces, which were the kind of powers that the Indian constitution had granted to its union territories. When Sri Lanka handed over a second set of revised proposals, the TULF immediately rejected the union territory model as falling short of the kind of devolution the Tamils wanted. In April 1986, following prolonged discussions with a high-powered Indian delegation in Colombo, President Jayewardene agreed to improve the devolution package with suitable institutional arrangements for the provincial councils, especially in the North and East, to consult with each other and act in coordination on matters of mutual interest and concern.

By January 1986, fratricidal warfare had erupted in Sri Lanka among Tamil militant groups. By the end of 1986, the LTTE had emerged as the dominant Tamil militant group, as the Tamil Eelam Liberation Organization (TELO), Eelam People's Revolutionary Liberation Front (EPRLF), and People's Liberation Organization of Tamil Eelam (PLOTE) were proscribed and chased out of the Tamil areas.

Rumors floated that the LTTE was to announce a unilateral declaration of Tamil Eelam (Tamil Homeland) by January 1, 1987. What the LTTE did that day was to declare its plan to license all motor vehicles in the Jaffna district, and to devise an elaborate plan to control traffic in the district in the absence of a civil administration—a prelude to the LTTE gradually taking over civil administration in the North and East. The government's immediate response was to introduce an economic embargo in January 1987, preventing the transport of fuel, food, and other essentials into the North, followed by an escalation of attacks by Sri Lankan security forces in the North and East. This led India to suspend its mediation efforts between the Sri Lankan government and the LTTE.

Many civilian lives were lost during the second half of April 1987. At least 127 Sinhalese were gunned down in the Trincomalee district, followed by a bomb explosion at the main bus station at Pettah, Colombo, resulting in the death of 113 people, with 295 injured. These attacks led the Sri Lankan government to conduct a full-scale military offensive in northeastern Jaffna peninsula—Vadamarachchy—between May 26, and June 2, 1987. The offensive, code-named Operation Liberation, resulted in the deaths of more than one thousand civilians and the arrest of one thousand or more youths, and successfully placed the Sri Lankan government in the driver's seat. The government forces took control of Vadamarachchy and ventured further into Jaffna.

India, concerned over the deteriorating situation in Jaffna, delivered a note to Sri Lanka on June 1, 1987, expressing concern over widespread starvation and food shortages due to the government's embargo.

The note added that India had decided to send relief supplies to the starving Tamil population in Jaffna by boat on June 3. Sri Lanka insisted that it was well able to feed its own people, and firmly rejected India's request. But on June 3, India sent a flotilla of nineteen fishing vessels with thirty-eight tons of provisions to Jaffna from Rameswaram. These vessels flew Red Cross flags and were escorted by a coast guard cutter carrying a battery of Indian and international media, with the discreet presence of an Indian naval craft in the background. The whole exercise, code-named Operation Poomalai, was doomed, with the Indian boats returning to Tamil Nadu after a six-hour standoff with the Sri Lankan Navy. India retaliated by threatening direct intervention. Sri Lanka was outraged. "It is a naked violation of our independence and sovereignty," was Sri Lanka's reply. Even though it appeared that the drama of the airdrop unfolded so swiftly, India had planned it all along in anticipation that Operation Poomalai would fail.

India gave less than an hour's notice in ordering an intrusion into Sri Lanka's airspace by launching Operation Eagle on July 4, 1987. The media were carried by five Antonov AN32 transport planes, accompanied by five Mirage 2000 jet fighters, to witness the dropping of some twenty-five tons of food in and around Jaffna city. The Tamils of Jaffna had a mixed reaction to Operation Eagle. The LTTE maintained silence, whereas other Tamil militant organizations and the Tamil United Liberation Front applauded India's direct intervention. Through its unprecedented action, India confirmed its regional supremacy by gesturing to the world that it would brook no nonsense in its backyard. The airlift was India's most direct intervention in a neighbor's affairs since 1971, when the country's troops were deployed in former East Pakistan to help Bangladesh win independence.

Indian High Commissioner J. N. Dixit held two meetings with President Jayewardene on July 18, reviving fresh hopes to end the ethnic turmoil in the country. India's new proposal was to join the North and East into a single regional unit to be administered by an elected council with wide powers. The agreement reached at the meeting signaled the end to the political impasse that had prevailed since independence.

The Indo-Lanka Peace Accord

Direct Indian intervention culminated in the signing of a peace accord on July 29, 1987, under deep controversy and curfew in Colombo, and without LTTE participation. The accord legitimized the deployment of the Indian military in Sri Lanka, with an assurance of a cease-fire within forty-eight hours, the surrender of Tamil militant weaponry within seventy-two hours, a referendum in the eastern province, devolution of power by establishing a provincial council, and Indian military assistance to implement the accord. India promised to take the required steps regarding the use of its territory by Tamils for terrorist activities.

In terms of the Accord, India was to prohibit the use of Indian territory for anti-Sri Lankan activities. It would close Tiger training camps, confiscate Tiger illegal arms, and shut offices and centers used for spreading separatist propaganda. The Accord also enabled India to tie up strategic interests, such as not allowing the deepwater port of Trincomalee to be used by other foreign powers, reaching an understanding with India about the employment and relevance of foreign military and intelligence personnel in Sri Lanka, and allowing for the review of agreements of foreign broadcasting organizations there. In return, India agreed to assist Sri Lankan security forces with military supplies and training facilities. The LTTE and other Tamil groups opposed the Accord because Tamil representatives were not consulted during the talks.

The Indo-Lanka Accord led to seventy thousand Indian troops landing on Sri Lankan soil, with the launch of Operation Pawan that began in the fall of 1987. Although Indian troops seized Jaffna (but not in the three days they had confidently predicted), the military offensive bogged down into a war of attrition—"India's Vietnam."

Anti-Indian Peace Keeping Forces (IPKF) Sentiments Herald New Chapter

The cumulative effect of hostile incidents between the IPKF and the LTTE provoked open warfare between them, and the IPKF realized soon enough that it was not easy to fight a guerrilla army like the LTTE. Ironically, the LTTE militants whom the Indian troops fought during the two years had been trained and armed by Indian soldiers in civilian clothes, affiliated to India's foreign intelligence agency, the Research and Analysis Wing (RAW). Thus, the LTTE knew the standard psychology, combat strategies, and weaponry of the Indian soldier, while the IPKF had no notion of the LTTE's strategies. Meanwhile, Jaffna Tamils, who earlier had favored Indian involvement in their lives, were now trying to get rid of them. The Indian troops had failed to disarm the LTTE. Anti-IPKF emotions went deep, convincing both the government and the LTTE that the Indian forces should be sent back.

What the IPKF intervention did was to destabilize Sri Lanka rather than bring peace. India ultimately was the main beneficiary of the Accord, securing its strategic interests and deciding Sri Lanka's fate in the light of its own security perceptions. The Accord changed India's position from mediator to guarantor of solution through its military intervention.

India learned lessons too. Deployment of the IPKF in Sri Lanka proved to be a total failure of Indian foreign policy. Renowned Indian defense analyst Ravi Rikhye estimates that the IPKF at its peak numbered as many as 150,000, including paramilitary forces.[1] However, it failed to disarm the LTTE and destroy its fighting capabilities while the LTTE continued to use safehouses in Tamil Nadu during the entire IPKF assignment in Sri Lanka. The IPKF, thus, lost not just its image as a peacekeeper but also about one thousand two hundred soldiers, with more than two thousand wounded. The whole exercise cost India approximately U.S. $1.25 billion.[2]

The Thirteenth Amendment of the Accord and Why It Failed

Political analyst Rohan Edrisinha says the Thirteenth Amendment of the Indo-Lanka Accord was fatally flawed in that "there was no clear division of power between the central government and provincial councils."[3] Dr. Neelan Tiruchelvam—a moderate Tamil, a leading Sri Lankan constitutional thinker, and a Member of Parliament until an LTTE suicide bomber assassinated him in 1999—agreed with Rohan Edirisinha's views. In fact, Dr. Tiruchelvam was involved in drafting the then current peace proposals when he was killed. This 1997 draft was partially federal in its devolutionary approach, but not explicitly so. Coordination between the periphery and the center was suggested, but without a judicial method to settle disputes over power and control. His compromise was to have a "second central legislative chamber to represent distinct regional views at the national level."

Jayadeva Uyangoda, a very vocal political analyst of current times, says that what is needed is "a futuristic political vision of an ethnically heterogeneous political association called a state"—a vision that needs to be shared by Sinhalese, Tamils, and Muslims. He also admits that sharing political power is the "most resisted" approach in Sri Lankan politics, and he "is profoundly skeptical whether a society steeped in violence, destruction, and hatred" has a "moral commitment to enmity," and is "a shell-shocked society, where reason and considered judgment in ethnic politics [have] given way to the politics of anxiety," can right itself easily. He firmly believes that compromise will come hard because "any solution acceptable to Tamil nationalists will almost certainly be unacceptable to Sinhalese nationalists and the Sinhalese people in general."[4]

In 1991, an LTTE female suicide bomber assassinated former Indian Prime Minister Rajiv Gandhi when he was on a campaign trail in South India. This marked a significant turning point in relations between India and the LTTE.

Premadasa–LTTE Talks

President R. Premadasa won the presidential election on December 19, 1988, replacing J. R. Jayewardene. Subsequently, his party, the UNP, won the ninth parliamentary election on February 15, 1989, held for the first time under a proportional representation scheme. His priority was to get Indian troops to withdraw from Sri Lanka, with the country facing another terrorist problem in the South in which the Maoist Janatha Vimukhi Peramuna (JVP) was taking to arms.

Government officials held secret talks with the LTTE in the northern jungles, allegedly even offering cash and weapons, with the aim of ridding the country of the IPKF. Official peace talks between the government and the LTTE began at the Hilton Hotel Colombo in February 1990, with LTTE representatives who were dressed in combat uniforms and were carrying arms flown by helicopter from the northern jungles. The Tiger delegation was led by Yogaratnam Yogi, head of the LTTE's political wing, and included Anton Balasingham (the Tiger's chief negotiator in the 2002 talks) and his Australian-born wife, Adele.

Bowing to Sinhalese extremist demands in ordering the withdrawal of the IPKF, Premadasa was a godsend for the embattled LTTE. With the IPKF gone, the LTTE wasted no time in wiping out rival militant organizations, to which President Premadasa turned a blind eye. His tolerance boomeranged on him when an LTTE suicide bomber assassinated him on May 1, 1993.

The LTTE used the fourteen-month cease-fire during the Premadasa talks to regroup, and the government was taken completely by surprise when the LTTE unilaterally broke the cease-fire on June 11, 1990, insisting that all police stations in the North and East must be closed, and that all police personnel who surrendered would be granted safe passage. Most police officers did just this under government orders. Instead, however, more than six hundred Sinhalese and Muslim police officers were taken to a jungle in the North, blindfolded with hands tied behind their backs, and brutally killed by spray upon spray of automatic fire. President Premadasa had made generous concessions to win the confidence of the LTTE, even to the extent of giving away vital strategic Army camps established by the military and providing arms to the LTTE. However, with the Tigers ruthlessly breaking the cease-fire on June 11, 1990, peace talks ended for the president in disaster and humiliation.

The Premadasa–LTTE peace talks failed over a number of issues, but mainly owing to accusations that both sides were arming themselves while talking peace. It has always been a ploy of the Tigers to use the respite given them by "peace talks" to further prepare for war. Thus, they recruited, forcibly conscripted, and trained fresh cadres, built up supplies, constructed bunkers, and made elaborate and extensive preparations for war, while denying what they were doing and accusing the army of preparing for war.

There were also rumors that Prabhakaran resumed the war because he felt let down. He thought that by helping Premadasa get rid of the IPKF, he would get control of the North and East.

Talking Peace After Premadasa

After President Premadasa was assassinated by a Tiger suicide bomber on May 1, 1993, parliament replaced him with Prime Minister Dingiri Banda Wijetunge. In June 1994, President Wijetunge, hoping to catch the Opposition off guard, called for early general elections in August 1994, which were won by the People's Alliance, ending the seventeen-year rule of the UNP. A visionary leader was very much in need, one who could extricate himself or herself from the dilemma of being the head of a Sinhalese political movement ultimately answerable to the Sinhalese voters and who could see the conflict at a more macro level.

The greatest hope for a negotiated settlement of the conflict came when Mrs. Chandrika Kumaratunga won election to the presidency in 1994 on a mandate promising to end the war. There were positive signs that the peace process would continue and bring about a lasting solution in 1995. Both regionally and internationally, there were also extremely positive responses to the peace process received from India, the United Kingdom, and the European Union (EU).

President Chandrika Kumaratunga and Peace Talks

At the end of 1994, President Chandrika Kumaratunga, who came into power on a mandate for peace, announced a government proposal for a cease-fire. A governmental delegation kept a dialog going with a delegation from Jaffna, and hopes of peace talks were maintained for the first three months of 1995. Negotiations finally broke down with the LTTE accusing the government of poor implementation of agreed-upon issues and stalling on further negotiations. Parity issues at the negotiating table were raised when the government chose to send "unknown" officials to the talks as opposed to major government officials. The Tigers declared an end to the truce and attacked two navy boats in Trincomalee harbor on April 19, 1995. Two planes were also shot down, and assaults by the LTTE on army and police bases as well as on rebel bases by the security forces resumed. Over the next month, the Tigers carried out a spate of attacks on the military, killing over two hundred fifty military personnel caught off guard.

The president initially declared this violence a temporary setback and tried to persuade the LTTE to return to the negotiating table. However, by late June 1995, the government declared it would militarily defeat the LTTE; and so began fierce battles between the Tigers and government troops. Colombo was not safe from Tiger attacks either: there was an explosion in August 1995 outside the Western Provincial Government Office. In October 1995, one of the two main oil refineries in the country was set ablaze. In November 1995, fourteen civilians and three Special Task Forces personnel were killed and fifty-nine people were injured when two LTTE suicide bombers blew themselves up during an attack on the Army Headquarters complex in Colombo. In October 1995, the government launched a major military offensive code-named "Riviresa" (Sunshine), with the clear focus of capturing Jaffna.

Truce Collapses and War Breaks Out Again

In 1996, there was heightened and relentless fighting both by the LTTE and government forces, with several major bomb attacks in Colombo once again bringing the conflict to the south of the country. On January 31, 1996, an LTTE suicide bomber detonated a truck-bomb weighing over one hundred kilograms at the entrance to the Sri Lanka Central Bank in the heart of the capital, killing more than one hundred people and wounding about fourteen hundred. It was the biggest bombing to date in the history of the conflict. Two more attacks occurred later in the year. The LTTE exploded two bombs in a packed commuter train in the evening rush hour in the suburbs of Colombo on July 26, 1996, killing 78 passengers and injuring 257. On April 18, 1996, Sea Tigers launched a suicide raid on the port of Colombo. Nine LTTE cadres were killed when the troops blew up their boats.

Harvard University's Program on International Conflict Analysis and Resolution (PICAR) on Sri Lanka's Conflict Resolution

Since 1994, PICAR, directed by Donna Hicks and William Weisberg, engaged in an unofficial problem-solving dialog to resolve Sri Lanka's conflict peacefully. The project collaborated with the American Friends Service Committee in organizing problem-solving workshops for Tamil, Sinhalese, and Muslim expatriates in the United States to discuss their needs, fears, and concerns, and to jointly develop resolution action.

In 1995, Hicks and Weisberg met with top government officials in Sri Lanka, LTTE leaders, and unofficial leaders with varied viewpoints on the conflict. "With the support of a grant from the United States Institute of Peace, PICAR intended to bring together influential persons affiliated with the government and LTTE in 1997 and 1998, using the interactive problem-solving approach, for discussions designed to lay the groundwork for effective official negotiations."[5] A second visit by Hicks and Weisberg to Sri Lanka led to a very productive meeting with Sinhalese political and civic leaders in Colombo. However, with an impending military offensive in the North, they could not travel to the North to meet with the LTTE leadership.

It was a stalemate once more. President Kumaratunga would consider further peace talks only after constitutional reform, while the LTTE wanted an official international mediator to negotiate, which the government consistently resisted. The LTTE insisted that high-level officials needed to participate, explaining that it could not work through conduits and must speak for itself. The government agreed to allow nonofficials to participate in problem-solving dialog but was unresponsive on the subject of official Sri Lanka government participation. The government wanted to discuss its proposed devolution of power to local regions, without international mediation, in talks attended by low-level government advisors.

Hicks and Weisberg concluded that "significant progress to end the conflict could only be made through face-to-face interactive processes."[6] (Press releases were not helping either party to fully understand the concerns and constraints of the other, "for the significant changes required to reverse protracted conflict.")[7]

In an environment of mistrust, with two past agreements and a cease-fire scuttled, Donna Hicks and William Weisberg said in their article that "strategic differences seem irreconcilable, and in the absence of interaction between the parties, any attempt to reconcile these differences backfires."[8] During the cessation of hostilities, President Kumaratunga unexpectedly suggested a mediator for the talks, an apparent concession to the Tigers. But the LTTE rejected this unilateral proposal as she had not consulted them and had out of the blue named a possible French mediator whom the Tigers did not know or trust. Probably, if the president had discussed the issue with the Tigers before announcing it publicly, there might have been a more positive reaction from the Tigers.

It was equally obvious that without direct communication between the two parties, each was not accepting the other's dilemma. The government had major political constraints in the form of pressures from the military, the Sinhalese nationalists, and parliamentary coalition partners. To the Tigers, the devolution package became irrelevant when they were not included in the process of developing it.

Terrorist Activity Steps Up

The LTTE continued its terrorist activities in 1997—attacking government troops, hitting economic targets, and assassinating political opponents. The LTTE naval faction attacked commercial shipping, including numerous foreign vessels, abducting the crew of an empty passenger ferry and setting it on fire. In September 1997, the LTTE used rocket-propelled grenades to attack a Panamanian-flagged, Chinese-owned merchant ship chartered by a U.S. chemical company to load minerals for export. Twenty people were killed, wounded, or missing from the attack. In August 1997, a group calling itself the Internet Black Tigers (IBT) claimed responsibility for email harassment of several Sri Lankan missions around the world. The U.S. State Department in *Patterns of Global Terrorism 1997* observed, "The Tigers claimed in Internet postings to be an elite department of the LTTE specializing in 'suicide email bombings' with the goal of countering Sri Lankan government propaganda disseminated electronically, stating the attacks were only warnings." At least thirty people were reported killed and two hundred fifty others were wounded when a suspected Tamil terrorist set off a bus bomb on March 5, 1998, outside a train station in the business district of the Sri Lankan capital. At least three children from two schools in the area and two police officers were among the dead victims.

International Banning of LTTE

The terrorist activities of the LTTE depended largely on the collection of funds abroad, specifically from Tamil expatriates in Western Europe and North America. One of the biggest successes of clamping down on terrorist activity in Sri Lanka was proscribing the LTTE internationally. The first major blow the LTTE received internationally was India's ban on it on May 14, 1992, following the assassination of former Indian Prime Minister Rajiv Gandhi. This was followed on October 8, 1997, when the United States designated the LTTE among thirty other groups as a Foreign Terrorist Organization (FTO), which greatly hampered the LTTE's ability to mobilize funds internationally. The money that the LTTE raised overseas at the time reportedly ranged between $5 million and $10 million per month. The LTTE fund-collecting activities in the United States had to go underground.

In October 2003, the United States redesignated twenty-five militant groups as FTOs, including the LTTE, and preserved its right to take action against them. The designation includes a ban on U.S. visas for group members, a freezing of assets in the United States, and a prohibition on any U.S. citizen or person under U.S. jurisdiction providing assistance to them. The United States officially supported the peace talks between Sri Lanka and the LTTE, but determined "that the LTTE continues to engage in terrorist activities."

On February 28, 2001, the United Kingdom designated twenty-one rebel groups as "terrorist organizations," including three Kashmiri organizations and Sri Lanka's LTTE. This designation was made under a new antiterrorism law designed to halt funding and support for United Kingdom–based terrorist groups. Britain's Terrorism Act replaced legislation aimed primarily at containing the thirty-year conflict in Northern Ireland. The new law made it an offense to belong to any of the banned groups and to support or to raise funds for them.

On December 21, 2001, the Australian government—complying with UN Security Council Resolution 1373 of September 28, 2001, to suppress the financing of terrorism—named twenty-five organizations, including the LTTE, as terrorist organizations whose assets must be frozen under the Charter of the United Nations (Anti-terrorism Measures) Regulations 2001. In February 1996, Malaysia made it a criminal act to support the LTTE, under which foreigners backing pro-LTTE rallies would face deportation. In November 2005, Canada became the latest Western country to declare the LTTE a terrorist organization and freeze its assets.

Thailand Admits LTTE Presence on Its Soil

For many years, Thailand refused to accept that it was a hub for the LTTE's gunrunning and fund-raising activities. Thai government officials denied the existence of any terrorist base, although former Army Chief General Surayud Chulanont said that the military had been aware of LTTE operations in southern Thailand for some time. Former Prime Minister Chuan Leekpai once said, "[Phuket] may be the smuggling route. . . . But there is no Tamil base in Thailand."⁹ In 2000, Thailand assured Sri Lanka that it would not tolerate Tiger activity on Thai soil any longer. A press release from the Thai government quoted Deputy Prime Minister and Minister of Interior of Thailand Banyat Bautadtan as saying, "It is not our policy to assist any terrorist group and there is no reason why we should allow LTTE terrorists to operate on our soil. We can assure you that we will be on the alert and take all precautions to bring them to book" and that "friendship between Sri Lanka and Thailand will be strengthened further."¹⁰

As the cumulative effect of these curbs and proscriptions, the LTTE was unable to raise funds or indulge in gunrunning on the scale it used to have.

LTTE Strikes Back

Just a week after the United States designated the LTTE as an FTO, the LTTE struck back with its most spectacular terrorist attack on October 15, 1997, with a truck bombing directed at the newly opened Colombo World Trade Center. The explosion injured more than one hundred persons, including many foreigners. Significant collateral damage was done to nearby buildings. This was the first time that the LTTE targeted foreign nationals.

At 6:10 a.m. on January 25, 1998, LTTE suicide bombers exploded a massive truck bomb at the entrance to the most sacred Buddhist temple and the United Nations Educational, Scientific, and Cultural Organization (UNESCO) World Heritage Site—the Sri Dalada Maligawa in the hill capital of Kandy—killing eight persons, including a two-year-old child, and injuring about twenty-five pilgrims. Following this attack, the LTTE was banned in Sri Lanka.

It has been a characteristic of the LTTE to ruthlessly and brutally eliminate opposition to its ideology and course of action. On July 29, 1999, moderate Tamil politician Dr. Neelan Tiruchelvam, a member of Parliament representing the Tamil United Liberation Front, who was also assisting in drafting peace proposals, was killed by a suicide bomber in a Colombo residential area while on his way to work. On December 18, 1999, there was a failed attempt by an LTTE female suicide bomber to assassinate President Chandrika Kumaratunga at an election meeting at the Town Hall in Colombo. Twenty-one persons were killed and more than one hundred were injured in this attack. The president lost one eye due to shrapnel injuries. The LTTE continued terror attacks on civilian and military targets right into 2001. In this pre-9/11 era, there was a certain daring in the type of attacks the LTTE carried out, especially in the airport attack of July 2001.

On July 24, 2001, despite ninety sentry points around the airport complex, and with more than five hundred men guarding it, a group of LTTE cadres in military uniform infiltrated the premises and destroyed half the fleet of Sri Lanka's national carrier and military aircraft. The cost to the country was estimated at more than $450 million. At the end of the confrontation with security forces, there were thirteen bodies of LTTE members, two having exploded bombs strapped on themselves. The economic cost of this attack, which was Prabakaran's brainchild, was much higher as it came at the height of the country's tourist season.

International Attention on Sri Lanka's Peace Talks

Sri Lanka's peace process drew international attention, and offers flowed in for facilitation. British broker Liam Fox paid three visits to Sri

Lanka since 1996 to facilitate the peace dialog between Chandrika and the UNP to pave the way to open negotiation with the LTTE. But this agreement was not implemented because the Sri Lankan government demanded that the LTTE meet certain conditions, such as the laying down of arms before talks could take place. It was thus a nonstarter.

In 1998, the Sri Lankan government invited Norway to facilitate peace talks, for the first time recognizing the need for a facilitator to the peace process, amidst hostility and suspicion on both sides. Oslo was approached simultaneously by Sri Lankan President Chandrika Kumaratunga, Foreign Minister Lakshman Kadirgamar, and LTTE leader Prabhakaran to assist in the many practical matters necessary to bring peace to Sri Lanka. Gradually, an official request from both sides emerged, and it was confirmed in 2000.

Norway's role was to help resolve differences and build a consensus on the devolution package, on LTTE's violent postures, on Sri Lankan troops in the northeast, and on the economic embargo of LTTE areas. In 2001, Norway suggested a one-year time frame to the Sri Lankan government to conclude negotiations with the LTTE, which was agreeable to Sri Lanka and India, too, but not to the LTTE.

In November 2000, British Minister of State for Foreign and Commonwealth Affairs Peter Hain warned the LTTE of dire consequences if it resumed violence: "they would be prosecuted in international war crimes tribunals to be set up in a year or two." The LTTE declared a unilateral cease-fire from December 25, 2000 to January 24, 2001, and extended it for another three months.

Implications of 9/11 for Terrorism and LTTE

With the new world order of post-9/11, the international political climate had little tolerance for terrorism, and this altered the balance of forces in Sri Lanka. Further, the Bush administration made it perfectly clear it would tolerate no impediment to U.S. interests on the Indian subcontinent. Thus, every major political party in Sri Lanka fell into line, backing the U.S.-led invasion of Afghanistan. For its part, India got an opportunity to voice its concerns regarding "terrorist activities" throughout South Asia. Thus, the peace talks unfolded in the backdrop of two particularly dramatic events: the LTTE attack on the Katunayake International Airport in July 2001 and the 9/11 terrorist attacks in the United States six weeks later. The airport attack might have made the government of Sri Lanka realize that there are limits to a military option to end the conflict, while the intolerance of international terrorism within the international community in the aftermath of 9/11 was a deterrent to the LTTE to carry on with violence.

Also, Sri Lanka looked to a greater Indian role to pressure the LTTE to continue peace talks. In May 2002, India extended its ban on the LTTE for a further two years and categorized it as a "terrorist group." As another negative for the LTTE, India offered Sri Lanka its technical and constitutional expertise "on aspects of the 13th Amendment to the Constitution." For the LTTE, to continue its terrorist activities would have been a path to self-destruction, as it would become a pariah in global politics. There was much bitterness to this state of events among the LTTE top rung. "Like blowing and spoiling a conch [shell], a madman called bin Laden clashed with America and now some countries have included us in their list of terrorists," was a bitter comment by LTTE theoretician Anton Balasingham, quoted in the article "Sri Lankan Peace-Talks: The LTTE Bows to International Capitals," featured on the World Socialist website.[11]

Ranil Wickremesinghe–LTTE Talks

Prime Minister Ranil Wickremesinghe, who won the national general elections in December 2001, signed a cease-fire agreement with the LTTE in February 2002. Peace talks, initially scheduled for May 2002, were repeatedly stalled, as the United National Front government came under pressure from Sinhalese nationalist groups to carry on with a military approach before negotiations. In this backdrop, the prime minister met President George W. Bush in Washington in July 2002 and was strongly pressured into scheduling talks. Shortly afterward, Wickremesinghe announced the dates for talks in Thailand, and in August declared he would lift the ban on the LTTE, which the LTTE demanded as a precondition for talks. Twelve days before the talks began, the LTTE was officially removed from the ban.

Peace Summits

The first round of formal peace talks between the Sri Lankan government and the LTTE took place at Sattahip, Thailand, from September 16–18, 2002, with priority given to humanitarian challenges in a step-by-step approach to peace. The assurance of safety, security, and identity of all communities, rehabilitation, resettlement, and reintegration of the displaced people were discussed as core issues. The Sattahip talks resulted in two agreements: a joint committee to deal with issues relating to high security zones and a joint task force for humanitarian and reconstruction activities. The joint committee on high security zones was to be made up of military personnel from both sides and work toward facilitating the return of the internally displaced people. The joint task force was to be a partnership between the government and the LTTE to handle identification, financing, and monitoring of urgent humanitarian and reconstruction activities in the North. The LTTE was accepted as the "sole representatives" of the Tamils, and the talks ended on an encouraging note.

The second round of talks was held in Sattahip, Thailand, from October 31–November 3, 2002. The issues discussed were the establishment of a Joint Task Force for reconstruction and rehabilitation and strategies to attract money for the peace process. Both sides broadly agreed on the need to win foreign aid, but there were sharp differences over the composition and the powers of a joint panel.

On April 14, 2002, U.S. Deputy Secretary of State Richard Armitage chaired a meeting in Washington, D.C., as a prologue to the Tokyo Summit held in June 2002 on aid for Sri Lanka's reconstruction and development, jointly organized by the U.S. State Department and the Sri Lankan government. The Washington meeting, also seen as increased U.S. interest in Sri Lankan affairs, was organized to coincide with the spring meetings of the World Bank and the International Monetary Fund (IMF) to ensure that key officials attending those sessions could also be present at this meeting. Over thirty countries, twenty-three international lending agencies, and two foundations participated in preparation for the Tokyo donor forum in June 2003. At the meeting, Indian Ambassador to the United States Lalit Mansingh reiterated India's commitment to the unity, sovereignty, and territorial integrity of Sri Lanka.

The third round of talks opened in Oslo, Norway, on December 2, 2002, and was praised by the international community, which pledged to provide about $70 million to bring normalcy to the conflict-ridden areas. The LTTE's chief negotiator Anton Balasingham participated. However, India sent a Third Secretary from its Oslo Embassy as an observer, instead of the Ambassador, Gopal Gandhi. In this context, Ambassador Manasingh's role at the Washington meeting is significant.

Differences on military issues began to appear with the fourth and fifth rounds of talks, which took place respectively in Thailand on January 6, 2003, and in Germany on February 7, 2003, with discussions centered on the federal model as a basis for the final solution. The LTTE rejected the government demand to surrender heavy arms before a final peace deal and withdrew from the Sub-Committee on De-escalation and Normalisation (SDN), a panel appointed by Norway in October 2002. The LTTE demanded a reduction in the size of the army camps to free private homes and property occupied by government forces, which led to a military deadlock, and the talks made no headway. The demand adversely affected the congenial atmosphere that prevailed throughout the peace process during the year 2002.

The sixth round of talks was held on March 18–21, 2003, at Hakone, Japan. It was hosted by the Japanese special envoy to Sri Lanka, Yasushi Akashi, who wanted to make the environment conducive to making progress. The issues that dominated the discussions were child abduction and recruitment as soldiers, devolution of powers, rehabilitation and re-construction, and the donors' conference scheduled for June 2003. The two sides agreed on a roadmap for devolution of power and a framework to ensure human rights and address the issue of child soldiers. But the talks did not conclude with any final peace deal.

The Tokyo Conference on Reconstruction and Development of Sri Lanka, sponsored by the Japanese government and attended by fifty-one nations and twenty-two international organizations, was held on June 9 and 10, 2003, with greater focus on longer-term financial assistance and donor coordination. There were four co-chairs at the conference repre-senting Norway, Japan, the United States, and the EU. The LTTE refused to participate, miffed by its exclusion from the April 2002 conference of donor countries in Washington.

LTTE's Negotiating Strategy

The LTTE's negotiating strategy during these six rounds of talks in-dicates certain constants that the LTTE fiercely adhered to without mak-ing any concession. One was its determination to project itself as having equal status to the government of Sri Lanka in all interactions with inter-national donors whose assistance was sought for reconstruction. Another was its resolve to get Sri Lankan troops to withdraw from Jaffna, which the LTTE regarded as the capital of Tamil Eelam, even before starting substantive discussions on the future political set-up of the country.

This withdrawal was projected as an essential component of the normalization process that needed to precede substantive political nego-tiations. The LTTE's repeated emphasis on this demand made apparent its perception of a de facto setup incomplete without Jaffna as the capi-tal. The LTTE also kept its perception of talks not as between the state of Sri Lanka and an organization that had taken up arms against it to achieve certain political objectives, but rather, as between the de jure state of Sri Lanka and a de facto state of Tamil Eelam on the modalities for retaining and adjusting the de facto setup, with its own administrative, police, judi-ciary, and military components, as part of an overall solution based on a federal facade for the two state entities: Sinhalese and Tamil.

The LTTE once again showed its haphazard attitude to a compro-mise by abruptly suspending talks with the Sri Lankan government in April 2003, and did not attend the donor conference in Japan in June 2003. In a letter to then Prime Minister Ranil Wickremesinghe, the LTTE said it was committed to a negotiated settlement to the two-decade-old war, but demanded that progress be made on the ground before proceed-ing. The LTTE suspended talks "for the time being."

Secession Within Secession

Things were falling apart for the LTTE in the meantime. In March 2004, the Tiger military leadership suddenly split, with the eastern commander, Vinyaramoorthy Muralitharan (a strategic genius known as Colonel Karuna), breaking with Prabakaran and requesting separate talks with the Norwegians and Sri Lankan political parties. This breakaway LTTE faction was fearful that its leader was being targeted for assassination and vowed to hit back. Government security forces went on red alert fearing factional fighting. Colonel Karuna formed his own political party—the Tamileela Peoples Liberation Tigers (TMVP)—thus creating one more impediment to the success of the LTTE's bloody quest to become the sole representative of the Tamil people.

This split has much significance because it drastically reduced the LTTE's strength. At a military level, the split created, for the first time, a territorial division within the LTTE fighting forces. Karuna controls a third of the LTTE's approximately eighteen thousand-strong cadre and is said to have considerable support in the East. He is seen as someone who has raised issues of concern to eastern Tamils. At the political level, it was a deadly blow to the idea of the inseparability of the North and East, for it has directly affected the LTTE's monolithic image. In a sense, it has made the armed struggle for a "Tamil Eelam" a nonstarter. Until the split, Karuna was in charge of the LTTE's Batticaloa-Amparai area. He is a hardliner, known for his military prowess and ruthlessness and credited with drawing up strategy for several Tiger operations against the Sri Lankan armed forces over the years. While the Sri Lankan government refrained from taking sides in the feud, it also rejected Karuna's request for a separate cease-fire agreement with him. Some situation analysts believe that the split in the LTTE is a positive development for the peace process, for a divided LTTE will be weaker, and thus, less intransigent, at the table talks.

Why Negotiations Led Nowhere

President Chandrika, who backed the negotiation process itself, was vocally critical of Prime Minister Wickremesinghe's negotiating strategy, which gave opportunity to the LTTE to exploit the process to consolidate its hold over the Tamil-inhabited areas and set up a de facto Tamil state, while proclaiming its willingness to consider a negotiated federal setup as a solution to the conflict. Prime Minister Wickremesinghe's obvious overeagerness to keep the process going by making one concession after another despite the LTTE's total intransigence on crucial issues gave an impression of negotiating from a position of weakness, which proved counterproductive.

Prime Minister Wickremesinghe could not proceed far with the peace process because of several wrong moves that he and his government had made. One was his unwise confrontational attitude toward the president, whose political affiliations were different from his, and his total alienation of her in the process. He failed to reach a national consensus on the negotiating strategy, and so kept the public in the dark about his government's talks with the LTTE, fueling fears among the people that he was selling the country to terrorists. This lack of transparency surrounding the peace talks and his reluctance to clearly state the government's position on negotiations were major reasons why he failed. Also, he wrongly believed that international support and pressure on the LTTE alone would keep the peace process going, along with a moderate LTTE stance, even with no domestic support for his strategy. On top of it all, he did not make it clear to the LTTE what points were negotiable and what were not.

The Sri Lankan Monitoring Mission (SLMM) set up under the leadership of Norway, the facilitator of the peace process, bent over backwards to humor the LTTE and closed its eyes to repeated LTTE violations of the provisions of the cease-fire agreement with the government. The SLMM sought to give the benefit of the doubt to the LTTE by exonerating it of any responsibility or playing down its responsibility for sea attacks by the Black Tigers, such as when the Sri Lankan Navy thwarted an attempt to smuggle anti-aircraft weapons and other arms and ammunition. The LTTE's sea cadres chose to scuttle the ship and go down with it to avoid being captured with their consignment. The SLMM decided to accept at face value the LTTE's denial of any responsibility. In a paper prepared for consideration by the government and the LTTE, the SLMM reportedly suggested that the LTTE's Sea Tigers be treated as a "de facto naval unit," while reiterating the "undebatable obligation of the Sri Lankan Navy's legitimate task of safeguarding sovereignty and territorial integrity."

LTTE Proposal for an Interim Self-Governing Authority (ISGA)

In October 2003, the LTTE proposed an elaborate plan for an ISGA, which divided the Sinhalese political parties on how much and in what form powers should be devolved to the Tamils. The ISGA proposals visualized setting up an interim administration with the LTTE representing the Tamils for the entire northeast province. Except for finance and foreign affairs, the ISGA would rule the entire province on its own terms, with powers to levy and collect taxes. It would create its own armed forces, navy, administration, and judiciary and control all eight districts that make up the province. It would have a minimum of four and a maximum of five years of life. In other words, this amounted to creating an Eelam as a part of Sri Lanka. Several of the ISGA conditions amount to an obvious blueprint for a separate state.

This is particularly evident in Clause 9, which states: "The ISGA shall have plenary powers for the governance of the 'Northeast' including powers in relation to resettlement, rehabilitation, reconstruction and development, including upgrading of existing services and facilities, raising revenue, levies and duties, law and order and over land. These powers shall include all powers and functions in relation to regional administration exercised by the GOSL [Government of Sri Lanka] in and for the Northeast." The commercial and strategic implications of such control overriding the jurisdiction of the Sri Lankan government are obvious.

The ISGA proposes to wield power and authority over not only the entire northeastern province, but also over the adjacent territorial waters stretching out to almost five hundred nautical miles. The ISGA's silence on disbanding the LTTE Army, Black Tigers, Sea Tigers, and Intelligence squads, and so on, indicates that the ISGA will legitimize LTTE's armed forces, including the Sea Tigers. This would result in Sri Lanka having two armies and two navies.

Clause 18 states that "the ISGA shall have control over the marine and off shore resources of the adjacent seas and the power to regulate access thereto." The consequences of exercising such power on Sri Lanka's national defense, shipping, and fisheries, and on exploiting mineral resources in nearly 70 percent of the territorial waters of Sri Lanka are obvious. Under this condition, the Sri Lankan waters in the Northeast would be under the jurisdiction of the Sea Tigers rather than the Sri Lankan Navy.

Clause 21 states that "all future agreements concerning matters under the jurisdiction of ISGA shall be made with the ISGA. Existing agreements will continue, but the GOSL shall ensure that all proceeds under such agreements are paid to the ISGA. Any changes to such agreements should be made with the concurrence of the ISGA."

In the absence of specific explanation, this implies that free trade agreements, defense agreements, trade and payments agreements, construction, supply, transport, and labor contracts, and so on, relating to any part of the Northeast and the territorial waters will have to be worked out with the ISGA rather than with the Sri Lankan government.

Financial Autonomy

The ISGA appears to be endowed with all the powers and authority of an independent and sovereign state, other than a separate currency, central bank, monetary board, and the membership of the multilateral lending agencies, such as the World Bank, Asian Development Bank, and the IMF. But there is a catch in Clause 12 of the ISGA on Powers to Borrow, Receive Aid, and Trade. It states: "The ISGA shall have powers to borrow internally and externally, provide guarantees, engage in or regulate internal and external trade." This means that the international community, including World Bank, IMF, Asian Development Bank (ADB), and others, will have to recognize the ISGA as a separate entity, which has the power, authority, and credibility to have direct dealings in relation to borrowing, debt servicing, and repayment. Further, the ISGA will be empowered to "engage in or regulate internal and external trade." The logical corollary of this is that it will regulate control of all ports and airports in its jurisdiction.

Why the ISGA Is Not Acceptable to the Government of Sri Lanka

The government of Sri Lanka considered the ISGA a blueprint for Eelam and was not agreeable to basing future peace talks on this proposal because the ISGA did not reflect the spirit of power-sharing in a federal format envisaged in the Oslo accord that paved the way for peace talks. It required that the government of Sri Lanka sacrifice three key elements of nationhood to the ISGA: territorial integrity, executive powers, and judicial powers. In other words, it was a de facto blueprint for an independent Eelam. In his annual policy speech broadcast over Tiger Radio in November 2004, Prabakaran challenged Sinhalese politicians to have a collective stand on peace talks and said, "The thirst of Tigers is Tamil Eelam—the motherland."[12] This statement appeared to be a move to prepare the ground to go back to a protracted war and give notice to international backers of the peace process that it was about to collapse.

The ISGA was meant to silence the international community by proclaiming LTTE's "pious" intentions of initiating moves for peace while the government of Sri Lanka was totally immobilized on the issue. Japanese Special Peace Envoy to Sri Lanka Yasushi Akashi failed to persuade the LTTE to resume peace talks without basing them on the ISGA.

The ISGA was presented by the LTTE at a time that the political environment among the major political parties was chaotic and confused. It then tried to pressure the government to accept the ISGA, threatening to return to its "freedom struggle" unless the government agreed to resume talks based on the ISGA to end the nineteen-month deadlock in talks. The ISGA was drawn up to prevent any negotiations on the core issue of federalism, which meant power-sharing. It assumed that the only thing to be negotiated any further was working out a schedule amending the constitution to legitimize the ISGA, rather than amend its form and content. Initially, the LTTE maintained that the ISGA would be open for negotiations, but then changed its mind and maintained that it should be the basis for negotiations.

The Sri Lankan government rejected the LTTE demand for an unconditional resumption of talks and accused the LTTE of using "threatening language" to undermine peace efforts. "A call, couched in threatening language, from the LTTE for a resumption of negotiations without conditions, while setting conditions itself by insisting unilaterally on a single agenda item is scarcely conducive to good faith negotiations," it said.[13]

With Norway as facilitators, the president and the government of Sri Lanka intended to discuss with the LTTE the peace process as a whole, not necessarily basing it on the ISGA proposals. The cease-fire monitors warned that Sri Lanka's fragile truce was becoming increasingly unstable because of escalating violence in the North and East, and urged a swift return to peace talks.

What Peace Talks Mean to the LTTE

The LTTE has always tried to use the peace process to secure its militaristic stance in its armed struggle for an independent Tamil Eelam. An analysis of the LTTE response to compromise and negotiation since the start of the war in 1983 shows that the LTTE has always used peace talks as an essential interval to reinforce its strength, recruit, rebuild, and rest. Once things were in place and the LTTE was ready to resume fighting, peace talks would be abandoned abruptly, and any existing truce would collapse like a house of cards. But the Sri Lankan government has consistently thwarted attempts at separation. However, neither side can prosecute a prolonged war; so peace talks are invariably resumed, only to be abandoned again.

The LTTE has used peace processes to secure three objectives: to advance the political cause of the Tamil people and lighten their economic burden, increase its own power as a monopolistic organization, and take further steps toward the ultimate goal of an independent Tamil Eelam. Thus, for the LTTE, peace processes are an integral part of an overall strategy to realize its short-term and long-term interests and objectives.

For its part, the government of Sri Lanka has always had as its aim to see that the LTTE does not consolidate itself and push for an independent Tamil Eelam. The government has time and again coerced the LTTE into a peace process, not with the aim of solving the Tamil problem and meeting the Tamils' aspirations built over the years, but to weaken the LTTE and force it to abandon its separatist agenda. With its concern to contain the LTTE and thwart its plans, the government has considered cautiously even the demands relating to the suffering Tamil population in the war-ravaged areas.

Even though the international community has been periodically urging the LTTE and the Sri Lankan government to resume peace talks, it always appears that the LTTE only pays lip service to assurances of negotiations. In the midst of the ongoing cease-fire, on July 7, 2004, an LTTE suicide bomber tried to assassinate prominent Tamil politician and former Cabinet Minister Douglas Devananda in his Colombo office. When being submitted to a body search prior to meeting with the minister, the bomber refused to be searched and subsequently exploded the bomb strapped on herself at a nearby police station, also killing four police and security personnel and injuring several others.

Successes and Failures of the Norwegian-Brokered Talks

The mistrust, suspicion, and hostility between the LTTE and the government of Sri Lanka made the role of a neutral, benign facilitator crucial to initiate peace talks. The biggest milestone of the Norwegian-brokered peace talks was the cease-fire agreement of February 23, 2002, between the LTTE and the Sri Lankan government. This was followed by a revival of dialog between the two, focused on issues of common interest such as rehabilitation and reconstruction, economic development and relief activities, whereas preceding peace talks mostly dwelt on political and military issues which only served to increase tension and hostilities rather than diffuse them.

While the Norwegian intervention drew much international attention to Sri Lanka's conflict and peace talks, Japan, the EU, and the United States also began exerting their influence on the peace process. During the 2003 peace talks in Tokyo, Japan pledged $1 billion to be disbursed over three years, the United States pledged $54 million, and Norway pledged $3 million, mostly for the Northeast. The Manila-based ADB promised $1 billion, and the World Bank pledged $200 million annually, while the EU committed $293 million over three years.

Norway's biggest failure as facilitator was its obvious leaning toward the LTTE, creating suspicions among the Sinhalese that the Norwegians were not trustworthy and that in the end, Norway would take the LTTE side and betray the government of Sri Lanka, which without doubt affected their public credibility. This mistrust, however, was not without cause. When LTTE pulled out its political workers from the East after attacks by anti-LTTE elements in the first week of August 2005, Hagrup Haukland, head of the EU Sri Lanka Monitoring Mission, was quick to say: "One of the cornerstones in the cease-fire agreement is that the LTTE should have the possibility to do political work in the North and the East and also have the freedom of movement of the cadres. If that cornerstone is removed, then it is jeopardy." However, in the immediate aftermath of Foreign Minister Kadirgamar's assassination, all he would say was, "The situation has deteriorated, it's a big, big blow to the cease-fire and the whole peace process irrespective of who is behind this."[14]

National Advisory Council for Peace and Reconciliation

President Kumaratunga faced a no-win situation, which she expressed at a press conference on September 3, 2004:

> With a group as intransigent and as ruthless as the LTTE and as one-minded and as focused as Mr. Prabhakaran . . . with a leader like that you cannot predict anything. He is in the habit of telling a lot of things to governments and going back on his word. The best example is what he did with President Premadasa. He promised him many things, got arms and money from him and then killed him off because he did not do exactly as the LTTE wanted. . . . But all I can say is that there is hope. I have not said this, in such a convinced manner before. Also, one must not forget that the LTTE is not just one person; the LTTE is a large number of people. The cadres are tired of this ruthless management of affairs—killing off people who don't agree with their ideas; killing off ordinary Tamil civilians. . . . So there is a time when the Tamil people will get tired of this kind of politics and will demand from the LTTE. I still hope that the LTTE also, like the other militant groups, will agree finally to come in to the democratic stream. That is our final objective.

The president of Sri Lanka aptly summed up the existing situation: "The LTTE's position is very simple—'no, we refuse talk about any final solution; we will only talk about the Interim Agreement; you have to set it up; it has to be operational; once that happens we will begin to discuss about the final solution.'"[15]

There was also the need to consider the impact of the peace process on the Muslims in the eastern province. There were clear indications of a growing radicalization of sections of the Muslim youth influenced by the Lashkar-e-Toiba (LET) of Pakistan, a member of Osama bin Laden's International Islamic Front (IIF), angry over the bypassing of Muslims in the entire peace process and over the government's inability to control the high-handed activities of the LTTE in their areas.

In this backdrop, President Kumaratunga launched the National Advisory Council for Peace and Reconciliation on October 4, 2004, as the official forum for consultation and guidance on issues of peace negotiations and for enhancing reconciliation and understanding among the communities. However, it was not supported by the key parties in parliament, whose support is essential for constitutional reform.

The Tsunami and the Heightened Expectations for Peace

As the peace process stagnated without much hope of immediate revival, a natural disaster in the form of a major tsunami struck South Asia on December 26, 2004, devastating entire areas. Sri Lanka was one of the worst affected countries, with the coastal areas completely devastated and thirty-one thousand people dead. The North and the East were very badly affected, too; and in the immediate aftermath of the tsunami, there were heightened hopes that the LTTE and the government would at last be united in the mutual need to rebuild after the natural disaster. The Tamil Rehabilitation Organization (TRO), a front organization of the LTTE, officially registered as a non-governmental organization (NGO) in Sri Lanka, internationally known as the LTTE fund-raising outfit and banned in several countries like the United States, United Kingdom, and Malaysia, came to the forefront in the areas temporarily controlled by the LTTE and handled tsunami relief efforts. A month after the tsunami, then Minister of Foreign Affairs Lakshman Kadirgamar said that the tsunami "has been a spur, or the trigger, which has accelerated the process" of the government and the LTTE working together on development issues.[16]

However, these positive expectations were short-lived. Before long it became clear that the LTTE was using the tsunami for propaganda purposes. Seizing the opportunity, the TRO rode on the international wave of sympathy and organized fund-raising campaigns even in countries like the United Kingdom where they are banned. The governments of these countries turned a blind eye to these activities, even though posters and other publicity material requested support only for the North and the East of Sri Lanka. At the same time, the TRO and the LTTE carried out a propaganda exercise against the Sri Lankan government claiming it had done nothing to assist the North and the East. On March 17, 2005, Foreign Minister Kadirgamar told a gathering at the prestigious International Institute for Strategic Studies in London that the LTTE should not be allowed to use the tsunami for propaganda purposes. The LTTE, in turn, accused the government of wanting to take control of the funds to use them as a bargaining point in the stalled peace process. The government, however, clearly stated that it has no intention of exploiting the relief issue for political gains, this being the largest humanitarian disaster the country had ever faced. So it became apparent that the tsunami, contrary to expectation, had driven the two parties even further apart.

LTTE Recruits Tsunami Child Victims and Other Children

Leader of the LTTE break-away faction, V. Muralitharan (Colonel Karuna) charged LTTE leader Prabakaran with "playing politics" in the provision of relief aid to the tsunami victims and accused him of "continued child conscription." The Human Rights Watch confirmed this through its report stating that the LTTE was recruiting children affected by the tsunami for use as soldiers. The report said that, "the Tamil Tigers, who were already recruiting large numbers of child soldiers, now may seek to replace forces lost in the tsunami with child recruits."[17] Meanwhile, the United Nations Children's Fund (UNICEF) reported three cases of children recruited by the LTTE from camps for tsunami survivors in Batticaloa and Ampara in the East of Sri Lanka.

In November 2005, the LTTE assassinated two respected Tamil principals in two schools in Jaffna for speaking out against recruiting children as child soldiers. Parents (even mothers) who complain to authorities are subjected to physical violence by the LTTE. Thus, it is quite clear that despite their adamant denials and superficial agreement to international protocols on child recruitment, the LTTE continues to recruit underage children as combatants, even while the cease-fire is enforced.

In February 2005, UN Secretary General Kofi Annan, in his report to the Security Council, accused the LTTE of child abuse, which includes recruiting children as soldiers; abducting, maiming, or killing them; and subjecting them to rape and other sexual violence. The LTTE was listed as one of fifty-four offending groups involved in the forced recruitment of underage children.

Post-Tsunami Operational Management Structure (P-TOMS)

With Norwegian facilitation, the LTTE and the Sri Lankan government signed a document on June 24, 2005, agreeing to a joint mechanism to disburse international tsunami aid in the tsunami-devastated areas of the North and the East. The document was termed a Memorandum for the Establishment of a Post-Tsunami Operational Management Structure, rather than an agreement. The signing took place after nearly six months of protracted discussions over the clauses in the memorandum. Subsequently, on July 15, 2005, the Sri Lankan Supreme Court blocked four sections of the P-TOMS Memorandum, ruling they were against Sri Lanka's constitution. Among the clauses termed illegal are the ones on locating the regional fund headquarters in Kilinochchi, the northern headquarters of the LTTE and the reference to the regional fund-sharing deal between the Sri Lankan government and the LTTE. The Supreme Court stressed that the entire memorandum was not suspended by the ruling, only parts of it. Close on the heels of the court order, the U.S. government, which had earlier urged the signing of the P-TOMS, withdrew from the fund, citing the terrorist status of the LTTE in the United States. The United States said it supported the P-TOMS but would not donate funds to it. Instead, the U.S. tsunami relief funds were to be directed to the Sri Lankan Treasury. Japan, too, having initially encouraged the signing of the P-TOMS, subsequently realized the implications of contributing money directly to the regional fund where the LTTE would have a managerial role in the fund. Following the Supreme Court stay order, the LTTE rejected the P-TOMS.

Assassination of Foreign Minister Kadirgamar

On the night of August 12, 2005, Foreign Minister Lakshman Kadirgamar, who carried out an extremely effective campaign to ban the LTTE internationally as a terrorist outfit, was assassinated by the LTTE. The denials that ensued from the LTTE were not taken seriously. Minister Kadirgamar was believed to have been on the hit list of LTTE as early as 1994. The LTTE initially issued a similar denial following the assassination of former Indian Prime Minister Rajiv Gandhi. Kadirgamar said not long before his assassination, "The Tigers have a record of systematically eliminating—by killing—their political opponents. All it requires is one well-timed killing somewhere, and the message spreads. The message is that it's very dangerous to speak up. Very few speak up and survive."[18] For more than a decade, Kadirgamar used his clout as Sri Lanka's foreign minister to warn the international community of the dangers of terrorism. While such atrocities were a Sri Lankan problem, the international community was content to ignore his vision of the future. However, everything changed following 9/11 and subsequent bombings in world capitals.

International Reaction to Kadirgamar's Assassination

U.S. Secretary of State Condoleezza Rice, who met Kadirgamar in June 2005, said, "This senseless murder was a vicious act of terror, which the United States strongly condemns." She praised Kadirgamar as a man of "dignity, honor, and integrity, who devoted his life to bringing peace to Sri Lanka." U.S. President George W. Bush's spokeswoman stated, "We condemn this outrageous and barbaric act." UN Secretary General Kofi Annan said, "Sri Lanka has lost a deeply respected statesman dedicated to peace and national unity." India condemned the assassination as a "terrorist crime" and offered its full support. Australia's Foreign Minister Alexander Downer said, "Lakshman Kadirgamar was an eminent statesman and a distinguished representative of Sri Lanka. He was a man of moderation who sought the path of peace and worked tirelessly for his country." Joschka Fisher, the foreign minister of Germany, said that it was a senseless and cowardly act of the LTTE terrorists and those responsible have to be arrested and brought before justice. Russia described the assassination as a "barbarous act of terror as a result of which an outstanding statesman has perished." Peace-broker Norway also condemned the assassination, with Foreign Minister Jan Petersen describing it as "an atrocious crime and a tragedy for Sri Lanka." Erik Solheim, leading Norwegian mediator, said the killing was "completely insane." Former U.S. Ambassador to Colombo Teresita Schaffer said, "This is not just because this type of murder is precisely what the cease-fire was supposed to prevent; it is not just because it quite understandably devastates whatever beginnings of trust had been created during the period since peace talks began. It is also because Sri Lanka needs leaders in order to move ahead, and it especially needs strong leaders in order to make peace. So killing Kadirgamar is a life-threatening wound to Sri Lanka's future." General Satish Nambiar, a former deputy chief of staff of the Indian Army, force commander and head of mission of the UN forces in former Yugoslavia and formerly an advisor to the government of Sri Lanka on certain aspects of the peace process, said, "His loss is certainly the LTTE's gain. The government of Sri Lanka will now have to look for a person who can articulate his views."

EU Travel Ban on the LTTE

On September 26, 2005, the EU in an extraordinary statement said, "The European Union is actively considering the formal listing of the LTTE as a terrorist organization" and that "in the meantime, the European Union has agreed that with immediate effect, delegations from the LTTE will no longer be received in any of the EU Member States until further notice."[19] The statement repeats the EU's "serious concern at the continuing recruitment and retention of child soldier cadres by the LTTE and reminds them that there can be no excuse whatsoever for this abhorrent practice to continue."[20] The travel ban prevents LTTE delegations from visiting EU countries. President Chandrika Kumaratunga's government requested the EU travel ban on the LTTE soon after the assassination of Minister Kadirgamar. The United States welcomed the EU decision to impose a travel ban on the LTTE and said that strong action should be taken against the LTTE to stop violence and killings.

The EU also declared that Sri Lanka's request to include the LTTE in the EU list of proscribed organizations was being actively considered. At a meeting in Brussels with the Confederation of Tamil Associations in Europe, an EU official assured that the travel ban on the LTTE would not be lifted. Upon being informed of LTTE intimidation, extortion, political killings, child abductions, and terrorist propaganda glorifying suicide bombers in violation of terrorism acts now in force in some EU member countries, the EU official requested regular briefings to make an effective case for proscription. It was the first time that expatriate Tamil democrats from all over Europe openly defied LTTE's threats and intimidation.

In the two and a half months following the Kadirgamar assassination, despite the many strictures and sanctions against it, the LTTE indulged in forty-four further killings, which by no means helped its quest to seek respectability in the eyes of the world.

U.S. Assistant Secretary of State for South Asian Affairs Christina Rocca said, "The EU ban reflected the international community's strongest message that acts of terrorism by the LTTE would not be tolerated. The United States, which has designated the LTTE as a terrorist organization, strongly felt that strong action should be taken against the LTTE to stop the growing number of killings, other forms of violence, and child recruitment."[21]

LTTE Threatens War Unless EU Removes Ban

The LTTE tried coercing Norway to lift the EU travel ban and threatened to resume war against the Sri Lankan government if it failed. A top-rung LTTE member, S. P. Thamilselvan, urged one of the four-member co-chairs, Norwegian Ambassador Hans Brattaskar, to make urgent representations on the LTTE's behalf to the EU. However, with human rights organizations urging the international community to follow the lead set by the EU, it is unlikely that the EU will change its stance in the near future. "The EU should continue to refuse LTTE delegations until political killings and child recruitment stop," said Jo Becker, children's rights advocacy director of the New York-based Human Rights Watch.[22] She also urged other UN member states to consider similar action. Casey Kelso, international director of the Coalition to Stop the Use of Child Soldiers, said,

"We welcome the recent EU agreement that LTTE delegations will no longer be received in [the 25] EU member states."[23]

"The two major democratic forces have to get together"

Outgoing Sri Lankan President Chandrika Kumaratunga, in an interview with the major Indian publication *Frontline* for its November 5–18, 2005, issue, said:

> I think internationalizing [the conflict] persuaded [Prabhabaran] to talk—on much lesser conditions than before. There were two things. One was the devastation they suffered because of the tsunami. Two, I would say, is the opening up of the whole process during Ranil's government, where large numbers of the LTTE [cadre] went abroad. They were able to come to Colombo, I continued to allow them to do that. They were able to see another world outside of their dark, little dingy holes and the tigers' den. And they began to see there is a better world outside than what is being promised by Prabakaran. I think there is pressure on Prabakaran from his people, "let us not go back to war, let us go for some negotiated thing." All these things made a huge difference and the qualitative difference.[24]

LTTE and Sri Lanka's Presidential Election

When the Supreme Court of Sri Lanka on August 26, 2005, ruled in favor of a presidential election in 2005, the LTTE took a nonchalant stance on the elections and said it did not care. Both the LTTE and its parliamentary proxy Tamil National Alliance (TNA) said that the Tamils need not take any interest in the candidates or in the election. Moreover, the LTTE publicly stated it would be neutral in the presidential stakes and would play no role in it. It gave the green light to the Tamil people to vote or to refrain from voting if they wished, and claimed that the Tamil people were politically mature and would act appropriately. So, the coast was clear for Tamil voters to back the candidate of their choice. The Tamils in the North and the East were happy about the cease-fire spearheaded by Ranil Wickremesinghe. On the other hand, Mahinda Rajapakse, the other main contender, targeted the majority community votes at the expense of the minorities and categorically ruled out separation and self-determination, and rejected the P-TOMS. It was only natural for the minority communities to back Wickremesinghe in such a situation. Against this backdrop, Tamil votes in enormous numbers were expected for Wickremesinghe without any LTTE-TNA involvement. The assumption was that a few days before the election, the LTTE would influence Tamil voters in favor of Wickremesinghe.

However, close to the day of the election, the LTTE that had assured "noninterference" in the poll broke its promise and launched a ruthless and relentless effort to prevent Tamils from voting. It severely dented Wickremesinghe's chances of victory. On Election Day, November 17, 2005, the LTTE burned tires, barred access to polling stations, and scared off voters through its intimidating presence. It fueled greater fear through surveillance of voters. It was clearly a call for a boycott, and the LTTE openly and actively engaged in preventing and obstructing people from voting. Almost no Tamils voted in LTTE-controlled areas. However, many Tamils in the East under Karuna's control voted despite the LTTE ban and the violence unleashed by it. Karuna, who broke away from the LTTE in March 2004 and has since been a major irritant for Prabhakaran's mainstream, encouraged the people in the East to come out and vote. As it happened, the voter turnout in the North was 1.2 percent of seven hundred thousand voters, while in eastern Batticaloa, also a predominately Tamil town under Karuna's authority, the voter turnout was 48.5 percent. In both areas, Wickremesinghe scored 70 percent or more of the vote.

In a message issued by the U.S. Department of State, the United States condemned the LTTE's interference in the democratic process and for denying "a significant portion of Sri Lanka's people" the opportunity to express their views. The EU's chief election monitor John Cushnahan, who headed an eighty-three-member observation mission of Sri Lanka's presidential elections, condemned the LTTE for blocking ethnic Tamils from voting. He observed that the voting process in the North and the East was "marred by violence" accompanied by an enforced boycott by the LTTE. He commented that the LTTE had used "unacceptable tactics" during the poll and that "they should be condemned for that."[25]

Mahinda Rajapakse Elected President

Mahinda Rajapakse won the presidential race with 50.3 percent of the vote while Ranil Wickremesinghe received 48.4 percent of the vote. At the swearing in ceremony of Sri Lanka's new president on November 19, 2005, Rajapakse promised to renew peace talks with the LTTE but reiterated his opposition to its demand for an independent state. "I will bring about an honorable peace to the country, respecting all communities," said the president, and added, "The government is ready to review the cease-fire agreement. This process can start as soon as the relevant parties are ready. Human rights violations, such as child abduction and murder that are happening despite the cease-fire, must come to an end."[26] Peace talks between the government and rebels have been deadlocked for more than two years. "I hope the LTTE will consider the peace offer seriously. Both parties can start the peace talks with an agreed time frame once the LTTE readies for the talks," the president said. Mr. Rajapakse hopes to take several measures to amend the cease-fire agreement with the LTTE to ensure no future hostile situations.

Reasons for LTTE Betrayal of Ranil Wickremesinghe

The LTTE's move close upon the eve of the presidential elections was totally unanticipated. While it was generally accepted that the LTTE would support the candidacy of Ranil Wickremesinge over Mahinda Rajapakse, ultimately the reverse took place, and Wickremesinghe lost a significant number of votes from the North he had been banking on. With the Tamils forced to boycott voting, the final result weighed in favor of Mahinda Rajapakse. Thus, in the final analysis, the LTTE helped the victory of Mahinda Rajapakse who, in comparison with Wickremesinghe, has taken a more hard-line approach to the peace process and has publicly rejected a separate state. In the same coin, the LTTE ensured the defeat of Ranil Wickremesinghe who has taken a softer approach to the issue of separatism and has been bending over backwards to please the LTTE. This turn of events mystified all political analysts.

A popular columnist, D. B. S. Jeyaraj, makes some pertinent observations in his column in *Tamiliana,* titled, "Why Is the LTTE Disappointed with Ranil Wickremesinghe?"[27] Jeyaraj says that the LTTE was unhappy over the slow progress in setting up an interim administration during Wickremesinghe's tenure as prime minister and equally angry that his election manifesto for the November 2005 presidential elections ignored the interim administration and made no meaningful commitment to a federal solution. The LTTE was also unhappy over the internationalization of the peace process, where the onus for progress in peace talks was placed on the international community. The LTTE was against such cultivation of the international community and felt that it would be trapped in an unproductive, prolonged cease-fire while its separatist movement became ever weakened by international involvement. The LTTE was hostile to Wickremesinghe signing a sixty-seven-point agreement with the leader of the Sri Lanka Muslim Congress, Rauf Hakeem, thus bestowing on Muslims a third-party status in peace talks and taking away from the LTTE the status of being the sole representative of Tamil-speaking people. The LTTE was annoyed with Wickremesinghe that he did not speak up on its behalf to lift the EU travel ban, which it expected Wickremesinghe would do. Having projected outgoing President Chandrika Kumaratunga as an enemy to the LTTE, Wickremesinghe then struck a deal with her during the presidential race. This incurred LTTE displeasure that was enhanced by the controversial comments close to the eve of the polls by Milinda Moragoda and Navin Dissanaike, party stalwarts of the UNP, that the UNP was responsible for the split in the LTTE. These comments were designed to win majority votes in the South but only drove the LTTE to heightened determination to teach Wickremesinghe a lesson by ensuring his defeat.

Does the LTTE Really Want Peace?

The real issue at stake here is: Does the LTTE genuinely want peace? All evidence points to the fact that it does not. At 11 p.m. on November 7, 2005, Sri Lanka's army bomb disposal unit took into custody a suicide bomber's kit from Colombo's residential Kollupitiya, after being tipped off by a telephone call of a suspicious-looking bag lying in the area. The suicide bomber's kit was packed with high-powered explosives of C4, sixteen hundred iron bullets, two detonators, and two switches and brought to Colombo to kill an important person during the November presidential election.

On November 19, 2005, with the help of Thai authorities, the Australian Federal Police (AFP) succeeded in preventing a people-smuggling effort to Australia by the LTTE. They seized a small vessel, the *MV Kosmo*, with a mainly Sri Lankan crew and carrying more than one hundred people, in the southern Thai port of Songkhla. The Royal Thai Police also arrested forty-nine Sri Lankans at an apartment in Chonburi Province near the seaside resort town of Pattaya. Human smugglers had transported 107 Sri Lankans to Pattaya to send them on to a third country. Other raids carried out in the far southern town of Hat Yai and on guesthouses close to Bangkok revealed clues of the LTTE's role in the people-smuggling. For instance, a passenger had to pay between U.S. $8,000 and U.S. $10,000 to agents, some even mortgaging land and houses to raise the funds. U.S. $2,000 of this money was for the LTTE. One hundred seven Sri Lankans had been brought to the Pattaya province in order to send them to a third country by the group of human-smugglers. Documents revealed that the instructions from the Pattaya-based Thai shipping company manager were to "carry the illegal immigrants to Australian territory [sic]."[28] They were then to be dropped off before the vessel would head back out to the open sea. The LTTE has long been known to use Thailand as a gateway to the West and also as a source of illegal arms trading.

In the fall of 2005, the LTTE carried out an intensely aggressive fund-raising campaign in European capitals, demanding large sums of money from Tamil expatriates living there. In London, the demand had been

£5,000 from individuals and £50,000 from businesses. LTTE operatives who visited expatriate Tamils had said, "After the elections, we are going for the war. This is the final and decisive attack to get our homeland. We need large sums of money urgently. We will return the money with interest in 3 years."[29] They had also encouraged people to obtain loans from banks and other sources. The expatriates were told if they did not contribute money, they would not be allowed to visit Eelam. Tamils threatened by the LTTE alerted the London Police about the illegal fund-raising by a banned terrorist group. The police responded by warning shopkeepers in Southall about the consequences of financing terrorist groups in the United Kingdom. However, police in other areas of the United Kingdom were unable to stop fund-raising for lack of specific information. In Switzerland, Germany, and France, LTTE operatives issued a questionnaire to Tamil residents, requesting details of all family members, work and income, and properties both in Europe and in Sri Lanka, and their contribution to the LTTE; and were instructed to apply for the "Tamil Eelam Identity" cards from the LTTE. Residents in Switzerland said that they were told that Tamil Eelam Identity cards would be required to visit Tamil areas in Sri Lanka.

However, it is now becoming clear that Tamil expatriates around the world, who have all these years helped fuel terrorism in Sri Lanka by funding the LTTE, are getting disillusioned and weary of extortion and threats. On November 23, 2005, a large group of Sri Lankan Tamil expatriates in Europe demonstrated against the LTTE opposite the parliament in Brussels, Belgium, and demanded that Europe ban the LTTE. This appears to be the first protest against the LTTE by Tamils themselves. The demonstrators pointed out that the LTTE, which continues to assassinate innocent Tamil civilians, could not be accepted as the sole representative of the Tamil people. They repeated that the LTTE is a terrorist organization and should be immediately banned in Europe. The protestors claimed that the LTTE atrocities were not only confined to Sri Lanka, but took place in European cities in such countries as the United Kingdom, Denmark, Norway, Netherlands, Switzerland, Germany, and France, where Sri Lankan Tamils live in significant numbers.

So it appears that the LTTE is in danger of losing its lifeblood, or at least a gradual erosion of funds, with the Tamil expatriates getting disillusioned with the organization and gradually, even reluctantly, accepting the true nature of the LTTE: the realization that it has no interest in looking after the rights of the Tamil people, but only a desire to terrorize and wield power. In fact, the LTTE desperately wants to achieve its goal of Eelam despite the hostile environment to terrorism in a post-9/11 world where once such action by the LTTE was viewed with great indifference. For all its threats to go back to fighting, the LTTE knows the world in which it carried out terrorist activity before has changed unexpectedly and permanently. The international categorizing of the LTTE as a terrorist group and its banning in nations of significance, and the curb on funding and weapons acquisition, have all weakened the LTTE's financial and fighting capability. Added to that, the newly emerging trend of disillusionment among Tamil expatriates who have been responsible for the major portion of LTTE funds is a positive element that the Sri Lankan government should use in forcing the LTTE toward meaningful peace talks in the coming days.

7

COUNTERTERRORISM STRATEGIES:
SUMMARY AND CONCLUSIONS

Yonah Alexander

More than two thousand years ago, the Chinese strategist Sun Tzu wrote in *The Art of War* about the significance of a surprise attack: "The enemy must not know where I intend to give battle, he must prepare in a great many places. . . . If he prepares to the front, his rear will be weak, and if to the rear, his front will be fragile. If he prepares to the left, his right will be vulnerable and if to the right, there will be few on his left. And when he prepares everywhere he will be weak everywhere."

If terrorism is a form of "warfare in the shadows," then the most spectacular and heinous manifestation of Sun Tzu's warning occurred on September 11, 2001, recalling Pearl Harbor's "Day of Infamy." The United States, the only power with unmatched conventional and un-conventional capabilities, was surprised when nineteen terrorists mounted an unexpected and unprecedented kamikaze operation considered to be the deadliest in recorded history.

Yet, 9/11 also underscores the reality that the built-in vulner-ability of modern societies and their infrastructures, coupled with the opportunity for the utilization of high-level conventional and mass-destruction weaponry, requires all nations, both unilaterally and in concert, to develop comprehensive strategies and capabilities to mini-mize future threats domestically, regionally, and globally.

The preceding chapters focused on the experiences of the United States, France, Germany, Italy, Egypt, and Sri Lanka in terms of the terrorist threats confronting them and the responses undertaken by their governments before and after September 11, 2001. The following discussion summarizes the experiences of these nations, highlighting some of the successes and failures of their respective strategies.

United States

The U.S. experience with terrorism did not begin with September 11, 2001. For over two centuries America underwent occasional outbreaks

190

of terrorism perpetrated in the country by both domestic and foreign groups. Some of the "homegrown groups" include the Ku Klux Klan, the Weather Underground, the Aryan Nations, and the Earth Liberation Front. Various ethnic and nationalist groups have also been active. In addition to these indigenous groups, foreign terrorists have operated in the United States, among them the Secret Army for the Liberation of Armenia, the Palestine Liberation Organization, Hamas, Islamic Jihad, Hizbollah, the Kurdistan Workers Party, and the Irish Republican Army.

Despite the proliferation of both American and foreign terrorist groups in the United States, the impact of their activities was "manageable." That is, even the approximately eight hundred terrorist attacks in the country in the 1970s and 1980s did not seriously disrupt the "American way of life" and the illusion of domestic security. But in the 1990s two major events influenced more than ever before the U.S. government's disposition toward, as well as the public's perception of, the terrorist threats within the country. First, on February 26, 1993, a powerful bomb explosion occurred in the parking garage of the World Trade Center in New York, killing six people, injuring 1,042 others, and causing widespread damage. This attack, considered the largest international terrorist incident in the United States up to that time, was perpetrated by a group of foreign terrorists from Egypt, Iraq, Jordan, and the Palestinian Authority. The second incident, labeled the largest act of domestic terrorism in American history, took place on April 19, 1995, destroying the nine-story Alfred P. Murrah Federal Building in Oklahoma City.

Notwithstanding these two unprecedented incidents, U.S. citizens and interests have been more affected by terrorism abroad than they have at home. Indeed, for some three decades before 9/11, American interests were major targets of terrorism overseas, including the attacks against U.S. citizens and property in Iran (1979), Lebanon (1983), Saudi Arabia (1996), East Africa (1998), and Yemen (2000). There are many factors contributing to this situation, including the fact that the United States maintains an extensive cultural, political, economic, and military presence abroad and that numerous foreign groups and governments oppose American values, policies, and actions.

In light of the pre-9/11 experience, it became clear that terrorism had a substantial impact on the way U.S. citizens lived, worked, and traveled abroad. During the same period, particularly in the 1990s, Americans in the United States became increasingly aware of the terrorist threats to their national security at home and abroad. The emergence of Osama bin Laden's al Qaeda, an international network of terrorist groups operating throughout the world, contributed greatly to U.S. concerns nationally and globally.

In the face of the terrorism threat to America in the pre-9/11 period, the U.S. government responses consisted of an elaborate organizational structure and various activities, including legislative, intelligence, law enforcement, military, diplomatic, and public affairs. Specifically, the Federal Bureau of Investigation (FBI) became the lead agency to deal with terrorism within the United States. The Department of State was responsible for coping with terrorism abroad. In addition, other governmental bodies, such as the Department of Defense, Department of Energy, Department of Treasury, and intelligence agencies, have had important roles in combating terrorism.

To be sure, each of these agencies has given its own slightly different characterization of what constitutes "terrorism." After struggling for many years to develop a uniform approach, a reality that has hampered the U.S. ability to formulate consistent policies, an official American definition emerged. It is contained in Title 22 of the United States Code, Section 2556f(d):

> The term "terrorism" means premeditated politically motivated violence perpetrated against noncombatant targets by subnational groups or clandestine agents, usually intended to influence an audience. The term "international terrorism" means any group practicing, or that has significant subgroups that practice, international terrorism.

Perspectives on terrorism have changed greatly since September 11. Once generally viewed as a type of crime, terrorism is now being seen as a new mode of warfare threatening the security interests of the United States and the world community. Yet certain basic principles that guided U.S. counterterrorism strategy before 9/11 endure in the post-9/11 era. These consist of four elements: First, make no concessions to terrorists and strike no deals. Second, bring terrorists to justice for their crimes. Third, isolate and apply pressure on states that sponsor terrorism to force them to change their behavior. And fourth, bolster the counterterrorist capabilities of those countries that work with the United States and require assistance.

The September 11, 2001, hijackings perpetrated by nineteen al Qaeda operatives killing and wounding thousands of Americans and nationals from more than ninety countries most graphically demonstrated the nature and intensity of the new global terrorism. It is not surprising, therefore, that President George W. Bush immediately began to develop and implement policies to improve homeland security and to form a global coalition to combat terrorism abroad.

Some of the notable domestic measures include providing emergency funding and other financial support to cope with nationwide needs; improving security at airports and expanding the Federal Air Marshal program; preparing for bioterrorism attacks and stockpiling emergency medicines; establishing a Foreign Tracking Task Force to deal with immigration issues; updating designation of foreign terrorist organizations in accordance with the Anti-terrorism and Effective Death Penalty Act; creating the Financial Institutions Hotline to report suspicious transactions related to terrorist activities; and detaining noncitizens suspected of being al Qaeda operatives and bringing them to military tribunals for terrorism trials.

Aside from these tactical steps, four dramatic actions have been undertaken in the post-9/11 era. First is the enactment of the Patriot Act, signed by President Bush on October 26, 2001. This measure, most recently known as the USA Patriot Improvement and Reauthorization Act of 2005 and signed by the president on March 9, 2006, allows intelligence and law enforcement officials to continue sharing information and using the same tools against terrorists already employed against criminals. This legislation strengthens the Department of Justice to better detect and disrupt terrorist threats.

The second important action was the establishment of the Department of Homeland Security (DHS) on July 16, 2003, consisting of twenty-two agencies for the purpose of providing a comprehensive counterterrorism strategy. This extraordinary structure, employing some 180,000 people, focuses on national, state, and local cooperation to assure shared responsibility for homeland security.

A third significant move was the creation on November 27, 2002, of the National Commission on Terrorist Attacks Upon the United States. Otherwise known as the 9/11 Commission, this group was charged with determining how the tragedy happened and how the United States can avoid future attacks. The Commission found that the U.S. government severely underestimated the gravity of the threats and did not adjust its policies to address them effectively. Their foremost recommendation was to design a balanced strategy, attacking terrorists from many different angles to prevent the groups from expanding. To assess if recommendations were implemented properly or not, an informal 9/11 Public Discourse Project was organized. After a series of public panels, it assessed that although some positive changes had occurred, there were still several instances of blatant failure requiring further reform.

The fourth critical measure undertaken by the United States relates to the role of intelligence in combating terrorism. The 9/11 Commission reported on the need for the intelligence community to improve information-sharing between governmental agencies and produce a central counterterrorism database. The Intelligence Reform and Terrorism Prevention Act of 2005 created the position of the Director of National Intelligence, bringing together about fifteen agencies under one structure.

On the international front, the United States initiated two major military operations against global terrorism that are currently continuing without an end in sight. President Bush declared war against al Qaeda after 9/11 and, together with an international coalition, launched in 2001 Operation Enduring Freedom in Afghanistan. With some twenty thousand

American troops in the country, the United States is still facing terrorist threats and an expanding insurgency of the Taliban. Similarly, the United States, in cooperation with like-minded countries, attacked Iraq in March 2003. After the defeat and capture of Saddam Hussein, the postwar security situation in that country has increasingly deteriorated. Terrorist attacks initiated by al Qaeda in Iraq, led by Abu Musab al-Zarqawi, and insurgent acts continue to plague some 140,000 American soldiers in the country. Indeed, sectarian violence has reached an unprecedented level and threatens to trigger a civil war in Iraq that U.S. forces apparently cannot prevent militarily.

In summary, it was not until September 11, 2001, that the United States and the rest of the world began to realize both the magnitude of the threat to international security terrorism represents and that terrorists consider themselves at war and will fight until total victory is achieved. As a result, the United States is now focusing heavily on homeland security and enacting new counterterrorism policies and legislation designed to protect the nation. Currently, the United States calls for defeating terrorist organizations, denying further sponsorship to groups, diminishing the underlying conditions that cause terrorism, and defending the United States, its citizens, and interests from future attacks. Only then will the U.S. position be secure. And yet, the debate regarding the "best practices" of U.S. counterterrorism strategies domestically and internationally will continue into the foreseeable future.

France

French society has been confronted with terrorism for more than one hundred years. The more recent manifestations of terrorism in France consist of a combination of domestically grown ideological terrorism, separatist movements, importation of foreign conflicts through immigration, and international terrorism. In confronting these threats, the French state has to contend with the contrasting requirements of democratic justice and efficiency. Since the 1970s, terrorism in France has assumed a number of fundamentally different forms. Separatist movements, such as the Liberation Front of Brittany (FLB), the National Liberation Front of Corsica (FLNC), and the Euskadi ta Askatasuna (ETA), have perpetrated numerous attacks against targets representing the French state. During the 1980s, the bloodiest decade in the history of French terrorism, ideological terrorism gained prominence, with groups such as *Action Directe* making the headlines. This was also the decade of imported conflicts, primarily the Israeli-Palestinian conflict, and of international terrorism emanating from the Middle East. State-sponsored terrorism increasingly began to take advantage of European logistical bases in the households of Muslim immigrants. The rise of the Algerian Muslim Islamist terrorist group Armed Islamic Group (GIA) during the 1990s signaled the arrival of radical Islamist terrorism in France. The waves of terrorist attacks in Paris of 1995 and 1996 were mainly linked to Algerian Islamist demands and exemplified a new type of terrorism: not state-sponsored but nevertheless international and religious in scope. During the 1990s, separatist movements again resorted to frequent violent attacks.

Terrorism has taken on new forms since the end of the Cold War. Terrorism is now structureless, shorn of ideology, and criminalized. For the most part, it is no longer directed by states. Terrorism has become a way to publicize economic, social, and cultural ills, and new terrorist actors, such as sects and ecologists, have emerged in France.

To counter these forms of modern terrorism, France has set up a system of prevention and repression based on the three principles of "specialization," "coordination," and "centralization": specialization of the services that form a complex whole, coordination at ministerial and operational levels, and centralization of the police and magistrates.

The Council for Home Security drives the political process. It evaluates threats and considers the means to deal with them. Resolutions are then confirmed within the Inter-ministerial Committee for Antiterrorist Liaison (CILAT), the overall coordinating committee. The Vigipirate contingency plan, the main tool in the battle against terrorism, is a uniquely French feature: it mobilizes the police, gendarmerie, and armed forces to ensure the protection of sensitive sites.

French legislation also targets terrorism specifically. Terrorism is defined as an infraction that is intentionally "linked to an individual or collective effort that intends to disturb public order through intimidation or terror." French law prohibits conspiracy to commit terrorism or ecological terrorism. Sentences for terrorism range from banishment, removal of civil rights, fines, and life imprisonment. The legal proceedings are handled centrally by the court of appeal (*Cour d'Appel*) of Paris, where the Central Antiterrorist Service (SCLAT) is based. A criminal court that is "specially constituted" (its jury is comprised of professional magistrates) delivers judgments.

Over the last thirty years, France has moved from a merely reactive policy to one of genuine prevention. Its goal has become to better anticipate the future developments of a phenomenon that is highly unpredictable in nature. Today's antiterrorist operations are a compromise between negotiation and repression.

During the 1970s, the population at large did not fully appreciate the seriousness of the threat posed by international and separatist terrorism, since terrorist acts occurred only sporadically. The government chose to depict these terrorist acts as serious criminal offenses, so as not to alarm the population and to deny terrorists the public audience they craved. The 1970s and 1980s were also a period of tolerance toward foreigners who pursued grievances in their country of origin. This policy meant leaving terrorists alone, so long as they did not break French law, which had the advantage of protecting France. May 1981 brought the left to power, whose view of security involved a structural reform of society and led to a "policy of openness" for a very short time. After 1982, the Airborne and Frontier Police (PAF) increased its surveillance of frontiers and several new services were created including CILAT, a minister responsible for public security, and a central databank of intelligence on terrorists (VAT). The Socialists' policy concentrated on change at the operational level. It sought to improve the organization of the different services, but neglected to specialize them. Sometimes, several services intervened at the same time, preventing the overall perspective essential for acting against a terrorist group.

Soon after the legislative elections of 1986, the newly elected Conservative government under Prime Minister Jacques Chirac sought to demonstrate its resolve. The government opted for offensive policies (e.g., multiple arrests, expulsions, and reinforced surveillance). Competition and rivalry between the services nevertheless still delayed inquiries. Finally expanded police modernization was undertaken, and genuine coordination between the services became reality, with the services recognizing UCLAT's authority.

The outbreak of the first Gulf War led France to adopt a preventive approach for the first time. In 1994, a White Paper on Defense presented terrorism as the main nonmilitary threat capable of affecting security. Religious extremists and nationalists were considered to represent other destabilizing threats. International surveillance of Islamist fundamentalists became the priority, and orders were given to dismantle any structure with radical Islamist connotations. The dismantling of the Chalabi network was an important success. By February 1995, the threat had become so important that France called for a European meeting of antiterrorist authorities.

After 9/11, the antiterrorist setup was reinforced, with additional involvement from the armed forces, integration of the health and medical chains into the alert mechanism, and additional measures to combat the funding of terrorism. Additional legislation expanded the list of possible terrorist offenses, and procedural requirements for prosecution were tightened. For the first time, the antiterrorist prevention mechanism was brought up to a level to include the nuclear, biological, and chemical weapons threats. France has also created a special unit to fight money-laundering and has proposed an international convention on the financing of terrorism at the United Nations. Cooperation between the French and American authorities on fighting terrorism has been exemplary: In 2002, a discrete counterterrorism intelligence center, code-named "Alliance Base," was set up in Paris by the Central Intelligence Agency (CIA) and French intelligence and has continued to function, even at the height of the French-American crisis of 2003. The mobilization against terrorism at an unprecedented international level since 9/11 has led to an increase in international cooperation that must be further strengthened and developed in the future.

Germany

National or domestic terrorism prevailed in the past when activists of the radical left-wing Red Army Faction (RAF) frightened the German people by hijacking persons or planes, especially during the 1970s. In total, thirty-five people died in RAF activities. In 1998, the group announced its dissolution. Today, right-wing extremist and Neo-nazi groups are the biggest problem in terms of domestic terrorism.

While international terrorism does not play an important role in present-day Germany, it did constitute a threat during the 1970s and 1980s—most notably when Palestinian terrorists took Israeli athletes hostage at the Olympic Games 1972 in Munich. In the 1980s, Germany suffered mostly from extremist Kurdish and Turkish groups that launched several explosive attacks. Today, groups such as Hamas use Germany, above all, as a base for fund-raising and recruitment.

Unlike international terrorism, transnational terrorism has affected Germany very strongly in recent years. This became obvious after 9/11 when intelligence agencies discovered that the 9/11 attacks were planned in Hamburg. In addition, three of the four suicide pilots had lived and studied there, including the mastermind of the attacks, Mohamed Atta. Other members of the so-called Hamburg cell involved in the planning of the attacks were later captured or are still being sought by security authorities.

Before 9/11, German police authorities managed to detect Islamist cells and prevent potential attacks. For instance, this was the case with the "Frankfurt cell" that had planned an attack on the Strasbourg Christmas fair. Additionally, the German minister of interior has outlawed other Islamist groups and extradited Metin Kaplan, the leader of the extremist Turkish Islamic group Caliphate State, which is based in Cologne and aimed at establishing an Islamic Caliphate. The group (eleven hundred members, including several suborganizations) was banned in 2001.

Since 9/11, the focus of German authorities has shifted toward Islamic extremism and foreign militant groups. According to an estimate by the domestic intelligence service, roughly thirty-one thousand members of radical Islamic organizations and three thousand to four thousand militant Muslims ready to use violence are living in Germany.

The German security authority structure differs from that in other countries, not least because it is a reaction to the events of the Nazi era. First, security authorities are organized along federal lines, that is, each of the sixteen federal states (*Länder*) has its own police forces as well as its own intelligence service and law enforcement institutions. Second, there exists a clear distinction between police and the intelligence service on the one hand, and between police (internal security matters) and the military (external) on the other.

The consequence of all these guidelines provided by the German Basic Law (*Grundgesetz*) is a very complex institutional setting of thirty-nine authorities plus various ministries that hold responsibilities in counterterrorism. Not only do different ministries supervise the federal institutions, but those institutions are spread across the republic, complicating their day-to-day interaction.

Homegrown groups largely shaped counterterrorism policy prior to 9/11. Therefore, the fight against terrorism was a domestic matter in which law enforcement and police measures played key roles. The experience with domestic terrorism since the 1970s led to the introduction of several antiterrorism provisions into the German criminal law, including the contact ban law, a special regulation for principal witnesses, and the "grid search" (a special scanning method). After 9/11, this grid search was used again to detect Islamist sleeper cells in Germany. This search failed, however, and people began to question whether scanning the data of millions of innocent people is justified or appropriate.

The German parliament and government reacted to the 9/11 incidents with several counterterrorism measures and new laws. At first, the government increased taxes to make more money available for the fight against terrorism. This special budget of 1.47 billion euros was mainly given to security authorities and the army in order to provide them with additional capabilities and new personnel. Additionally, the parliament passed two "security packages," each of them reforming security-related laws. The first package allows authorities to ban religious organizations if their purpose or activities violate the criminal law, are directed against the constitutional order, or disregard the idea of international understanding. This was not possible before because the German law included a privilege for religious groups, guaranteeing special rights and protection. The second reform included in the first security package makes it a punishable offense to support or be a member of a terrorist organization based abroad. Before 2002, conviction was only possible when someone was a member of a terrorist organization with a formal base in Germany.

The main goal of the second security package was to strengthen the rights of security authorities. Police institutions, intelligence service, and law-enforcement agencies can now, under certain circumstances, access information from public and private services, such as mail, air traffic, and bank accounts. Another important new provision relates to immigration of foreigners. Persons who constitute a threat to democracy and freedom or to the security of the Federal Republic (including members or supporters of an organization that supports terrorism) shall not be granted entry visas or residence permits.

Apart from these security packages, other terrorism-related laws have been passed, such as the Immigration Law of 2005 that allows federal or *Länder* institutions to deport persons with a suspected terrorist background or persons who may threaten the public order (including people who propagate hate or violence in public).

Traditionally, Germany is in favor of strong multilateral institutions and international organizations. Therefore, it supported the UN efforts to combat terrorism by ratifying several terrorism-related conventions. Beside this more "diplomatic" approach, Germany shifted its policy in terms of deployment of military force for counterterrorism purposes. Now, under certain conditions, armed forces' missions are considered necessary to combat terrorism. For that reason, Germany supports the U.S.-led Operation Enduring Freedom. Originally, Germany contributed thirty-nine hundred troops to that operation. The special forces worked together with United States and other international forces to hunt terrorists.

As far as long-term efforts are concerned, Germany is broadly engaged in Afghanistan and supports the reconstruction and state-building process with military and civilian personnel. Germany has sent twenty-two hundred troops to Afghanistan, which are part of the International Security Assistance Force (ISAF), a component of the North Atlantic Treaty Organization. Moreover, it has established two Provisional Reconstruction Teams with four hundred fifty personnel. Besides these military efforts, Germany spends significant amounts of money on Afghanistan's reconstruction and has become the "lead nation" in this effort after hosting the Bonn peace conference. Generally speaking, Germany has also tried to foster a dialogue with the Muslim world after 9/11. Another effort made by the Federal Republic is to prevent the spread of political extremism by, for instance, supporting international initiatives for solving regional conflicts, fostering democratization processes, emphasizing poverty reduction, and supporting state building.

Some open questions remain. First, the balance between civil liberty and security concerns is not yet solved. Security is without doubt a precondition for liberty, but the yearning for security should not become a threat to these liberties. Second, there are conflicting objectives in domestic and foreign policies, for instance, as far as the access to Germany is concerned. While it has to be restricted for security reasons, freedom of trade and the possibility to travel should not be limited for external policy reasons. Third, the distinction of internal and external security can hardly be sustained against the background of transnational threats. A closer linkage between police, military, and civilian protection services might therefore seem sensible, but it is prohibited by the Basic Law. Fourth, fragmentation of the security apparatus, as described above, is an issue because this decentralized structure creates barriers to information-sharing and common sense.

In summary, one can conclude that despite the range of activities, there still exists no cross-governmental strategy for counterterrorism that systematically links the various issues and measures. One step could be to integrate operational policies (combating and arresting terrorists, destroying their bases, etc.) and structural counterterrorism policies (focusing on the societal and political causes of terrorism). The approaches should not contradict each other but rather reinforce each other.

Italy

Terrorism is not a new threat to Italy. Since the 1970s, it has evolved from a bilateral threat comprised of right- and left-wing factions to a multilateral one involving Mafia organizations as well as foreign terrorist groups, principally Islamic fundamentalists. This evolution caused difficulty in developing an effective Italian counterterrorism policy.

Initially, terrorism in Italy was purely political in nature, supporting either the extreme right or extreme left. The left began with extra-parliamentary political groups that sought revolution, and quickly resorted to violence to subvert Italian democratic society. In the early 1970s, many groups, supported by young workers or college students, were formed. The *Brigate Rosso* would eventually emerge as the most prevalent.

Right-wing organizations were also formed, seeking an anticommunist authoritarian government. These movements would commit several large-scale indiscriminate massacres to ensure a strong psychological impact upon the Italian populace. The two leading organizations, the *Ordine Nuovo* and the *Avanguardia Nazionale*, had direct ties to the *Repubblica Sociale Italiana*, founded by Benito Mussolini during the waning years of the Second World War.

Violent demonstrations throughout the 1970s soon led to direct guerrilla-style confrontations, and the terrorist groups would grow more hostile to include bombings and murdering of people who did not agree with their strategies. Later, during a second phase of violence, these organizations would commit several high-profile robberies and kidnappings to not only generate finances, but also to seize the political spotlight. However, kidnapping was found to have an adverse effect on popular support, as the *Brigate Rosso* discovered after murdering hostage Aldo Moro, the leader of the Christian Democratic party and former Prime Minister of Italy.

The first counterterrorism agency in Italy was founded in 1974, and quickly attempted to integrate all counterterrorist efforts under one central command. It focused on infiltrating security forces into various terrorist organizations in order to gain knowledge about their leaders and to identify their support bases. Soon, police began arresting the leaders and uncovering cells across the country.

The Italian Parliament also assisted in fighting terrorism by passing several laws giving counterterrorism forces a freer hand in conducting operations. For example, in urgent cases, searches could be conducted without a warrant. Among these new laws, the counterterrorism forces also relied on legal instruments that were tested while combating organized crime, specifically the Mafia. However, success was limited, and attacks still occurred on occasion, principally because the government sometimes tightened this "judicial leash" out of a desire to maintain control over the counterterrorism forces. This inconsistency greatly hampered the abilities of the counterterrorist forces.

Toward the end of the 1970s, counterterrorism forces began utilizing a new method. Increasingly, government officials found that the terrorists they captured were willing to cooperate in exchange for reduced sentences. The tactic of *repentance* greatly assisted the Italian authorities in discovering names, locations, political links, and financial support. While the tactic was mostly successful against left-wing organizations, it greatly reduced overall amounts of subversive activities.

The actions taken by the Italian government and the vigorous rejection of terrorism by the Italian population brought about a sharp decline in terrorist activity in the 1980s. Between 1981 and 1983, fifty-four percent of all suspects related to terrorist activities were arrested, and by the end of 1987, around four thousand had been captured, one-third of whom were members of right-wing organizations. These tactics would continue to be successful into the 1990s, when they began to be used against the Mafia, who, it was discovered, had been collaborating with terrorists.

Despite the best efforts of the Italian counterterrorism forces, many organizations were able to reorganize and set up new bases with the assistance of foreign groups. For example, *Brigate Rosso* survived with the assistance of the French group *Action Directe* and from the German group *Rote Armee Fraktion*. The international climate of the Cold War greatly influenced the terrorist struggle in Italy, and international sources provided financial and logistical support as well as arms and training.

The left-wing groups enjoyed a much wider scope of international support. This ranged from arms provided by Arab terrorist-supporting nations such as Libya to training in Lebanon facilitated by left-leaning Arab organizations such as Front of Refusal, to direct support provided to the *Brigate Rosso* by the Soviet KGB. Right-wing groups were supported by the dictatorships of Spain, Portugal, and Greece. This influx of assistance from abroad increased the number of terrorist organizations to 269 by 1979, 217 of which were left wing.

Although the two have historically been mutually exclusive entities, terrorism and the Mafia have developed links particularly during the mid-to-late 1980s. The relationship became apparent to the Italian government when *Brigate Rosso* bombed ex-mayor of Florence, Lando Conti, during a high-profile Mafia trial. *Brigate Rosso* subsequently made a statement that by prosecuting the Mafia, the Italian government was diverting "public opinion from the real problems of the country."

In order to combat these activities, the Italian government formed the *Direzione Investigativa Antimafia* in 1991. The organization relied on the methods of repentance and dissociation that had been fostered by the counterterrorism efforts of the 1970s. In addition, the Italian government defined a new type of crime, the "Mafia criminal conspiracy." The country also adopted counterkidnapping strategies, offered greater protection to repentants, and set up a system to combat illegal financing.

As the twenty-first century began, new Italian terrorist groups have appeared in Italy and are operating in two directions, by attacking state institutions directly and attacking representations of the ruling powers. These new forms of terrorism emphasize their international impact and play off the suffering social sectors, largely in southern Italy.

During the 1990s, Italian security forces also became aware of the presence of fundamentalist Islamic "cells" operating within their country's borders. Given the high volume of immigration, the entrance of such cells comes not as a surprise, but remains a high priority security risk. Due to Italy's centrality in the Mediterranean such cells have provided a jumping-off point to the rest of Europe. However, these groups are a threat because they traffic arms, which may provide offensive capabilities to local Italian terrorists, and spread propaganda capable of inciting future terrorist attacks.

Financial support is a basic necessity for all terrorist organizations and, as such, it represents a key vulnerability to be exploited by counterterrorism officials. Many of the foreign terrorist elements in Italy already fund their operations through arms trafficking, drug trading, and money laundering. However, more recently, terrorists have increasingly adopted more traditional methods, such as robbery and kidnapping, to support their new operations. Despite successes in combating terrorism, which have resulted in fewer attacks, there has been a marked increase in funding through both traditional and international means. Consequently, financial institutions illustrate an increasingly important threat.

The question that must be asked now is: "How can repentance, proven successful in the 1980s, be used today when the threat is much more varied?" The modern terrorist generally resides outside of common culture, unlike the repentant terrorists of the 1980s who were members of a common Italian society. For this reason, intelligence from modern repentant terrorists may be used but should not be considered completely credible. Instead, a greater integration of international and national organizations, both vertically and horizontally, is needed. Specialized organizations must be created to deal with all aspects of dynamic international criminal systems.

September 11 placed renewed emphasis on Italy's historical fight against various forms of domestic terrorism and organized crime. It has seen the terrorist threat assume two distinct forms: traditional domestic terrorism and Islamic fundamentalist terrorism. On the domestic terrorism front, links have been discovered connecting extreme fringe groups within the antiglobalization movement such as the Sardinian Autonomy Movement (MAS), the Revolutionary Front for Communism, and the *Brigate Rosso*.

Islamic fundamentalists represent the other major terrorist threat facing Italy, a fact that was highlighted by the March 2004 Madrid train bombings. Prior to this event, Italy was considered only a logistical base from which terrorists recruited fighters, raised funds, and forged documents. However, the Madrid attacks compelled Italian authorities to significantly expand their counterterrorism efforts. This improved intelligence revealed an active informal network of Islamist terrorist cells within Italy, comprised of groups such as the Algerian Armed Islamic Group, the Egyptian Gama al-Islamiya, and the Iraqi Ansar al-Islam. In addition, there exist growing links between terrorists and common criminals, as suggested by collaboration between Camorra members who have converted to Islam while in prison. These discoveries have led Italian authorities to conclude that the country, because of its geographical position, has become a selected target for terrorist groups and individual radicals bent on jihad.

Additional Italian counterterrorism efforts have included strengthening antiterrorism legislation such as Decree-Law 374/2001, which codified the crime of conspiracy to commit acts of international terrorism and permits prosecution of anyone promoting, creating, organizing, managing, or financing terrorism as well as extending judicial police powers to include preemptive, court-authorized wiretaps. Moreover, Italian authorities passed legislation to freeze and/or seize the financial assets of suspected terrorist organizations.

Post-9/11 Italian government structural changes also enhanced the country's counterterrorism capabilities. Interdepartmental coordination bodies and ad hoc units have been created to provide an operational framework able to coordinate counterterrorism efforts. International cooperation has been streamlined via the Coordinating Structure for International Counter-Terrorism Cooperation within the Ministry of Foreign Affairs. Finally, at the operational level, the government has integrated the military into homeland defense, guarding high-risk Italian infrastructure and ensuring transportation safety.

New Italian legislation passed in July 2005 provides that suspects can be detained for up to twenty-four hours without charge and interrogated without the presence of legal counsel. In addition, it expands the definition of prosecutable terrorist activity to include "public provocation to commit terrorist offences," "recruitment for terrorism," and "training for terrorism," as well other accessory crimes, the cumulative effect of which has been to allow Italian authorities to "cast a wider net" to prevent potential terrorist acts. Additional preventative measures have included improved intelligence gathering, information-sharing, training, and investigation strategies, particularly between other European countries. An example of this cooperation is the recent introduction of the "European arrest warrant," which has noticeably streamlined traditional extradition procedures while maintaining grounds for extradition refusal such as extraditing persons to countries in which they could be subject to torture or the death penalty.

These enhanced counterterrorism measures have created a concurrent concern for the balance between increased state power designed to more effectively combat terrorism and the maintenance of individual rights and freedoms, both of potential terrorist suspects and civilians living in Italy's heightened security environment. Another human rights issue of concern is that of asylum-seekers, particularly those who may pose a risk to Italian national security. Italian law No. 133 allows for the circumvention of normal expulsion procedures and the immediate expulsion of aliens believed to pose a security threat. Overall, the Italian government remains committed to both enforcement within the bounds of international human rights law and strict internal judicial oversight, allowing the balance between security and civil liberties to be constantly readjusted as circumstances change.

Current Italian laws do not define terrorist offenses beyond the definitions included in existing international antiterrorism conventions, and instead reference those treaties in force that condemn specifically defined criminal offenses as "acts of terrorism." Therefore, a case exists for creating a new umbrella counterterrorist convention that clearly and unequivocally articulates requirements and norms of counterterrorism law and policy. However, after attempting to arrive at a consensus, an Italian government working group refused to propose its own definition, deciding instead to recognize the progress made by United Nations Security Council Resolution 1566 and to agree that terrorist acts are never justifiable on political, ideological, racial, ethnic, religious, or other grounds. Essentially, the group concluded that acts specifically targeting civilians or noncombatants, whatever the context or motive, must be outlawed.

Egypt

Terrorism erupted in Egypt in the late 1970s and early 1980s with the assassination of President Anwar Sadat. It peaked in the mid 1990s before trailing off to its current low levels. However, the phenomenon is still very real, with recent major attacks such as the ones in Luxor,

Taba, and Sharm el Sheik. Terrorists based in Egypt often initiate these acts of terrorism, but they work in conjunction with leaders residing abroad. With most of the attacks targeting tourists and economic establishments, their objectives are clearly to destabilize Egypt's society, politics, and the economy. The cause for terrorism in Egypt can be internal (poverty, political weakness, lack of cultural consciousness) or external (foreign funding, foreign terrorist networks). The common methods of terrorism are assassination of political figures, religious violence against churches and mosques, attacks against economic targets, social violence, and incitement against the government. In fighting terrorism, Egypt utilizes counterterrorism strategies on numerous levels: police action, nonviolent religious propagation, legal and legislative opposition, use of the media, and socioeconomic measures such as education.

More specifically, Egypt's strategy to counter terrorism has been pursued on both the international and national levels. On the wider international level, Egypt has signed and ratified numerous international conventions on multiple aspects of terrorism, such as aviation, bombing, punishment, financing, maritime issues, hostage-taking and kidnapping, and nuclear terrorism. When these conventions are signed, they become law in Egypt. Egypt is also an active participant in international conferences on terrorism for the purposes of preventing, studying, and combating international terrorism. Furthermore, Egypt is a member of, and active participant in, the International Criminal Police Organization (INTERPOL), through which information and data on international terrorism is shared.

Egypt is also committed to regional cooperation in combating terrorism. As an important member of the League of Arab States (LAS), it has signed numerous treaties and conventions enacted by the LAS. In addition, Egypt has also pushed for antiterrorism agreements with the Organization of Islamic Conference and the Council of Arab Ministers of Justice.

Along with broader international and regional agreements to combat terrorism, Egypt has been involved in numerous bilateral agreements relating to terrorism. Most of these instruments center on a few major issues: prevent aid and sanctuary to indigenous terror groups, isolate the perpetrators, prevent acts of terrorism, and extradite the terrorists.

It is evident that on the domestic level, legislation is one of the most effective tools in combating terrorism. A critical legal instrument is law No. 277, adopted in 1992, which clearly defines the meaning of terrorism and lists specific terrorist offenses. Significant responses are the strict laws against financing terrorist groups, which provides the government access to personal bank accounts and money transfers. In addition, Egypt's counterterrorism policies cover a wide range of areas. One major principle is no negotiation with, or concessions to, terrorists. Furthermore, Egypt also has a policy of preventing terrorism before attacks occur rather than merely responding to attacks already sustained. This includes securing borders and import points, enforcing ID cards, restricting possession of firearms, prohibiting military or paramilitary groups, and enacting the surveillance of terrorist communications.

One of the key policies of the government is to accept repentance from terrorists as a way to create conflict within terrorist organizations, obtain information, and also encourage terrorists to return to the right path. However, this does not mean that terrorists are not subject to severe penalties. It is a policy that no amnesty shall be granted and no safe haven shall be permitted for perpetrators of terrorist crimes.

In order to implement the various counterterrorism policies, Egypt established some specific structures, such as the Financial Action Task Force (FATF), to deal with money-laundering issues. Moreover, in 1998, the National Committee for International Cooperation in Combating Terrorism was established, bringing together experts from the Ministries of Justice, Interior, Foreign Affairs, and Intelligence Service to prepare legal rules, propose agreements, and prosecute terrorists.

In summary, Egypt has effectively acted against terrorism in all its forms and manifestations, wherever and by whomsoever committed as well as any attempt to encourage, instigate, organize, or engage in the preparation and/or commission of terrorist acts. Thanks to this overall policy, terrorism no longer represents a significant threat to Egypt. In fact, violent acts have decreased precipitously since 1994–1995. In response to these and more recent terrorist attacks, Egypt wholly cooperates with the Security Council Counter-terrorism Committee (CTC) through its regular reports in which complete replies are given to all questions.

Sri Lanka

The Liberation Tigers of Tamil Eelam (LTTE) is a Sri Lankan Tamil rebel group that seeks a separate nation within Sri Lanka for the Tamil minority. It was covertly supported by the Tamil United Liberation Front (TULF), the political party representing the Tamil community in Colombo's political establishment. The LTTE's battle for a separate state has been relentless since the violent communal riots of July 1983. These riots, an outgrowth of the ethnic conflict that was gathering momentum and escalating into a major wave of terrorism, concluded on December 21, 1984, as plans were made for peace talks in 1985; the talks never materialized, however. The next attempt at peace talks with the LTTE was with Indian mediation, held in Thimpu, Bhutan, in July and August 1985, which ended abruptly and unexpectedly in failure, after a walkout by the LTTE and TULF leaders. By January 1986, fratricidal warfare erupted among Tamil militant groups and by the end of the year, the LTTE had emerged as the dominant Tamil militant group.

Direct Indian intervention culminated in the signing of a peace accord between Sri Lanka and India on July 29, 1987, without LTTE participation. Per the terms of the accord, seventy thousand Indian troops landed in Sri Lanka in the fall of 1987. Deploying Indian Peace Keeping Forces (IPKF) in Sri Lanka proved to be a total failure of Indian foreign policy, for they were unable to disarm the LTTE or destroy its fighting capabilities while the LTTE continued to use safe houses in Tamil Nadu. The IPKF lost its image as a peacekeeper, and about twelve hundred soldiers were killed with over two thousand wounded. In 1991, a female LTTE suicide bomber assassinated former Indian Prime Minister Rajiv Gandhi while he was campaigning for reelection in South India. This was the turning point in relations between India and the LTTE.

President R. Premadasa, who won the presidential election on December 19, 1988, replacing J. R. Jayewardene, had as a priority the withdrawal of Indian troops from Sri Lanka. Government officials held secret talks with the LTTE in the northern jungles, allegedly even offering cash and weapons, with the aim of ridding the country of the IPKF. With the IPKF gone, the LTTE wasted no time in wiping out rival militant organizations, to which President Premadasa turned a blind eye. This policy of tolerance toward terrorist violence backfired when an LTTE suicide bomber assassinated him on May 1, 1993.

The greatest hope for a negotiated settlement of the conflict came when Chandrika Kumaratunga became president in 1994 on a mandate promising to end the war. There were positive signs that the peace process would continue and bring about a lasting solution in 1995. Both regionally and internationally, there were also extremely positive responses to the peace process from India, the United Kingdom, and the European Union. At the end of 1994, President Kumaratunga announced a government proposal for a cease-fire. Negotiations finally broke down, however, and the LTTE declared an end to the truce by attacking two navy boats in Trincomalee harbor on April 19, 1995. In October 1995, the government launched a major military offensive, code-named "Riviresa" (Sunshine), with the clear focus of capturing Jaffna. The following violence of 1996 and 1997 saw relentless fighting between the LTTE and government forces.

The proscription of the LTTE by foreign countries in the 1990s helped to undermine the group and decrease terrorist activity in Sri Lanka. Meanwhile, Sri Lanka's peace process drew international attention, and offers flowed in for facilitation. British negotiator Liam Fox paid three visits to Sri Lanka since 1996 to facilitate the peace dialogue between Chandrika and the LTTE. However, this agreement was not implemented because the Sri Lankan government demanded that the LTTE meet certain conditions, such as the laying down of arms before talks could take place. In 1998, amidst hostility and suspicion on both sides, the Sri Lankan government invited Norway to facilitate peace talks, for the first time recognizing the need for a third-party facilitator for the peace process. An official request from both sides emerged, and it was confirmed in 2000. Thus, the peace talks unfolded against the backdrop of two particularly dramatic events: the LTTE attack on the Katunayake International Airport in July 2001 and the 9/11 terrorist attacks in the United States six weeks later.

Prime Minister Ranil Wickremesinghe, who won the national general elections in December 2001, signed a cease-fire agreement with the LTTE in February 2002. Peace talks in 2002 and 2003 took place in Thailand, Norway, Germany, and Japan. In October 2003, the LTTE proposed an elaborate plan for an Interim Self Governing Authority (ISGA) which detailed how power should be devolved between the Sinhalese political parties.

President Kumaratunga launched the National Advisory Council for Peace and Reconciliation on October 4, 2004, as the official forum for consultation and guidance on peace negotiations and enhancing reconciliation and understanding among the communities. However, the key parties in parliament, whose support is essential for constitutional reform, did not support it.

As the peace process stagnated without much hope of immediate revival, a natural disaster in the form of a major tsunami struck South Asia on December 26, 2004, devastating entire areas of the country. Sri Lanka was one of the worst affected countries, with the coastal areas completely devastated and 31,000 people dead. In the immediate aftermath of the tsunami, there were heightened hopes that the LTTE and the government would at last be united in the mutual need to rebuild after the natural disaster. However, these positive expectations were short-lived. Before long, it became clear that the LTTE was using the tsunami for propaganda purposes.

On August 12, 2005, Foreign Minister Lakshman Kadirgamar, who carried out an extremely effective campaign to ban the LTTE internationally as a terrorist outfit, was assassinated by the LTTE. On September 26, 2005, the European Union imposed a travel ban on the LTTE, preventing LTTE delegations from visiting European Union countries. The United States welcomed the European Union decision and said that strong action should be taken against the LTTE to stop violence and killings.

Despite LTTE relentless effort to prevent Tamils from voting in the 2005 elections, Sri Lanka's new president, Mahinda Rajapakse, promised to renew peace talks with the LTTE but reiterated his opposition to the LTTE demand for an independent state.

Does the LTTE genuinely want peace? All evidence points to the contrary. Tamil expatriates around the world, who have for years helped fuel terrorism in Sri Lanka by funding the LTTE, are becoming disillusioned, weary of extortion and threats, and are reluctantly accepting the true nature of the LTTE: it has no interest in promoting the rights of the Tamil people, but only desires to terrorize and wield absolute power.

Successes and Failures: Selected Lessons for Future Counterterrorism Strategies

The foregoing summaries of the counterterrorism strategies of these six nations reveal both successes and failures of policies and actions. The following discussion highlights selected examples of what worked and what did not work for the purpose of considering a "best practices" framework for combating both conventional and unconventional future terrorist threats.

As we have seen, the basic principles guiding U.S. policy consisted of four key elements: making no concessions to terrorists and striking no deals; bringing terrorists to justice; isolating and applying pressures on state sponsors of terrorism and forcing them to change their behavior; and bolstering the counterterrorism capabilities of those countries that work with the United States and require assistance in combating terrorism.

While these principles are sensible and should be considered as "best practices," unfortunately, American policymakers have not always implemented them in reality, resulting in adverse unintended consequences. For instance, the arms and financial deals struck in the aftermath of the seizure of the U.S. embassy in Tehran in 1979 encouraged further attacks against American targets abroad. Following 9/11, while the United States was successful in tracking down hundreds of terrorists abroad, it failed to prosecute those apprehended and held under harsh conditions in Guantanamo Bay and other reportedly secret locations, thus eroding international confidence in prompt American justice.

Furthermore, American experience in combating state sponsors of terrorism are only partially successful. Afghanistan, Iraq, and Libya are no longer in the terrorist camp. But other states, such as Iran and Syria, continue to sponsor terrorism, and the Sudan, Cuba, and North Korea are still on the State Department's terrorist list. The threat, then, from rogue states that support and provide sanctuary to terrorists is still intact.

On the other hand, positive results have stemmed from U.S. efforts to develop strong cooperation with the international community in forging a global consensus to combat terrorism. Under the Antiterrorism Assistance Program, for example, Washington provides training and related assistance to law enforcement and security services of selected foreign governments. Increased unprecedented collaboration and coordination are also evident on the diplomatic, intelligence, and economic levels.

What appears to be problematic, however, is the initiation of the Bush preemptive doctrine, unveiled on September 20, 2002, in the aftermath of 9/11 and before the invasion of Iraq. This policy, which shifted American strategy from its traditional deterrence and containment approach toward a more pro-active and aggressive disposition, allows the

United States to act alone and preemptively, if necessary, to exercise the right of self-defense in confronting global terrorism and threats from hostile states seeking weapons of mass destruction. Despite the continuing U.S.-led multilateral coalition efforts to prosecute the war against terrorism in both the "front-lines" of Afghanistan and Iraq, the likelihood of a military victory in the short term is doubtful, particularly in the current insurgency environments.

Nevertheless, the Bush administration reaffirmed the 2002 preemptive doctrine in the release of a new "National Security Strategy of the United States," dated March 15, 2006. In this White House document, the most controversial element, namely, the elevation of preemptive strikes to a central component of American strategy, is still proclaimed. But beyond the need to project military power in order to prevent terrorist attacks before they occur and to deny the terrorists opportunities to control nations from which they could launch operations, there is a recognition that there is a long-term need to focus on "the war of ideas" and to expand human rights and democratic infrastructures.

Now almost four years after the "National Security Strategy" was initiated, the key question is whether the United States is as safe as it needs to be in light of the conventional and unconventional challenges to homeland security. The defense gaps, ranging from adequately protecting the nation's critical infrastructure to first responders' preparedness, call once again for learning the lessons of the past and focusing more realistically than ever before on the structures, resources, and implementation of the counterterrorism recommendations offered by various commissions over the past three decades.

It is obvious, of course, that despite the fact that the United States, thus far at least, is the only superpower, it must conduct the global counterterrorism campaign in close partnership with European allies, such as France, Germany, and Italy, and other like-minded nations in the developing world, including Egypt and Sri Lanka. While these countries feature both success and failure in confronting security challenges, their collective experiences can serve as useful guideposts for effective future responses. Naturally, each nation reflects its distinct history and challenges. In France, in the face of escalating threats, both left- and right-wing governments had to respond to public outrage over continual attacks. They initiated more aggressive measures, such as increased surveillance of suspected Islamic terrorists, authorizing car searches, and introducing plans for biological, chemical, and nuclear threats.

While this record must be acknowledged for its positive elements, the counterterrorism balance sheet also contains failures in addressing the challenges of modern terrorism. For example, France did not prevent the Algerian uprising in the 1950s and 1960s, the terrorist activities of the 1970s and 1980s, the rise of Islamists in the 1990s, and the expansion of al Qaeda networks in the post-9/11 period. Many factors have contributed to this situation. For instance, the policy of toleration that provided "safe haven" for terrorists as long as they broke no national laws has undermined public and international confidence in France's capability to cope with expanding threats. Moreover, governmental confusion over how to reconcile the perception of terrorism as a criminal conduct or consider it as an act of war; the turf wars between the various agencies responsible for combating terrorism, such as jurisdictional conflicts; and rivalries among personalities within the security services have also hampered more successful responses.

Germany, like France, had to face both domestic and international terrorism for decades. But unlike the French experience, the domestic challenge to Germany developed initially in the late 1960s and 1970s, partly as a result of "under-identification" with the postwar democracy because of its Nazi past. Right-wing political violence, particularly against foreigners in Germany, also challenged national security. Moreover, the country had to cope with Middle Eastern spillover terrorism, including Iranian, Palestinian, Kurdish, and Algerian threats. Thus, as early as the 1970s, Germany established a computerized police and intelligence apparatus. The domestic databases, used for "grid searching," were adjusted in the post-9/11 period in an effort to prevent future attacks on the country.

Since 2002, the government also allocated substantial funding to combat terrorism and provide a strong legal framework to deal with multifaceted needs, including the "First Security Package" (e.g., banning the Hamas-related charity al-Asqa) and the "Second Security Package" (e.g., marshals on civilian airliners). Additionally, in 2005, other policy changes improved German counterterrorism capabilities, such as greater centralization of the security services.

These efforts apparently resulted in expanded investigations of suspects and the arrest of numerous suspected Islamist extremists. It is noteworthy that a German court became the first to convict an al Qaeda terrorist linked to the 9/11 attacks.

Another particularly significant development in Germany's strategy is the shift from considering terrorism as a law-enforcement challenge to a strategic threat warranting military involvement. The government, therefore, deployed military forces in counterterrorism roles, as illustrated in Germany's contribution to Operation Enduring Freedom in Afghanistan and to that country's reconstruction. In addition, Germany became a major participant in the antiterrorism naval task forces off the Horn of Africa and the Mediterranean whose mission is to ensure the security of shipping lanes and to disrupt supply and escape routes used by terrorists. In Iraq, Germany provides training to the country's police force and contributes humanitarian and reconstruction assistance.

Despite its mostly positive record, some discernable failures of German policies and actions are evident. For example, the preemptive "grid search" capabilities have, thus far, proven ineffective. Many of the expanded surveillance efforts in the post-9/11 period eroded some civil liberties. The fact that counterterrorism agencies within the government (e.g., police, intelligence, and the military) are administered separately creates difficulties of information-sharing, coordination, and operational response effectiveness. Clearly, the political rivalry between federal and state authorities has prevented the integration of the various security services. The absence of a comprehensive cross-governmental organizational structure has seriously limited effective counterterrorism capabilities. Moreover, cooperative efforts between German authorities and the European Union have proven to be difficult due to different threat perceptions, legal traditions, and security architecture approaches.

The history of Italian terrorism is particularly complex compared to the problems facing other European countries, such as the Spanish Euzkadi Ta Azkatasuna or the Irish Republican Army, which are based on ethnic or religious aims.

The Italian authorities have had difficulty in defining coherent counterterrorism strategies because of the different and antithetic aspects of the subversion activities. A first question is whether repentance, which worked so well against terrorism in the 1980s, can be proposed as a means to fight subversion today, when organized crime, as well as terrorism of all kinds, work together to destabilize established order. The repentant terrorists of the 1980s came from factory and university backgrounds. They fought for a final revolution inspired by ideologies. Hampered in these aims by the authority's response, terrorists could repent or dissociate, deciding to settle their own account with justice. However, such action seems not worthwhile for a member of the new foreign terrorist groups operating from Italy to the rest of Mediterranean areas. This is most evident in the case of terrorists belonging to Muslim fundamentalism.

The repressive measures against this new terrorist phenomenon must include those structures and means that were used both at the national and international level to fight organized crime successfully. They must not depend on "good luck" or on the "good will" of questionable repentant terrorists, but on efficient organization, such as the cooperation of different police forces, and greater specialization and concentration in investigations. So it has become indispensable to work in a context that has no frontiers, with support from international police authorities that enables the local authorities to be aware of and to value the different criminal phenomena. Specialized organizations are needed to fight crime and terrorism. An efficient counterterrorist and anticrime system must pass the test of being legal, efficient, and transparent.

The danger of terrorist activities can be limited by guaranteeing stable economic growth, adequate employment for an expanding labor force, human rights, democracy, and the rule of law, to those countries that are the sources of the most serious threats to international security.

At the same time, Italy always emphasized that the fight against terrorism should be accompanied by measures aimed at promoting stronger government institutions, safeguarding the human, civil, economic, and cultural rights of all communities, fostering the return of refugees to their homes, and rebuilding the social and economic fabric. It has been fundamental for Italy to participate actively in the international efforts to strengthen the bases of collective security and to prevent regional conflicts.

In reviewing the specific experiences of Italy's counterterrorism strategies, the record of successes include the rescue of kidnapped U.S. Gen. James Dozier; the establishment in 1974 of the first antiterrorism agency centralizing the counterterrorism efforts of Italy's police corps; the 1991 formation of the Anti-Mafia Investigative Agency; the dismantling in 2004 of the new Red Brigades-Communist Combatant Party (BR-CCP); the introduction of governmental structural changes (e.g., Financial Security Committee), operational counterterrorism measures (e.g., military control of sensitive targets), and intelligence-judicial cooperation programs; and the investigation, detentions, prosecutions, and expulsion of terrorist suspects, particularly linked to the al Qaeda networks in the country.

On the other hand, Italy's counterterrorism efforts also failed throughout the years in particular areas. Among the problems that emerged were the following: lack of coordination between intelligence services and territorial police forces; instructional bureaucratic interferences; lack of intra-European coordination; underestimating the magnitude of Italy's Islamist network; and the inability of the judicial system to offer an acceptable definition of terrorism.

Despite Egypt's important leadership role in the Arab and Moslem world, this country was not immune from terrorism at home and abroad. What is particularly significant is that while Islam does not condone terrorism, the perpetrators against Egypt utilized theological rationalizations to justify their acts.

Gama al-Islamiya (Islamic Group), for example, advocated since the late 1970s the violent path to be a proper way of "liberating" the Islamic nation of an "infidel" government and the community of "nonbelievers." Cells of Islamic revolutionaries, of which Islamic Group members were a part, were involved in the 1981 assassination of President Anwar Sadat. Among the better-known leaders of the group are Sheikh Abdel-Rahman (currently imprisoned in the United States for his role in the 1993 attack on the World Trade Center) and Ayman al-Zawahiri (cofounder and second in command of al Qaeda now hiding somewhere in South Asia). This movement, jointly with the relatively new faction called Talaa'al al-Feteh (Vanguards of Conquest), are dedicated to overthrowing President Hosni Mubarak's government and replacing it with an Islamic state based on Sharia (Islamic law).

In general, Egypt was successful in monitoring and rooting out old and new terrorist cells. In the post-9/11 period, the government's "zero tolerance" toward terrorism resulted in the arrest of many suspects and bringing them to justice. It also instituted more stringent airport and port security measures.

Internationally, Egypt initiated bilateral treaties focusing on judicial matters such as extradition and information-sharing. Regionally, Egypt has become a signatory to several treaties with the League of Arab States, such as the Arab Antiterrorism Agreement of 1998. It also serves as a counterterrorism hub for other Middle Eastern and North African countries. Moreover, Egypt expanded its counterterrorism activities beyond the region. It developed close cooperative relationships with the United States on a broad range of law enforcement and judicial matters and is actively involved with other countries to extradite Egyptian terrorists from abroad. It supports the efforts of the United Nations, became a party to nine international conventions and a signatory to an additional two, and exchanges intelligence and police information with INTERPOL.

And yet, these accomplishments provide no guarantee that future terrorist attacks will not occur. Apparently missing from Egypt's counterterrorism strategy are long-term efforts to address some of the root causes of terrorism in the country, including political, social, and economic dislocations. Expanded international support will be required to achieve this end.

Sri Lanka has been victimized by intense levels of terrorism for decades. A separatist group, Liberation Tigers of Tamil Eelam (LTTE), relies on a guerrilla strategy that includes the use of terrorist tactics. What makes the security situation more complicated than the cases of the other countries analyzed in this study is the fact that the LTTE controls most of the northern and eastern coastal areas of Sri Lanka. Moreover, LTTE receives both political and financial support from the large Tamil communities in Asia, Europe, and North America.

Examination of the counterterrorism experience indicates successes in three major areas. First, the ceasefire established in the country since 2001 is still holding despite numerous recent violations. Second, backlash against LTTE terrorism resulted in a significant decrease in sympathy and support from abroad. Third, the international designation of LTTE as a terrorist organization led to the freezing of its financial assets in many countries.

However, despite numerous rounds of peace talks initiated by Norway and other international mediation efforts, thus far at least, diplomatic moves have failed to produce a consensus between the parties on political and military issues. On the other hand, both sides realize the requirements for economic development and reconstruction, particularly after the extraordinary suffering caused by the tsunami disaster.

The foregoing summaries of the counterterrorism strategies of these six nations reveal both successes and failures. Regardless of the different experiences and lessons of each individual country, several realities with policy implications emerge:

First, the vulnerability of modern societies and their critical infrastructures, coupled with the exploitation of conventional and unconventional weapons, require all states, both unilaterally and in concert, to develop credible responses and capabilities to minimize future threats.

Second, there are no simplistic or ideal solutions to the dangers posed by terrorism. As the challenges to the security of states continue to evolve, current and future counterterrorism instruments utilized by sovereign nations must adjust to respond accordingly.

Third, patience, resolve, perseverance, political will, and relentless pursuit of terrorists and their supporters are critical elements in a counterterrorism strategy. Nations must also be cautious to avoid the kind of overreaction that could lead to repression and violation of civil liberties and ultimately to weakening of the very democratic institutions that we seek to protect.

Fourth, "best practices" approaches to combat terrorism—nationally, regionally, and globally—are founded on a broad range of actions, including apprehension or elimination of operatives and their leadership; destruction of command, control, and communications; disruption of infrastructures and sanctuaries; denial of material support and funding; and infliction of severe punishment on state sponsors and collaborators.

And fifth, the following policies need to be adopted or strengthened:

- develop coherent governmental and intergovernmental policies;
- establish efficient organizational structures to conduct, coordinate, and implement policies;
- introduce new legal instruments to close gaps in domestic and international law;
- produce quality human and technological intelligence and enhance sharing within and among nations;
- strengthen law enforcement capabilities at all levels and encourage regional and global cooperation;
- wage an intensified campaign to disrupt the flow of funds ;to terrorist movements in concert with financial and economic institutions worldwide;
- prevent the proliferation of weapons of mass destruction to rogue states and terrorist groups;
- initiate new concepts, doctrines, training, and missions for military forces tasked to combat terrorism in different environments such as urban insurgencies;
- increase cooperative relationships and alliances with like-minded nations through diplomatic efforts and provide counterterrorism technical assistance to those nations in need of support; and
- expand the involvement of civic societies, such as religious,

professional, and educational bodies, in participating in the battle against terrorism.

To be sure, the implementation of the foregoing approaches guarantees neither a prompt defeat nor an achievable total victory over terrorism. The challenge facing the international community must be constructed on a long-term, realistic, and integrated war strategy of both weapons and ideas not dissimilar to the twentieth century experiences fighting Fascism, Nazism, and Communism. Whether the post-September 11 world learns the lessons of the past and is successful in eliminating the globalization and brutalization of modern terrorism requires heeding the advice provided in Proverbs 3:25, "Be not afraid of sudden terror."

NOTES

Chapter 1: United States

Some parts of this chapter are based on unclassified research and reports prepared by the author in his capacity as academic advisor to several U.S. government agencies and Congress during the past thirty years. He alone is responsible for the content and interpretation of the material presented.

1   Material drawn from an open source database developed and administered by the Inter-University Center for Terrorism Studies in Arlington, VA and Washington, DC.

2   Bernard K. Johnpoll, "Perspectives on Political Terrorism in the United States" in Yonah Alexander, ed., *International Terrorism: National, Regional, and Global* (New York: Praeger Publishers, 1976), p. 30.

3   See generally *1–8 Terrorism: An International Resource File 1986–1990 Index* (Yonah Alexander, ed., Ann Arbor, MI: UMI, 1991) (defining issues of terrorism and providing literature on the general topic of terrorism).

4   Arkansas Code Ann. § 5-13-301 (Michie, 1997).

5   Ohio Rev. Code Ann. § 5747.023 (Anderson, 1996) (providing for tax abatements for certain victims of terrorism).

6   42 U.S.C §§ 5195–5197f (1994). See generally *Legal Responses to Terrorism: U.S. State Legislation* (Yonah Alexander and Edgar H. Brenner eds., Dobbs Ferry, NY: Oceana Publications, 2000).

7   U.S. Department of Justice, FBI, *Terrorism in the United States* 34 (1988), and 28 C.F.R. Section 0.85.

8   *Terrorism in the United States* 1999 (FBI, Counterterrorism Division, 1999).

9   "Pattern of International Terrorism: 1980," a research paper prepared by the National Foreign Assessment Center, Washington, DC, p. ii. (This is a Central Intelligence Agency publication.)

10 Report of the Department of Defense Commission on Beirut International Airport Terrorist Act, October 23, 1983 (December 20, 1983), p. 122.

11 Ibid. Executive Summary.

12 Address before the Jonathan Institute's Second Conference on International Terrorism, Washington, DC, June 24, 1984, p. 2.

13 Address by Secretary George Shultz before the Park Avenue Synagogue, New York, October 25, 1984, p. 1.

14 Ibid., pp. 1–2.

15 Address by Secretary George Schultz before the American Society for Industrial Security, Arlington, VA, February 4, 1985, p. 2.

16 "Public Report of the Vice President's Task Force on Combatting Terrorism," (Washington, DC: U.S. Government Printing Office, February 1986), p. 1.

17   Ibid.

18   22 U.S.C. § 2656f(d) (1994).

19   U.S. Department of State (Office of the Coordinator for Counterterrorism), *Country Reports on Terrorism* 2004 (April 2005).

20   22 U.S.C. § 2656f(d) (1994).

21   22 U.S.C. § 2656f(d) (1994), cited in *17 Terrorism: Documents of International and Local Control,* 170–71 (Yonah Alexander and Donald Musch, eds., Dobbs Ferry, NY: Oceana Publications 1999) [hereafter *17 Terrorism*].

22   Cited in remarks prepared by the Attorney General Alberto R. Gonzales on "Intercepting Al Qaeda: A Lawful and Necessary Tool for Protecting America," presented at the Georgetown University Law Center, January 24, 2006, p. 3.

23   An oversight hearing on terrorist threats to the United States was held by the Subcommittee on Immigration and Claims, see *U.S. House of Representatives, Comm. of the Judiciary, Subcomm. on Immigration and Claims, Witness List* (January 26, 2000) http://www.house.gov/judiciary/im12500.htm [hereafter *Hearings*]. For earlier legislative moves, see e.g., H.R. 2507, 101st Congress (1989) (a bill initiated to establish a commission on aviation security and terrorism, seeking to investigate the destruction of Pan Am 103 on December 21, 1988, and KAL on August 31, 1983).

24   Congressional Record, vol. 130, no. 35 (March 22, 1984), p. 2.

25   98th Congress, 2nd Session, H.R. 562.

26   Public Law 92-539, October 24, 1972, amended the Criminal Code (Title 18, U.S.C.).

27   Public Law 93-366, August 5, 1974.

28   Public Law 98-473, October 10, 1984.

29   Cited in *29 Terrorism: Documents of International and Local Control*, p. 521 (Yonah Alexander and Donald Musch, eds., Dobbs Ferry, NY: Oceana Publications, 2001).

30   U.S. Department of State, *Fact Sheet: The Charges Against International Terrorist Usama bin Laden*, available at www.usembassy.state.gov/posts/af1/wwwh0001.html.

31   Ibid.

32   Ibid.

33   Ibid.

34   See, for example, Ann Scott Tyson, "Ability to Wage 'Long War' Is Key to Pentagon Plan," *Washington Post,* February 4, 2006.

35   Information for this section is primarily drawn from various open databases at the Inter-University Center for Terrorism Studies, the Rand Corporation, and the FBI.

36   Department of Justice, FBI, *Terrorism in the United States 1988*, op. cit. See also statement by Oliver B. Revell, Associate Deputy Director-Investigations, FBI, before an open session of the Committee on Government Affairs, U.S. Senate, September 11, 1989. For an overview of the domestic and international terrorist threat to the United States, see "Public Report of the Vice President's Task Force Combating Terrorism," February 1986, and "Report on the Brinks Incident" in *Terrorism: An International Journal*, vol. 9, no. 2, p.169–206.

37   FBI, *Terrorism in the United States* (1999).

38   See, for example, City of Oklahoma, *Final Report*, 1996.

39   Associated Press report, April 28, 2003.

40   *San Diego Union-Tribune* report, November 30, 2005.

41   See, for example, Edward F. Mickolus, et al., *International Terrorism in the 1980's / A Chronology of Events* (Ames: Iowa State University Press, 1989), and U.S. Department of State, *Political Violence Against Americans, 1999*.

42   U.S. Department of State, *Patterns of Global Terrorism: 1990* (April 1991).

43   See, for instance, "Terrorist Incidents Involving U.S. 1981–1990 (A Chronology)," Congressional Research Service, December 7, 1990.

44   See, for example, Yonah Alexander and Allan Nanes, eds., *The United States and Iran: A Documentary History* (Frederick, MD: University Publications of America, 1980).

45 Report of the Department of Defense Commission on Beirut International Airport Terrorist Act, October 23, 1983 (December 20, 1983), p. 141.
46 See, for example, Mickolus, et al., *International Terrorism in the 1980's*, and U.S. Department of State, *Political Violence against Americans, 1999*.
47 See, for instance, U.S. Department of State, *Patterns of Global Terrorism: 1990* (April 1991).
48 See, for example, Yonah Alexander and Michael S. Swetnam, *Usama bin Laden's al-Qaida: Profile of a Terrorist Network* (Ardsley, NY: Transnational Publishers, 2001). See also a more recent publication, Yoram Schweitzer and Sari Goldstein Ferber, "Al-Qaeda and the Internationalization of Suicide Terrorism," Tel Aviv: Jaffee Center for Strategic Studies, Memorandum 78, November 2005.
49 See, for example, "Conceptual and Structural Analysis of Assassinations," Staff Report of the National Commission on the Causes and Prevention of Violence (October, 1969).
50 State Department Fact Sheet, heroes@clark.net.
51 Task Force Report, February 1986, p. 9.
52 Statement before the Institute of International Education and the World Affairs Council, Denver, CO (reprinted in *American Foreign Policy*, 1987, doc. 1).
53 Gore Commission Report, February 12, 1997. See also *Los Angeles Times*, October 6, 2001.
54 See, for example, the Terrorism Prevention Act, House of Representatives, 104th Congress, 2nd Session, Report 104-518, April 15, 1996.
55 See, for instance, Center for Non-Proliferation Studies, http://cns.miis.edu/research/cbw/120city.htm.
56 For subsequent Gilmore reports see, for example, Prentice Hall's Cybrary and the EIIP Virtual Forum.
57 See, for instance, www.emergency.com/2001/21stcentury.rpt.htm.
58 Report by the National Commission on Terrorism. Washington, DC: Government Printing Office, June 2000.
59 See, for example, Yonah Alexander and Donald J. Musch, *Terrorism: Documents of International and Local Control* (Dobbs Ferry, NY: Oceana Publications), vols. 29–35.
60 "Uniting and Strengthening America by Providing Appropriate Tools Required to Intercept and Obstruct Terrorism," USA Patriot Act of 2001, H.R. 3162, signed by President Bush on October 26, 2001.
61 Executive Order 13228, October 8, 2001.
62 *The 9/11 Commission Report: Final Report of the National Commission on Terrorist Attacks upon the United States* (New York: W. W. Norton, 2004).
63 Commission Report, p. xvi.
64 Ibid.
65 "Final Report on 9/11 Commission Recommendations," December 5, 2005, www.9-11pdp.org, and Remarks of Chairman Thomas H. Kean and Vice Chairman Lee H. Hamilton, December 5, 2005, p. 2.
66 For numerous documents on intelligence issues, see, for instance, Alexander and Musch, op. cit., vols. 29–35; The 9/11 Commission Report, op. cit.; and the Commission on the Intelligence Capabilities of the United States Regarding "Weapons of Mass Destruction," Report to the President of the United States, March 31, 2005.
67 9/11 Public Discourse Project, Final Report, and Remarks of the Chairman and Vice Chairman, op. cit. December 5, 2005. For an excellent CIA insider's perspective on the broad issues before 9/11 see Paul R. Pillar, *Terrorism and U.S. Foreign Policy* (Washington, DC: Brookings Institution Press, 2001).
68 *Washington Times*, December 15, 2005.
69 See, for example, http://en.wikipedia.org/wiki/UAS_Patriot_Act.
70 For comparison with the pre-9/11 perspectives see, for example, "National Security Strategy of the United States," (The White House, January 1993) and Yonah Alexander

and James S. Denton, *Governmental Responses to Terrorism* (Fairfax, VA: HERO Books, 1986).

Chapter 2: France

*   The author would like to acknowledge the invaluable research assistance for this chapter provided by Marie-Hélène Chals. Thanks also to Ruth Lambertz who helped with the updates.

1   The Foundation for Strategic Research (FRS) in Paris has put together a comprehensive database on terrorist activities in France since the 1950s that represents an extremely useful, indeed unique, instrument for terrorism scholars and counterterrorism practitioners. At this stage, the database is in French only, available at https://bdt.frstrategie.org.

2   Dana Priest, "Help From France Key In Covert Operations; Paris's 'Alliance Base' Targets Terrorists," *Washington Post,* July 3, 2005; and Jeff Stein, "Meet the United States' Unlikely Ally in the Terror Wars," *Congressional Quarterly Homeland Security*, October 28, 2005.

3   The OAS demonstrated its opposition to Algerian independence with beatings, leading to some deaths, in districts of Paris with large proportions of Muslim immigrants, attacks on the headquarters of the French Communist Party, and several attempts to assassinate General de Gaulle in 1961, 1962, and 1963.

4   Thierry Vareilles, *Encyclopédie du terrorisme international,* coll. Culture du renseignement (Paris: l'Harmattan, 2001).

5   Convicted then amnestied under François Mitterrand in 1981, the movement broke up with some of its members even participating in the Breton Democratic Union, a group that promotes independence but condemns violence and participates in national elections.

6   Outlawed in 1978, the organization took on its present identity in 1980.

7   August 3, detonation of car bombs in front of l'Áurore, Minute, and Arche, Paris-based newspapers.

8   The St. Germain drugstore bombing, two dead, thirty-four wounded; attacks at Orly Airport on an El Al plane, twenty wounded; assassination of two inspectors of the *Direction de la Surveillance de la Territoire* (DST) and a Lebanese informant.

9   Bombings of the Socialist and the RPR Gaullist party headquarters, the Defense ministry, the European Space Agency, the IMF, Interpol, the Maison Diocésaine in Paris, the Hispano Bugatti Society in Montrouge, the Dassault headquarters in St. Cloud, the Elf-Aquitaine building, the *Minute* newspaper, the Maison de la Radio, and Antenne 2 television station.

10   The perpetrator of this attack was Habib Maamar, sentenced to life imprisonment on December 15, 1989.

11   August 17, detonation of a bomb on the Avenue de Friedland in Paris; August 26, a bomb is defused on the Paris to Lyon high-speed railroad line; September 3, the bombing of the Richard Lenoir marketplace in Paris; September 4, a bomb is defused in Paris; September 7, a car bomb is detonated in front of a Jewish school in Paris; October 6, a gas cylinder explodes at the Maison Blanche subway station in Paris; October 17, another gas cylinder is let off in the high-speed subway network in Paris.

12   Nathalie Cettina, *La coordination policière et judiciaire dans la lutte contre le terrorisme en France*, March 1997, Paris, IHESI, p. 1.

13   "Major terrorism and security of critical infrastructure: new threats, new stakes." Assises nationales, HCFDC, 1999.

14   In 1999 the spokesperson for the ARB stated that the "only effective way to get France to yield was the armed struggle." Thierry Vareilles, *Encyclopédie du terrorisme international*, p. 70.

15   Marianne Lefevre, *La dérive de la Corse, une dérive économique, sociale, politique*, in Herodote no. 80, 1st trimester 1996, p. 24, cited in Xavier Cretiez and Jérôme

Ferret, eds., *Le silence des armes, l'Europe à l'épreuve des séparatismes violents*, coll. La sécurité aujourd'hui (Paris: IHESI, 1999).

16 Beurs is a slang term for Arabs, which originated in working-class suburbs and is now used by young Arabs to refer to themselves.

17 "Judge warns of Iraq 'Black Hole'," *BBC News*, October 20, 2005.

18 John Ward Anderson, "France says Extremists are Enlisting its Citizens," *Washington Post*, October 19, 2005.

19 "France is 'Enemy No. 1,'" *News 24*, September 27, 2005 and "Report: Islamic Terror Suspects to Appear before Magistrate," *MIPT Terrorism Knowledge Base*, The Associated Press, September 30, 2005.

20 Territorial Surveillance Bureau, information service, see II. A, Information Services.

21 Alexandre Del Valle: *Le totalitarisme islamiste à l'assaut des démocraties* (Paris: Editions des Syrthes, 2002).

22 Lionel Dumont, who belonged to the Roubaix gang, is one such example: a native Frenchman, living in the north of France, he converted to Islam with the sponsorship of a friend. He then fought in Bosnia in a brigade made up of Afghan, Arab, and foreign fundamentalists and approached the al Qaeda network. Upon his return, he was recruited into the GIA, and formed the "Roubaix gang" with several young extremists. While RAID, a counterterrorist intervention group made of police and gendarmerie, killed or arrested a number of its members, Dumont managed to escape to Bosnia.

23 France has gone from being a sanctuary to becoming a target, as the 1995 attacks and the failed attacks of 1998 and 2000 show. According to the experts, various factors have convinced the GIA to alter its strategy: France's continued, though decreasing, support for the regime in Algeria, the dismantling of the GIA's arms-sourcing networks, and its fast-growing implantation in France, which have given the organization a sufficient number of bases and recruits to bring the "holy war" to French soil.

24 Revue de Défense nationale, quoted in Roland Jacquard, *Fatwa contre l'Occident* (Paris: Albin Michel, 1998), p. 119.

25 The role of the Defense Ministry in counterterrorism is described in: Ministère de la Défense, "Defence Against Terrorism, A Top Priority of the Ministry of Defence Paris, 2005." www.defense.gouv.fr/sites/defense/english_contents/files/defence_against_terrorism120.

26 The Ile de France (that is to say Paris and the seven administrative departments that surround it): Hauts de Seine, Seine Saint Denis, Val de Marne, Val d'Oise, Yvelines, Essonne, and Seine et Marne.

27 Lille, Rennes, Marseilles, Lyons, Metz, Tours, Bordeaux.

28 Since 1994, it is called the Directorate for Immigration Control and for Operations Against Illegal Workers (DICILEC). It reports to the minister of the interior.

29 The law passed on July 22, 1996, stipulates that a terrorist act occurs when a person "participates in a group in which there is a specific purpose or a tacit agreement that has committed one or several terrorist acts that fall under previous articles" (Article 422-1 CP).

30 Irene Stoller, the former representative of the public prosecutor in charge of the 14th section. Report of conference "Large-scale terrorism and security of critical infrastructure: new threats, new stakes." Assises nationales, HCFDC, 1999, p. 34.

31 The DST and the 6th DCPJ (which became the DNAT) were brought in to examine jointly the DC-10 attack; the 6th DCPJ and the Lyons SRPJ were brought in to look at the Kelkal affair; the DNAT and the SPRJ cooperate in the Basque country.

32 Created in 1961 during the Algerian war in response to OAS activity, this special court had enlarged powers, including extending the period of detention without charge to fifteen days.

33 Nathalie Cettina: *Les enjeux organisationnels de la lutte contre le terrorisme* (Paris: LGDJ/Montchretien, 1995), p. 216.

34   Nathalie Cettina, op cit., p. 26.
35   Taken from a television interview with President François Mitterrand on August 17, 1982, on TF1.
36   A special antiterrorism unit under the control of President Mitterrand's antiterrorism advisor attempted to frame several Irish people who were later proved innocent in court.
37   "The cream of the cream of the antiterrorist division" according to Daniel Burban, *9 ans à la division antiterroriste* (Paris: Robert Laffont, 1990), p. 71.
38   The presumed leader of FARL (Lebanese Armed Revolutionary Forces).
39   A memo of the General Directorate of the National Police, March 29, 1976.
40   Philippe Madelin. *La galaxie terroriste* (Paris: Plon 1986), p. 384.
41   Thanks to their source, the Tunisian Lofti Ben Khala, who infiltrated the Faoud network, the DST was able to bug the Koranic school of Fouad Ali Saleh, which allowed it to record the information necessary to confirm his responsibility for the attacks.
42   Roger Auque and Jean-Louis Normandin.
43   Both services have a number of complementary advantages: the DGSE has a number of contacts abroad, some of which were activated more than twenty years ago. The general intelligence services have a network that covers the whole territory, and the Paris information services have a comprehensive knowledge of the Paris suburbs.
44   A movement that supports the Armed Islamic Group (GIA) responsible for much of the bloodshed that has wracked Algeria since 1992.
45   Interview on the televised news, France 2, September 5, 1995.
46   The SNCF and the RATP begin a communication campaign whose main slogan is "*Attentifs, Ensemble,*" or "Be on your guards, each of us."
47   "French Official Presents Anti-Terror Bill," *Washington Post,* October 16, 2005.
48   General Secretariat for National Defense, placed under the prime minister's authority.
49   Le Figaro, "*Le recit d'un exercice secret simulant un attentat chimique dans le metro,*" October 8, 2001.
50   Paul Wilkinson, *International Terrorism: The Changing Threat and the EU's Response,* Chaillot Paper no. 84, EU Institute for Security Studies, October 2005.

Chapter 3: Germany

1   Richard Clutterbuck, *Terrorism, Drugs and Crime in Europe after 1992* (London: Routledge, 1990), pp. 48–51.
2   For example, the RAF and *Action Directe* tried to establish a common platform with other left-wing extremists. The groups issued a joined communiqué in 1985 that called for the "unity of West European revolutionaries."
3   According to Katzenstein, between 1970 and 1979, German security authorities registered 649 attacks, with 31 people killed and 79 injured. In addition, 163 people were taken hostage. The vast majority of these incidents were caused by left-wing terrorism. See Peter Katzenstein, "Same War–Different Views: Germany, Japan, and Counterterrorism," *International Organization* 57 (Fall 2003), p. 740.
4   On German left-wing terrorism, see in particular Stefan Aust, *The Baader-Meinhof Group* (London: The Bodley Head, 1987); Clutterbuck, *Terrorism,* 46–60; Adrian Guelke, *The Age of Terrorism and the International Political System* (London/New York: I. B. Tauris, 1995), 88–104; Alexander Straßner, *Die dritte Generation der "Roten Armee Fraktion"* (Wiesbaden: Verlag für Sozialwissenschaften, 2003); Klaus Pflieger, *Die Rote Armee Fraktion—RAF* (Baden-Baden: Nomos, 2004); Butz Peters, *Tödlicher Irrtum: Die Geschichte der RAF* (Berlin: Argon, 2004).
5   Federal Office for the Protection of the Constitution [Bundesamt für den Verfassungsschutz], *Verfassungsbericht 2003* (Köln, 2004), p. 53.
6   In May 2005, the leader of the Neo-nazi organization, the 29-year-old Martin Wiese, was sentenced to seven years in prison for heading a "terrorist group."

Notes

Notes 223

7   This definition is used by the *RAND–St. Andrews Chronology of International Terrorism*.

8   Ilich Ramirez Sanchez, alias Carlos, was finally arrested in 1994 in Sudan and convicted in France. His closest partner, the German Johannes Weinrich, was arrested in 1995 in Yemen and convicted in Germany.

9   For the "Group Carlos," see in particular Oliver Schröm, *Im Schatten des Schakals: Carlos und die Wegbereiter des internationalen Terrorismus* (Berlin: Ch. Links, 2002).

10 Because of their violent actions, the minister of the interior has forbidden both, the PKK in 1993 and the DHKP-C in 1998.

11 According to the 2003 report of the Federal Office for the Protection of the Constitution, the LTTE has about 750 supporters in Germany, the MEK about 900, Hamas about 3,000, and Hizbollah about 800. In 2002, German authorities closed down the Islamic association Al Aqsa for supporting Hamas with money and logistics. See German Embassy, Washington, DC, at http://www.germany-info.org/relaunch/politics/new/pol_terr_alaqsa.html. In December 2004, the Federal Administrative Court finally approved this decision.

12 Ulrich Schneckener, *Netzwerke des Terrors: Charakter und Strukturen des transnationalen Terrorismus* (Berlin: Stiftung Wissenschaft und Politik, Studie 42, December 2002); Ulrich Schneckener, *Transnationaler Terrorismus: Charakter und Hintergründe des "neuen" Terrorismus* (Frankfurt A.M.: Suhrkamp, 2006).

13 El-Motassadek was first sentenced to fifteen years in prison by the Higher Regional Court of Hamburg (2003), the first person worldwide convicted in relation to 9/11. However, Mzoudi was finally released in February 2004 due to a lack of evidence. In June 2005, the Highest Court of Appeal (Bundesgerichtshof) confirmed that decision and, subsequently, ordered a retrial of the el-Motassadek case since he was convicted on the basis of the same evidence. However, in August 2005 the Hamburg court came again to the conclusion that el-Motassadek was a member of a terrorist organization and sentenced him to seven years. Nevertheless, the charges of assisting in the 9/11 plot could not be confirmed. Throughout both trials, one problem was that the testimony of the arrested Binalshibh and others had been withheld by U.S. authorities for security reasons and could not be used in its entirety in front of German courts. See Kirstin Hein, "Die Anti-Terrorpolitik der rot-grünen Bundesregierung," in *Deutsche Sicherheitspolitik. Eine Bilanz der Regierung Schröder*, eds., Sebastian Harnisch, Christos Katsioulis, and Marco Overhaus (Baden-Baden: Nomos, 2004), p. 163.

14 In 2002 Zammar was seized in Morocco, secretly flown to Syria, and questioned by interrogators of Syria's General Security Directorate (GSD) and, presumably, by U.S. specialists. Since 9/11, Darkanzanli was observed and questioned several times by German authorities without finding compelling evidence for the charges. Based on a Spanish request and an EU arrest warrant, he was finally arrested in 2004. He is accused by Spanish investigators of being involved in the Madrid train bombing of March 2004 and other activities in Spain linked to al Qaeda. However, in July 2005 the Constitutional Court finally decided that the way German authorities implemented the EU warrant arrest violates the Spanish constitution. The immediate effect was that Darkanzanli had to be released.

15 In October 2005, after 20 months of court proceedings, four Al-Tawhid members (three Palestinians and one Algerian) were found guilty for planning attacks against Jewish establishments. They were sentenced to five to eight years in prison.

16 The Caliphate State had been under surveillance by the German security authorities since its foundation in 1984. In 2000 Kaplan was sentenced to four years in prison for inciting the murder of a rival. Finally, in 2004 Kaplan was handed over to Turkish authorities, who wanted him for treason charges. See Markus Rau, "Country Report Germany," in *Terrorism as a Challenge for National and International Law: Security versus Liberty?*, eds., Christian Walter, Silja Vöneky, Volker Röben, and Frank

Schorkopf (Berlin/Heidelberg: Springer, 2004), p. 19, online at http://edoc.mpil.de/conference-on-terrorism/index.cfm.

17 In April 1949, in a letter to the Parliamentary Council, which worked on the new German constitution, the Allies demanded that the powers of police and intelligence be separated. See Hein, "Anti-Terrorpolitik," p. 153.

18 Christian Leggemann, "Der Einsatz von Streitkräften zur Terrorismusbekämpfung—die aktuelle Debatte in Deutschland," in *Der Kampf gegen den Terrorismus: Strategien und Handlungserfordernisse in Deutschland*, eds. Kai Hirschmann, Christian Leggemann (Berlin: Berliner Wissenschafts-Verlag, 2003), pp. 261–63.

19 In 2003 fifty-nine BKA liaison officers worked in forty-eight countries. See Federal Criminal Police Office, Facts and Figures, online at www.bka.de/profil/broschueren/bka_zahlen_fakten_engl.pdf

20 Among the new criminalized acts were: membership in a terrorist organization or public advocacy of terrorism, supporting a terrorist organization, nonreporting of a terrorist crime, glorification of violence, inducement to criminal acts, approbation and rewarding of criminal acts, threatening criminal acts, and feigning a criminal act.

21 Rau, "Country Report," pp. 3–5.

22 Clutterbuck, *Terrorism*, p. 59.

23 Katzenstein, "Same War," p. 741.

24 According to Katzenstein, during the 1980s about five percent of the West German adult population were covered by some form of surveillance system. See Katzenstein, "Same War," pp. 741–42.

25 Rau, "Country Report," 33–38; Verena Zöller, "Liberty Dies by Inches: German Counter-Terrorism Measures and Human Rights," *German Law Journal* vol. 5, no. 5 (2004): pp. 487–88.

26 See Klaus Jansen, "Polizeiliche Terrorismusbekämpfung: Eine kritische Auseinandersetzung," in *Der Kampf gegen den Terrorismus: Strategien und Handlungserfordernisse in Deutschland*, eds., Kai Hirschmann and Christian Leggemann (Berlin: Berliner Wissenschafts-Verlag, 2003), pp. 153–90; Wolfgang Hoffmann-Riem, "Freiheit und Sicherheit im Angesicht terroristischer Anschläge," *Zeitschrift für Rechtspolitik* vol. 35, no. 12 (2002): pp. 497–501; Gert-Joachim Glaessner, "Internal Security and the New Anti-Terrorism Act," *German Politics* vol. 12, no. 1 (April 2003): pp. 43–58.

27 See Antwort der Bundesregierung [Response of the Federal Government], *Fortführung der Maßnahmen zur Bekämpfung des Terrorismus*, Deutscher Bundestag (15. Wahlperiode), May 14, 2004, DrS 15/3142, pp. 2–6.

28 In this regard, it is not without irony that Otto Schily, one of the lawyers defending RAF members and prominent critic of antiterrorism laws in the 1970s, now, as member of the government, takes a tough stance against extremism and terrorism.

29 The fall 2005 elections in Germany brought to power a "great coalition" comprised of Christian Democrats and Social Democrats under the chancellorship of Angela Merkel.

30 See Rau, "Country Report"; Hein, "Anti-Terrorpolitik"; Kai Hirschmann, "Wie voll ist das Glas? Terrorismusbekämpfung in Deutschland," *Der Mittler Brief: Informationsdienst zur Sicherheitspolitik* vol. 19, no. 3 (2004); Peter Roell, "Deutschlands Beitrag zur internationalen Terrorismusbekämpfung," in *Der Kampf gegen den Terrorismus*, eds., Kai Hirschmann, Christian Leggemann (Berlin: Berliner Wissenschafts-Verlag, 2003), pp. 125–42; Katzenstein, "Same War," pp. 748–52; Glaessner, "Internal Security," pp. 49–55; Berthold Meyer, *Im Spannungsfeld von Sicherheit und Freiheit. Staatliche Reaktionen auf den Terrorismus* (Frankfurt: Hessische Stiftung Friedens- und Konfliktforschung, HSFK Standpunkte no. 1, 2002). See, in addition, Germany's Report to the Security Council Committee established pursuant to Resolution 1373 (2001) concerning Counter-Terrorism (S/2002/11).

31 Due to increased tax revenues, the government expected for the following years an increased counterterrorism budget (2003: 1.62 million euros, 2004: 2 million euros, 2005: 2.1 million euros).

32 This change was also necessary due to prior decisions of the European Union. Back in 1998 the European Council had adopted a joint action to ensure that the involvement of someone in a criminal organization based in an EU country could be prosecuted in any member state. See Rau, "Country Report," pp. 42–43.

33 The subjective element is only reflected by the nonbinding working definition of the Office for the Protection of the Constitution. The Office describes terrorism as "the persistent struggle for political goals, which are to be attained with the help of attacks against the physical integrity, life, and property of other persons, in particular through serious criminal offenses as defined in section 129a paragraph 1 in the Criminal Code, or through other offenses, which serve as preparation for such crimes." See Rau, "Country Report," pp. 11–13; Zöller, "Liberty," pp. 477–79.

34 These involved the Federal Constitution Protection Act, the Military Counterintelligence Service Act, the Federal Intelligence Service Act, the Federal Border Guard Act, the Federal Criminal Police Office Act, the Passport Act, the Personal ID Card Act, Civil Aviation Act, the Aliens Act, the Alien Central Registration Act, and the Security Screening Act.

35 See in particular new sections 3 and 8 of the Federal Constitution Protection Act, which expanded significantly the rights of the Federal Office of the Protection of the Constitution. Most of these provisions, however, will expire automatically after five years ("sunset provisions") and have to be renewed by the parliament.

36 Details, however, are subject to a separate federal law. So far, the new possibilities have not been implemented for German citizens. See Rau, "Country Report," pp. 29–30.

37 Excluded from these provisions are associations whose members are mainly citizens of other EU member states. See new section 14 of the Act Governing Private Associations.

38 Substantially new is the reference to international terrorism. Other provisions were already implicitly or explicitly stipulated by old sections of the law. See Rau, "Country Report," pp. 49–50.

39 With regard to asylum-seekers, fingerprints and other identification-related information will now be preserved for a period of ten years after asylum is granted. It will also be possible to compare fingerprints taken automatically with fingerprint records of the Federal Criminal Police Office. See new section 16 of the Asylum Procedure Act.

40 The above-mentioned Kaplan case triggered this regulation. The extremist Metin Kaplan was able to postpone his deportation for several months due to the elaborated German appeal proceedings.

41 See Leggemann, "Terrorismusbekämpfung," pp. 265–68.

42 In February 2006, however, the Federal Constitutional Court declared Article 14 of the Aviation Security Law unconstitutional. It did so for essentially two reasons: because the Basic Law does not allow the use of military force for domestic purposes except for defense matters, and because the disputed paragraph was seen as incompatible with the fundamental right to life (Article 2 of the Basic Law) to the extent that the use of armed force affects persons on board the aircraft who are not participants in the crime. According to the Court, by the state's using their killing as a means to save others, they would be treated as mere objects, which would deny them the value that is due to a human being for his or her own sake. This decision triggered a debate within the Grand Coalition Government whether a terrorist attack should be understood as a case of defense, which would then allow for the use of the *Bundeswehr*, at least in instances where no innocent persons are involved (e.g., a sea or air attack without kidnapping others).

43 A similar incident happened in June 2004 when a Turkish man, apparently due to personal problems, hijacked a Turkish airliner in Munich and forced the pilot to return to the airport.

44 See Rau, "Country Report," pp. 38–39.

45 See Antwort der Bundesregierung, *Maßnahmen*, pp. 11–12.

46 See Rau, "Country Report," pp. 45–46.

47 See, in particular, "Fourth Financial Market Promotion Act" (June 2003) and "Law for the Improvement of the Fight Against Money Laundering and the Fight Against the Financing of Terrorism" (August 2002). The latter implemented the second money-laundering directive of the EU from December 2001. See also Germany's Report to the Security Council Committee established pursuant to Resolution 1373 (2001) concerning Counter-Terrorism (S/2002/11), pp. 4–5.

48 See Antwort der Bundesregierung, *Maßnahmen*, pp. 9–11.

49 In addition, Germany is participating in NATO's Operation Active Endeavour, which aims at observing the Eastern Mediterranean Sea and safeguarding the civilian sea traffic. In March 2003 the mission was supplemented by NATO's Operation Strait of Gibraltar (STROG), which controls the entry into the Western Mediterranean Sea.

50 See Martin Wagener, "Auf dem Weg zu einer 'normalen Macht'? Die Entsendung deutscher Streitkräfte in der Ära Schröder," in *Deutsche Sicherheitspolitik. Eine Bilanz der Regierung Schröder*, eds., Sebastian Harnisch, Christos Katsioulis, and Marco Overhaus (Baden-Baden: Nomos, 2004), pp. 94–97.

51 Despite the German position not to support the U.S. invasion in Iraq, the NBC teams were left in Kuwait during war and would have helped Allied Forces in cases of emergency, at least on Kuwaiti soil. Moreover, the intelligence cooperation between the BND agents in Baghdad and U.S. authorities was kept during the war.

52 The mandate was renewed in 2004 and in 2005 without changing the contingent.

53 The German PRTs differ legally and politically from the U.S. and the British PRTs, which act under the combat operation Enduring Freedom. By opting for the ISAF mandate, the German government wanted to underline that its PRTs should be regarded by the Afghan population as part of a peacekeeping mission. The German PRT concept also involves an independent development and aid component.

54 Until 2003, Germany spent 690 million euros for its military participation in ISAF; in 2004, 320 million euros have been envisaged.

55 In each of 2002 and 2003, Germany spent 5.1 million euros for the dialogue program.

56 See Federal Government, *Action Plan: "Civilian Crisis Prevention, Conflict Resolution and Post-conflict Peace-Building,"* May 12, 2004, p. 9.

57 Ibid., p. 9.

58 See Meyer, *Sicherheit und Freiheit*; Zöller, "Liberty."

59 See Zöller, "Liberty," pp. 487–93.

60 The charges of corruption or fraud involved in particular the visa departments of the German representations in Kiev, Moscow, Tirana, and Pristina (Kosovo).

61 See Christoph Gusy, "Die Vernetzung innerer und äußerer Sicherheitsinstitutionen in der Bundesrepublik Deutschland," in *Herausforderung Terrorismus: Die Zukunft der Sicherheit*, ed. Werner Weidenfeld (Wiesbaden: Verlag für Sozialwissenschaften, 2004), pp. 197–221.

62 One main advocate for using the *Bundeswehr* domestically is Wolfgang Schäuble (CDU/CSU), since fall 2005 the successor of Otto Schily as Federal Minister of the Interior.

63 Some of these issues, however, may be resolved within the framework of a general reform of the federal system, which will be one major project of new government.

64 The result is that the implementation for the EU arrest warrant into national law has been further delayed. Originally, the European Council had concluded that the arrest warrant should be implemented by all member states until the end of 2003.

Chapter 4: Italy

1   From the statements of BR terrorist Antonio Savasta, it seemed that emissaries of some Eastern European countries, particularly Bulgaria, tried to contact the BR because they were interested in managing the Dozier kidnapping "politically," in exchange for money and arms. Although this money would have been useful to an organization in decline, the individuals in charge of the kidnapping did not want to surrender control to others. Giorgio Galli, *Il partito armato. Gli "anni di piombo" in Italia, 1968–1986* (Milano: Kaos Edizioni, 1984), pp. 332–33.

2   Oronzo Reale was the Minister of Justice and draftsman of the law.

3   This practice was made public during the trial of some members of a terrorist group early in 1985 when they issued a document signed by 170 terrorists in custody.

4   This aspect emerged in particular during the investigations into the kidnapping and killing of Aldo Moro.

5   It was revealed, in fact, that the person in charge had been Giuseppe (Pippo) Calò, one of the most important members of a Mafia "family" in Palermo; he was sentenced to life imprisonment for that massacre. Sergio Zavoli, *La notte della Repubblica* (Milano: Mondadori, 1995), 433.

6   Some copies of a letter bearing the symbols of the BR terrorist group, and vindicating D'Antona's murder, were found to have been sent by mail from Naples. In this city there are many unemployed and temporary workers, and it is easy to get people involved in violent forms of protests, even terrorist attacks, organized by radical groups.

7   In Italy, this phenomenon is socially and territorially rather limited: the target of eco-terrorist attacks has usually been sabotage of the construction sites of the high-speed railway and the high-tension grid. For some groups, people speak also of "environmentalist and animalist radicalism" that has been mainly in the form of "food sabotage" actions. There was an escalation during the days of the World Trade Organization (WTO) summit in Seattle (November 1999), and the raison d'être of the extremist ecological groups was the struggle against globalization and against economic liberalization.

8   See Article 10, paragraph 2.

9   See Article 15.

Chapter 5: Egypt

1   This part is essentially based on two important reports, namely: "Confronting Terrorism," Report no. 14, Consultative (Shoura) Council, Commission for Arab, External, and National Security Affairs, Cairo, 1994 (in Arabic), hereafter, referred to as Report no. 14; and "External Dimensions of Terrorism Phenomenon" (second part of the report on confronting terrorism), Report no. 18, Consultative (Shoura) Council, Commission for Arab, External and National Security Affairs, Cairo, 1997 (in Arabic), hereafter referred to as Report no. 18.

2   It has been maintained that Egypt was and will remain "a homeland for security and an oasis for stability" (Report no. 14, p. 9).

3   Report no. 14, pp. 24–26; Report no. 18, pp. 1 and 44. Before 1992, violent and terrorist operations were only "temporary explosions" (Report no. 18, p. 58).

4   Report no. 18, pp. 2 and 49.

5   Statement of the Egyptian Minister of Interior, in Report no. 14, p. 136; see also Report no. 18, p. 50.

6   Report no. 14, pp. 26–28; Report no. 18, pp. 52–56.

7   Report no. 14, pp. 92–93. The Egyptian Minister of Interior also said, "Terrorism is attacking the capabilities of the country and people." League of Arab States: A Report on the Work and Results of the Joint Meeting of the Arab Councils of Ministers of Interior and Justice, Cairo, 25/12/1418 H–22/4/1998 G, pp. 6–7 (in Arabic).

8   Report no. 14, pp. 36–46; Report no. 18, pp. 52–53.
9   The existence of "widespread extreme poverty inhibits the full and effective enjoyment of human rights and breeds intolerance and violence" (UNESCO and Human Rights, Paris: UNESCO, 1996, p. 358).
10 See Report no. 18, p. 90.
11 Report no. 14, pp. 33 and 136.
12 See Report no. 14, pp. 29–33; Report no. 18, pp. 54–55.
13 Report no. 14 maintains that in Egypt, terrorism follows a new pattern and manifestation "aiming at attacking tourism as well as trying to threaten investment climate, in order to affect Egypt's economy and its international status." Moreover, terrorism aims at "destabilizing the society through the wide use of violence and assassination of innocent people with a view to creating a state of general chaos" Report no. 14, pp. 10 and 92.
14 Report no. 14, pp. 47–89; Report no. 18, pp. 79–80; Arab Republic of Egypt National Report, Ninth UN Congress on the Prevention of Crime and the Treatment of Offenders, Cairo, 28 April–8 May 1995, p. 49. Moreover, Egypt's strategy to address violent crimes has been outlined as follows:

    (1) Addressing the phenomenon of violence: "The policy adopted by the government . . . focuses on the improvement of conditions of life to foster social stability. Social and housing projects, services to deprived and overcrowded areas are ongoing efforts. New housing agglomerations are replacing squatters. Industrial centers are providing employment and alleviating overcrowdedness. Economic plans are envisaged to improve effective exercise of democracy in an environment of plurality. Those are means adopted to relax tensions, which generate political strife and violence in society. Efforts of the Ministry of Interior to restrict the possession of weapons and to tighten security to deter drug smuggling are of paramount importance in the prevention of crime."

    (2) Addressing terrorism: "Egypt's policy to address terrorist crime revolves around a number of axes. On the preventive axis, it strives to involve the population in detecting terrorist elements; and on another axis, it mobilizes religious teachers to propagate sound religious doctrine. On the legislative axis, penalties for terrorist crimes have been stiffened, and penitent terrorists are given a chance to repent. The security policy and international cooperation are effective factors in curbing terrorist crimes." Arab Republic of Egypt National Report, Ninth UN Congress on the Prevention of Crime and the Treatment of Offenders, p. 79.

    (3)Additionally, a detailed description of the antiterrorist strategy applied by Egypt is set forth in the fourth report submitted to the Security Council Counter-Terrorism Committee (S/2004/343, pp. 7–10).
15 Report no. 18 states that there are some difficulties that impede international cooperation for combating terrorism, namely: (1) resistance or hesitation of some governments to cooperate in combating terrorism for reasons, in their view, of national security; (2) some measures for combating terrorism may involve violation of human rights; (3) differences among laws of various states may result in obtaining the status of political refugee in some states; (4) vagueness of the distinction between organized crime and terrorism may hinder the operation of some mechanisms for combating terrorism (Report no. 18, p. 112).
16 In fact, Egypt "has participated in the study and discussion of all topics raised in international conferences, meetings and committees on action against organized crime." Moreover, Egypt "has participated in the formulation and adoption of the resolutions and recommendations of the General Assembly and the Economic and Social Council which have been incorporated in the draft of Naples Political Declaration and Global Action Plan against Organized Transnational Crime" (Arab Republic of Egypt National Report, Ninth UN Congress on the Prevention of Crime and the Treatment of Offenders, p. 41).

17 Egypt signed the Geneva Convention of 1937 (as is well known, the convention did not enter into force, due to nonratification by states; only India had ratified it) and the International Convention for the Suppression of Terrorist Bombings. (See *Journal Al-Ahram*, December 16, 1999, p. 1, in Arabic.)

Egypt is a party to a great number of the above-mentioned conventions, such as those of 1973 and 1979 ("Multilateral Treaties Deposited with the Secretary General" UN, New York, 1999, pp. 656 and 662; Report no. 18, pp. 196–97.)

Egypt is now considering the provisions of the International Convention for the Financing of Terrorism and the International Convention for the Suppression of Terrorist Bombings (Report of Egypt to the Security Council Counter-Terrorism Committee, S/2004/343, p. 3).

18 Fifth report submitted to the Security Council Counterterrorism Committee, S/2005/288, p. 5.

19 As for the convention on the physical protection of nuclear material of 1979, Egypt is not a party to it for the following reasons: "There is an imbalance in the convention between the state through which the material passes and the state transporting such material in terms of the division of financial responsibilities in protecting nuclear material. This imposes an enormous financial and technical burden on Egypt in ensuring the security of and protecting this material, especially given the possibility of it passing through the Suez Canal, which is located in Egyptian territory. Egypt addresses the problem of protecting nuclear material passing through its territory on the basis of an agreement with the transporting State on a case-by-case basis" (Reply to the preliminary comments/ questions on the report of Egypt on measures to combat terrorism submitted to the Counter-Terrorism Committee pursuant to Security Council resolution 1373 [2001], S/2002/601, p. 12).

20 Ahmed Abou-el-Wafa, *Public International Law* (Cairo: Dar Al-Nahda Al-Arabia, 2004), p. 118 (in Arabic).

21 See also the statement of the Egyptian Minister of Foreign Affairs, in Report no. 18, p. 196.

22 Report no. 18, p. 105.

23 Report no. 18, pp. 147–48.

24 Thus, for example, the Ninth UN Congress on the Prevention of Crime and the Treatment of Offenders (held in Cairo in 1995) has approved and adopted many proposals put forward by Egypt, such as: (1) condemnation of all forms and practices of organized and terrorist crimes; (2) calling upon all states to adopt national effective measures for the prevention and suppression of terrorist and transboundary crimes; (3) inciting states to enhance international cooperation with a view to combating terrorist and transboundary organized crimes; (4) calling upon all states to exchange technical information; (5) calling upon competent organs of the UN to gather information about links between transboundary organized crimes and terrorist crimes; (6) calling upon centers and institutes for the prevention of crime and criminal justice to duly study the relationships between transboundary organized crimes and terrorist crimes, effects resulting therefrom, and methods to confront them (see Report no. 18, pp. 102–4).

Moreover, Egypt participated in the Counter-Terrorism International Conference held in Riyadh (Kingdom of Saudi Arabia) February 5–8, 2005 (Fifth report submitted by Egypt to the Security Council Counter-Terrorism Committee, S/2005/288, p. 5).

25 Report submitted by Egypt to the Security Council Committee established pursuant to resolution 1373 (2001), S/2001/137, p. 9.

26 S/2001/1237, S/2002/601, S/2003/277, S/2004/343, S/2005/288.

27 See also Ahmed Abou-el-Wafa, *The League of Arab States* (Cairo: Dar Al-Nahda Al-Arabia, 1999), p. 699, in Arabic.

28 "League of Arab States: A Collection of Treaties and Conventions," Secretariat General, Tunis, 1985, pp. 101–6 (in Arabic). Egypt was the first Arab state to deposit its

instrument of ratification. The convention prohibits extradition in political crimes. However, extradition is mandatory in the following crimes (Article 4): (1) offenses against the kings and presidents of states, their spouses, ancestors, or offspring; (2) offenses against crown princes; (3) premeditated murder; (4) terrorist offenses. In its instrument of ratification Egypt made a reservation on the aforementioned four offenses set forth in Article 4, which include terrorist offenses. Egypt maintained that in such offenses, extradition is not mandatory (ibid., p. 102 at note 1).

29   Ibid., pp. 92–95.

30   Ibid., pp. 92–97.

31   The agreement has been signed by the ministers of interior and justice of all Arab members of the LAS (twenty-two member states). It has been ratified by the following member states: Palestine (June 3, 1998); Bahrain (June 28, 1998); United Arab Emirates (December 9, 1998); Arab Republic of Egypt (December 14, 1998); Kingdom of Saudi Arabia (January 28, 1999); Algeria (March 9, 1999); Jordan (April 7, 1999); Tunisia (April 22, 1999); Sudan (May 24, 1999); Libya (June 10, 1999); Yemen (August 8, 1999); and Oman (October 25, 1999).

   According to Article 40, the agreement "shall enter into force thirty days after the deposit of instruments of ratification, approval or acceptance by seven Arab states." Accordingly, with the deposit by Jordan, on April 7, 1999, of its instrument of ratification, the agreement entered into force May 7, 1999. See text of the agreement, in *Arab Republic of Egypt Official Journal* (hereafter referred to as *Official Journal*), no. 18, May 6, 1999, pp. 1312–38 (in Arabic).

32   Thus, paragraph 3 of Article 1 provides that a terrorist crime means "Any crime or attempted crime committed in execution of a terrorist purpose in any one of the signatory states or against their nationals, properties, or interests in a way punishable by their national laws." The crimes stipulated in the following agreements, except those excluded or unratified by the signatory states, are considered terrorist: (1) Convention on the Offences and Certain Other Acts Committed on Board Aircraft (Tokyo, 1963); (2) Convention for the Suppression of Unlawful Seizure of Aircraft (The Hague, 1970); (3) Convention for the Suppression of Unlawful Acts Against the Safety of Civil Aviation (Montreal, 1971) and the Annexed Agreement signed at Montreal on 10.5.1984; (4) Convention on the Prevention and Punishment of Crimes Against Internationally Protected Persons, Including Diplomatic Agents (New York, 1973); (5) International Convention Against the Taking of Hostages (New York, 1979); (6) The United Nations Agreement on the Law of the Sea (1982), the Part Concerning Maritime Piracy; (7) the 1988 Convention for the Suppression of Unlawful Acts Against the Safety of Maritime Navigation; (8) the 1988 Protocol for the Suppression of Unlawful Acts Against the Safety of Fixed Platforms Located on the Continental Shelf; (9) the 1991 Convention on the Marking of Plastic Explosives for the Purpose of Detection.

   Article 2 of the agreement provides that all acts of struggle by different means, including military struggle against foreign occupation and aggression for liberation and self-determination, in accordance with the principles of international law, are not considered crimes, save any act posing threat to the territorial integrity of any Arab state. The agreement also provides that the crimes set forth by Article 1 are not considered as political crimes. Additionally, the following crimes are not to be considered as political crimes, even if they were politically motivated (Article 2 paragraph B): (1) any offense against the kings, presidents, and rulers of the signatory states as well as their spouses, ancestors, and offspring; (2) any offense against crown princes, vice-presidents, prime ministers, and ministers of the signatory states; (3) any offense against the internationally protected persons, including diplomats in the signatory states or those accredited in them; (4) premeditated murder or forced robbery of individuals, authorities, or means of transport; (5) sabotage of public properties and those dedicated to public service even if owned by another signatory state; (6) crimes or manufacturing, smuggling, or possessing weapons, ammunition of explosives, or any other substances intended for use in terrorist crimes.

33 Those measures are the following: (1) measures for the prevention and combating terrorist crimes (Article 3); (2) the Arab cooperation for the prevention and combating of terrorist crimes (Article 4); (3) conditions and procedures for the extradition of terrorists (Articles 5–8, 22–28); (4) judicial delegation (Articles 9–12, 29–33); (5) cooperation (Articles 13–18); (6) seizure and forfeiting of objects and articles resulting from the crime (Articles 19–20); (7) exchange of evidence (Article 21); (8) measures for the protection of witnesses and experts (Articles 34–38); (9) impossibility to put reservation by a contracting state, which implies a breach of the provisions of the convention or its objectives (Article 41); (10) possibility for a contracting state to withdraw from the Agreement after the lapse of a six months notice (Article 42).

34 "Resolutions of the Council of the League of Arab States," Secretariat General, LAS, Department of the League Council Affairs, Cairo, March 1993 (in Arabic).

35 See "Resolutions of the Council of the League of Arab States," Secretariat General, LAS, Department of the League Council Affairs, Cairo, September 1999, pp. 57–58 (in Arabic). Additionally, Egypt approved Resolution no. 2 (second and third) of the first meeting of the joint ministerial commission of the councils of Arab interior and justice ministers, in which Arab states decided: to incite regional and international organizations to prepare treaties for combating terrorism, like the Arab antiterrorism agreement, for the sake of enhancing cooperation among states in security and judicial matters in order to combat that phenomenon; and to request the Arab group in the Organization of Islamic Conference and the Organization of the United Nations to take knowledge of the Arab antiterrorism agreement and to apply it on the Islamic and international levels (ibid., pp. 59–60).

36 Resolutions adopted by the Council of the League of Arab States, regular session 120, 9/9/2003, p. 67 (in Arabic).

37 Report no. 18, pp. 93–97.

38 Ibid., pp. 97–99.
    Moveover, Egypt participated in the Arab Regional Symposium on Combating Terrorism, held in Cairo within the framework of the League of Arab States on February 16–17, 2005 (Fifth report submitted to the Security Council Counterterrorism Committee, S/2005/288, p. 5).

39 Ibid., p 100. It had been maintained that Arab cooperation to combat terrorism was far from achieving its objectives. This is due to the following reasons: (1) the attitude of some Arab states with regard to the taking of religion as a coverage, in general; (2) differences of views about how to deal with the phenomenon; (3) and the Arab differences, which hinder Arab cooperation in general (Report no. 18, pp. 100–1).

40 Ibid., p. 149.

41 In this regard, two salient factors characterize the Egyptian conduct, namely: the cooperation with states that harbor terrorists, with a view to ensuring their extradition; and nonacceptance of the "direct treatment choice" of terrorist elements, aimed at capturing and eliminating them on the territories on which they reside. This choice is in conflict with the traditions of Egyptian foreign policy, based on nonintervention in domestic affairs of other states and the necessity to conserve strong relations with states of the world (Report no. 18, pp. 106–7).

42 The most important of which are the following: (1) agreement relating to judicial cooperation in criminal matters and extradition between Egypt and Turkey (*Official Journal*, 1991, pp. 3304–21, in Arabic); (2) agreement relating to cooperation in criminal matters between Egypt and Greece (ibid., 1992, pp. 579–89, in Arabic); (3) agreement relating to judicial cooperation in criminal matters, the transfer of convicted persons and extradition between Egypt and Poland (ibid., 1993, pp. 501–24, in Arabic); (4)

agreement relating to judicial cooperation in civil and criminal matters between Egypt and Libya (ibid., 1993, p. 1779, in Arabic); (5) agreement relating to judicial and legal cooperation in civil and criminal matters between Egypt and Cyprus (ibid., 1994, pp. 3056–76, in Arabic); (6) agreement relating to judicial cooperation in civil, commercial, and criminal matters between Egypt and China (ibid., 1995, pp. 1872–89, in Arabic); (7) agreement relating to cooperation in criminal matters between Egypt and Morocco (ibid., 1997, pp. 2833–49, in Arabic); (8) agreement relating to the transfer of convicted persons between Egypt and Spain (ibid., 1995, pp. 2474–81, in Arabic); (9) agreement relating to drugs and organized crime between Egypt and Malta (ibid., 1998, pp. 969–76, in Arabic); (10) agreement relating to security cooperation concluded between Egypt and Cyprus (ibid., 1995, pp. 952–56, in Arabic); (11) agreement relating to the transfer of convicted persons concluded between Egypt and Great Britain (ibid., 1996, pp. 520–31, in Arabic); (12) agreement relating to security cooperation between Egypt and Yemen (ibid., 1997, pp. 274–77, in Arabic); (13) an understanding for security cooperation between Egypt and Sri Lanka (ibid., 1998, pp. 846–51, in Arabic); (14) agreement relating to security cooperation between Egypt and Pakistan (ibid., 1998, pp. 2806–11, in Arabic); (15) agreement relating to cooperation in the suppression of organized crime concluded between Egypt and Hungary (ibid., 1999, pp. 554–62, in Arabic); (16) agreement relating to judicial cooperation between Egypt and Lebanon (ibid., 1999, pp. 1276–79, in Arabic); (17) agreement relating to cooperation in the field of the suppression of crime between Egypt and Russia (ibid., 1999, pp. 1736–41, in Arabic); (18) agreement between Egypt and Panama for the cooperation in combating crime (ibid., no. 14, April 2000); (19) the extradition agreement concluded between Egypt and South Africa (ibid., no. 1, January 2004, p. 6); (20) agreement between Egypt and Slovakia concerning cooperation in the suppression of crime (ibid, no. 34, August 25, 2004, in Arabic).

43 This means that in case of conflict, national legislation shall prevail over the international agreement. See also, the agreement relating to cooperation in security matters between Egypt and Cyprus (Article 3).

44 Article 53 of the Egyptian constitution of 1971 states: "The state shall grant the right of asylum to any Foreign person persecuted on account of his defense of the rights of peoples or of human rights, or for the cause of peace or justice. The extradition of political asylum seekers is prohibited."

However, Egypt maintains that "an important development in the legal meaning of a political offense was precipitated by the mounting tide of terrorist action. Violence and terrorism targeted international civil aviation in particular. As a result of the high incidence of hijacking, the capture of hostages and other such crimes, which result in virtual disasters, the international community decided to strip such crimes of the protection accorded to political offenses, even if they be perpetrated for obvious political objectives. Egypt adopted this understanding, and joined several agreements for judicial cooperation in this area" (Arab Republic of Egypt National Report, Ninth UN Congress on the Prevention of Crime and the Treatment of Offenders, p. 19).

Moreover, "'the Egyptian Ministry of Justice has made it a practice, with regard to the legal cooperation agreements concluded by it on crime and the extradition of criminals, to provide that crimes of terrorism are not to be considered political crimes for which extradition will be denied" (Report submitted by Egypt to the Security Council Counter-Terrorism Committee established pursuant to resolution 1373 [2001], S/201/ 1237, p. 14).

See also, for example, the agreement relating to legal and judicial cooperation between Egypt, Iraq, Yemen, and Jordan. This agreement provides for the possibility for extradition of criminals, except in political crimes. However, the agreement excludes from the ambit of political crimes, inter alia, some of the offenses provided by the Arab antiterrorism agreement (*Official Journal*, 1990, pp. 962–63, in Arabic).

45 Under such agreements, some states extradited twenty-nine persons accused of terrorist acts in 1994 (Report no. 18, p. 91). An example of the above-mentioned agreements was concluded with Lebanon. Under that agreement, there are three kinds of extradition, namely:

(a) Obligatory extradition (Article 35): extradition is mandatory if the following conditions are satisfied: (1) if the requested person is charged with a crime punishable for a period of not less than one year, or convicted of prison for a period of not less than two months; (2) if the crime was committed in the territory of the requesting state, or outside the two contracting states provided that their laws would have punished it if it had been committed therein; (3) in any case, the crime should be punishable under the laws of the requesting and requested states.

(b) Voluntary extradition (Article 26): the requested state may refuse extradition: (1) if the requested person is a national; (2) if the offense occurred on the territory of the requesting state and the requested person is not one of its nationals and for acts not punishable under the law of the requested state; (3) if the offense was committed outside the territories of the two contracting states and is not punishable under the laws of the requested state, and the requested person is not a national of the requesting state; (4) if the offense or punishment lapsed according to the laws of the requested state, unless the requested person is a national of the requesting state.

(c) Prohibited extradition (Article 27): extradition is prohibited in the following cases: (1) if the offense is a political one; (2) if the offense was committed in the requested state; (3) if the requested person enjoys diplomatic immunity; (4) if the requested person is one of the officials charged with an official mission abroad and the crime occurred during or because of the exercise of that mission; (5) if the kinds of penalties set forth in the laws of the requesting state are not determined, as to their kinds, by the laws of the requested state; (6) if the requested person had been tried or is under trial or investigation; (7) if the offense or punishment lapsed according to the laws of the requesting state and those of the state on whose territory the offense occurred.

46 In this context, it should be recalled that: "The Egyptian government has historically adopted cautious approach towards extradition agreements with other countries. The only extradition agreement concluded by Egypt was with the Sudan on May 7, 1902. A temporary agreement was also concluded with the government of Palestine in 1921 and with Iraq in 1931" (Arab Republic of Egypt National Report, Ninth UN Congress on the Prevention of Crime and the Treatment of Offenders, p. 17). See also limitations and conditions of extradition of offenders in Egyptian law, ibid., pp. 18–24.

47 The Egyptian penal code was adopted in 1937 and criminal proceedings were issued in 1950. However, until 1992, the "Egyptian legislation did not know the terrorist crime as an independent crime, different from any ordinary offence" (Report no. 14, p. 72).

48 "The specificity of the law resides in that it introduced legislation to address terrorist crimes engendered by terrorist doctrines. New procedures were established governing inquisition, prosecution and trial" (Arab Republic of Egypt National Report, Ninth UN Congress on the Prevention of Crime and the Treatment of Offenders, p. 79).

49 Report no. 14, p. 16. Moreover, the Minister of Interior affirmed that the established principles of the Egyptian security policy are "the early prevention, the immediate deterrence, the refusal of bargaining and the abiding by legal measures." (See *Al-Ahram Journal*, December 21, 1999, p. 13 [in Arabic].) In 1993, the Minister of Interior also maintained that "those who insist on using fire arms and bombing . . . will pay with their lives in these resistances in accordance with the right of legitimate defense" (Report no. 14, p. 137).

50 Arab Republic of Egypt National Report, Ninth UN Congress on the Prevention of Crime and the Treatment of Offenders, pp. 54 and 71. Twelve percent of the Egyptian TV programs deal, in one way or another, with the terrorist phenomenon (Report no. 14, p. 80, note 1).

51 See, for example, a decision published in *Al-Ahram Journal*, December 8, 1999, p. 14 (in Arabic).

52 See, especially, some decisions, in this regard, published in the *Official Journal* from 1993 to 1999. The president's decision usually refers to the military court, the crime in question, as well as any other crimes annexed to it, which "may be attributed to the criminals or others."

53 Fifth report submitted by Egypt to the Security Council Counter-Terrorism Committee, S/2005/288, May 4, 2005, pp. 3–4.

54 Arab Republic of Egypt National Report, Ninth UN Congress on the Prevention of Crime and the Treatment of Offenders, p. 43. Moreover, the laundering of funds may "be considered a crime of concealment of the truth prescribed by Article 44 bis of the Egyptian penal code. The prescriptions of the criminal code pertaining to the crime of holding funds of an illicit source may be applicable to the laundering of funds" (loc. cit.).

Provisions of law No. 97 of 1992 criminalize the financing of terrorism, regardless of whether the terrorist act was actually committed. Moreover, the scope of Egyptian law extends to raising and providing funds for terrorist purposes, regardless of whether the funds have been transferred from one country to another. "The financing of terrorism is punishable even if the funds used are of legal origin. If the funds are of illegal origin, the perpetrator of the acts in question is also liable to other penalties provided for under penal law for this type of offence" (Fourth report submitted to the Security Council Counter Terrorism Committee, S.2004/343, p. 4).

Finally, Article 208 bis (a) of the Code of Criminal Procedure (as amended by law No. 174 of 1998) provides for freezing of funds. This applies to funds of persons who commit, attempt to commit, participate in, or facilitate the commission of terrorist acts.

55 The opening of accounts is subject to some conditions, which include the prior approval of the national competent authorities. Under law No. 34 of 1971, as amended by law No. 95 of 1980, the socialist public prosecutor has the right to impose custodianship over an individual's property and assets if there is evidence that his assets grew as a result of unlawful operations. See, also, economic measures taken by the Central Bank of Egypt on October 2001, in response to Security Council Resolution 1373 (2001), in Report Submitted by Egypt to the Security Council Committee Established Pursuant to Res. 1373 (2001), S/2001/ 1237, pp. 8–9.

56 *Official Journal*, no. 22 bis A, June 5, 2002, p. 27 (in Arabic). The above-mentioned law is an application of what has been recommended by the General Assembly of the UN in its resolution 51/210 (1996). In that resolution, the General Assembly called upon all states "to investigate, when sufficient justification exists according to national laws . . . , the abuse of organizations, groups or associations including those with charitable, social or cultural goals, by terrorists using them as a cover for their own activities."

57 See also guidelines adopted by the committee set up by the minister of justice, in Report Submitted by Egypt to the Security Council, S/2001/1237, pp. 5–7.

58 Other Egyptian laws may concern the same matter. Those laws include Act no. 54 of 1964 on Reorganization of Administrative Control, amended by Act no. 112 of 1983; the Illicit Gains Act (no. 193 of 1951) and the amendments thereto; the Administrative Prosecution Body Act (no. 117 of 1958) and the amendments thereto; the Central Auditing Agency Act (no. 144 of 1988).

59 *Official Journal*, no. 25 bis, June 24, 2002, p. 4 (in Arabic). See also: "Reply to the Questions on the Supplementary Report in Measures to Combat Terrorism," submitted by Egypt to the Security Council's CTC, S/2003/277, pp. 4–8.

60 Fifth report submitted to the Security Council Counter-Terrorism Committee, S/2005/288, p. 14.

61 Ahmed Abou-el-Wafa, *The Law of Diplomatic and Consular Relations in Law and in Practice, with Special Reference to What Is Applied in Egypt* (Cairo: Dar Al-Nahda Al-Arabia, 2002), p. 265 (in Arabic).

62 Thus, the "strategy of the police is designed to realize the following objectives: (1) to combat all forms of crime and to cleanse the society of wrongdoers; (2) to protect the national security against elements which seek to undermine legality and the rule of law; (3) to protect individual's safety and to safeguard his personal freedom, rights and property; (4) to protect and safeguard institutions and public facilities. The strategy is based on the following foundations: (1) to protect the society against crime, harmful and subversive conceptual trends, and deviate behavioral patterns; (2) to modernize law enforcement organs by upgrading their mechanisms, improving their cadres and providing them with up-to-date technical facilities; (3) to adopt scientific methods in police operations; to develop police techniques and support scientific research in relevant specialized areas; (4) to promote regional and international cooperation and to establish mutual security relations in order to develop social control mechanisms, upgrade human capabilities and benefit from the exchanges of experiences with other countries for combating crime" (Arab Republic of Egypt National Report, Ninth UN Congress on the Prevention of Crime and the Treatment of Offenders, p. 52). See also other measures, in "Reply to the Preliminary Comments/Questions on the Report of Egypt on Measures to Combat Terrorism Submitted to the CTC Pursuant to Security Council Resolution 1373 (2001)," pp. 7–8.

63 *Official Journal*, no. 39, September 1995, pp. 2427–28.

64 Ibid., no. 42, October 1996, pp. 2571–72. The above-mentioned order provides that it is issued in order to "safeguard the country's security and vital interests and the necessities of safeguarding public order."

65 Ibid., no. 28 bis A, July 12, 1998, pp. 2–3. The order states that it aims at "safeguarding the country's security vital interests and public order and moralities as well as protecting citizen's privacy."

66 See law No. 394 of 1954 concerning weapons and ammunitions, as amended recently by the law No. 162 of 2003. For a person to apply for a license, he shall be at least 21 years old; not have received a criminal sentence or a minimum prison term of one year for injury to a person, to assets, or to honor, and shall not have been sentenced more than once to a term of imprisonment, even for less than a year, for one of these offenses; not have been sentenced to a custodial penalty for receiving stolen goods, theft or attempted theft, drug trafficking, or an offense involving explosives; not have been sentenced for attempts to harm the government committed in national territory or abroad; not be a homeless person, a suspect, or a person under police surveillance; be of sound mind; be physically able to carry a weapon; be aware of the necessary precautions to take when handling a weapon.

67 See also the various measures adopted by Egyptian authorities, in Report Submitted by Egypt to the Security Council, S/2001/1237, p. 7. Additionally, Egypt has adopted several measures to deal with and prevent attempts to import and smuggle weapons and explosives of all kinds (see more details, in fifth report submitted to the Security Council Counter-Terrorism Committee, S/2005/288, p. 7).

68 *Official Journal*, no. 22 bis A June 5, 2002, pp. 27–29 (in Arabic).

69 Supplementary report submitted by Egypt to the Security Council Counter-Terrorism Committee, S/2004/343, April 20, 2004, pp. 12–13.

70 From May 1994 until 1997, about 2,500 repentants have been released (statement of the Minister of Interior, in Report no. 18, p. 187). Moreover, 500 repentants from the jihad organization, Gama al-Islamiya, who have rejected violence, have been released from prisons. The overwhelming majority of those persons are from Upper Egypt. (*Al-Ahram*, July 24, 2000, p. 19, in Arabic).

71 See also Article 15 paragraph 2 of the Egyptian code on criminal proceedings.

72 Article 57 of the Egyptian constitution; the explanatory memorandum of law No. 97 of 1992, in "Annex to Verbatim Records of the Session No. 101, July 15, 1992." People's Assembly, p. 66 (in Arabic).

73 *Official Journal*, no. 1 bis, January 6, 2000, pp. 4–5 (in Arabic).

74   See as well measures taken by Egypt, in Report Submitted by Egypt to the Security Council, S/2001/1237, p. 10.
75   *Official Journal*, no. 48, November 26, 1981.
76   Ahmed Abou-el-Wafa, "A Study of Some Aspects of the Phenomenon of International Terrorism," *Journal of Diplomatic Studies*, Institute of Diplomatic Studies, Ministry of Foreign Affairs, Riyadh, no. 6, 1410 H.–1990 G., p. 89 (in Arabic).
77   It has been said that the terrorist problem "occupies an advanced position in the priorities of the Egyptian national activity at present" (Report no. 14, p. 11).
78   However, legislative amendments are not the sole remedy to combat terrorism. Every citizen has his role to play. So, too, political parties, educational establishments, popular organizations, mass media, youth centers, and the clergy (Report no. 14, p. 74).
79   Report no. 18, p. 116.
80   Ibid., pp. 60, 62–65, 67, 68, 84, 90, 91–92, 116, 185, 185–86.
81   Since 1997, it has been maintained that "terrorism no longer represents a real phenomenon or an important problem in Egypt" (ibid., p. 115).
82   See Ahmed Abou-el-Wafa, *The International Protection of Human Rights* (Cairo: Dar Al-Nahda Al-Arabia), 1425-2005, pp. 96–98 (in Arabic).
83   As regards Islam, it has been said that, "with regard to religious tolerance, Islam seems to have a better record than Christianity." H. Bielfldt, "Muslim Voices in the Human Rights Debate," *Human Rights Quarterly*, vol. 17 (1995) p. 597.
84   Thus, in *Terrorism: How the West Can Win* (Benjamin Netanyahu, ed., New York: Farrar, Straus and Giroux, 1986), we can find the following articles: M. Khadduri, "Political Terrorism in the Muslim World"; Lewi, "Islamic Terrorism"; Vatikiotis, "The Spread of Islamic Terrorism." See also, An-Naim, "Islamic Ambivalence to Political Violence—Islamic Law and International Terrorism," *German Yearbook of International Law*, 1988, pp. 307–36. Moreover, a writer speaks of "the threat of Islamic fundamentalism" and of "the increasing and menacing threat posed by Islamic fundamentalists" (M. Curtis, "International Law and the Territories," *Harvard International Law Journal*, vol. 32 [1991] pp. 467–68). Another article says: "The term (Islamic revivalism) evokes various associations: antiwestern sentiment, terrorism, factional struggles, a return to traditions, the veil, the Koran" (K. Hamlin, "The Impact of Islamic Revivalism on Contract and Usury Law in Iran, Saudi Arabia and Egypt," *Texas International Law Journal*, vol. 22 [1987] p. 352).
85   I have said, "In sum, Islam's purpose is to keep the absolute value of life for its precious character: human life must be always respected and protected in every case where there is no valid reason justifying a contrary attitude. It is in reality a donation which concerns humanity in its entirety. This necessitates, from the point of view of Islam, the inviolability of human bodies with a view to preserving the individual's life and, through it, the whole humanity" (Ahmed Abou-el-Wafa, "Le devoir de respecter le droit à la vie en droit international public," *Revue Egyptienne de droit international*, vol. 40 [1984] p. 69).
86   If some Muslims "'are fanatics or even terrorists, that does not mean that Islam should be held responsible for their actions" (M. Zakzouk, "Islam Exposes the Biased Attempts to Discredit It," Supreme Council for Islamic Affairs, Cairo, 1419–1998, p. 44).
87   In this context, a western author says: "An appeal to the Shari'ah doctrines might well provide an effective counter method to international terrorism." He adds: "Islamic law condemns terror-violence, and a terrorist who invokes that law may be legally wrong." This is mainly because "respect for human life and property is a fundamental principle of the Shari'ah." He concludes, "Islamic law coordinates, integrates and legislates against that which western jurists have so far failed to control. The Shari'ah is a resource the west must no longer overlook" (D. A. Schwartz, "International Terrorism and Islam," *Columbia Journal of Transnational Law*, vol. 29 [1991] pp. 630, 650–51, 652).

88   Ahmed Abou-el-Wafa, "Le devoir de respecter le droit à la vie en droit international public," op. cit., p. 69. See also Ahmed Abou-el-Wafa, "The Islamic Shari'ah and the Phenomenon of International Terrorism," *Journal of the Institute of Arab Researches and Studies*, vol. 19 [1991] pp. 5–37 (in Arabic). *A Book Relating to Rules of International Law and Relations*, vol. 12, *Islam and the Phenomenon of International Terrorism* (Cairo: Dar Al-Nahda Al-Arabia, 2001), in Arabic.

Chapter 5 Concluding Note

Egypt has sent, as mentioned above, five reports to the CTC. In resolution no. 6289, the Council of the League of Arab States called upon all members of the League to send to the contact unit, in the Secretariat of the League, with the CTC all views and proposals about measures to combat terrorism in order to ensure Arab coordination (Decisions of the Council of League of Arab States, session 119, 24/3/2003, p. 58, in Arabic).

Even Egypt usually declares its strict adherence to rules of international law concerning terrorist acts. Thus, upon signature, Egypt formulated two reservations on the "International Convention for the suppression of terrorist bombings" (1997), concerning Article 6, paragraph 5 and Article 19 paragraph 2, by saying that it is bound by those two articles insofar as there is no contradiction or violation of rules and principles of international law.

Thus, Egypt declared that it is bound by Article 6 paragraph 5 "in so far as the domestic laws of states parties do not contradict the relevant rules and principles of international law." As for Article 19 paragraph 2, Egypt declared that it is bound by it "in so far as the military forces of the State, in the exercise of their duties, do not violate the rules and principles of international law." (See text of the reservations in: "Multilateral treaties deposited with the Secretary General," UN, New York, 2005, p. 131.) Moreover, upon signature, Egypt declared that it "does not consider itself bound by Article 35 paragraph 2 of the UN Convention Against Transnational Organized Crime (2000); Ibid., p. 178.

Chapter 6: Sri Lanka

1   K. M. de Silva, *Reaping the Whirlwind* (New Delhi: Penguin Books, 1998).
2   de Silva, *Reaping the Whirlwind*.
3   Rohan Edrisinha, "Constitutionalism, Pluralism, and Ethnic Conflict: The Need for a New Initiative," p. 174, Chapter 11 in *Creating Peace in Sri Lanka: Civil War & Reconciliation*, Robert Rotberg, ed., (Washington, DC: Brookings Institution Press, 1999).
4   Jayadeva Uyangoda "Sri Lanka Conflict and SAARC" Online issue of *South Asian Journal* (August–September 2003), http://www.southasianmedia.net/Magazine/ Journal/srilanka_conflict.htm.
5   William Weisberg and Donna Hicks, *Sri Lanka Problem-Solving Project,* PICAR (October 15, 2004), http://www.tamilcanadian.com/northeastern_herald/ pageview.php?ID=2580&SID=40.
6   Ibid.
7   Ibid.
8   Ibid.
9   AFP, "Tigers Set up Base in Thai Island." Indian Express Newspapers, Ltd. (June 3, 2000), www.indianexpress.com/ie/daily/20000605/iin05008.html.
10   "Thailand Says No to LTTE," (July 21, 2000), priu.gov.lk/news_update.
11   Editorial Board "Sri Lankan Peace Talks: The LTTE Bows to International Capital," World Socialist Website (September 21, 2002), http://www.wsws.org/articles/2002/ sep2002/sril-s21.shtml.

12   AFP "Sri Lanka Rejects Tamil Tigers' Demand for Talks," (December 2, 2004), http://www.dailytimes.com.pk/default.asp?page=story_2-12-2004_pg4_15.

13   Daily News, "Government: LTTE Call Scarcely Conducive to Good Faith Negotiations," (December 2, 2004), http://www.priu.gov.lk/news_update/Current_Affairs/ca200412/20041202gosl_response_ltte_statement.htm.

14   CTV.ca News Staff, "Sri Lanka Declares Emergency after Assassination," CTV News with Lloyd Robertson, (August 12, 2005) http://www.ctv.ca/servlet/ArticleNews/story/CTVNews/20050812_srilanka_assassination_ 20050812/.

15   Col. R. Hariharan (ret.), "LTTE'S ISGA Proposals and Security Implications for India," Paper no. 1115, (September 13, 2004), http://www.saag.org/papers12/paper1115.html.

16   Opinion—Leader Page Articles, "We Will Not Discriminate Against LTTE-held Areas: Kadirgamar," *The Hindu* (January 28, 2005), www.hindu.com/2005/01/28/stories/2005012804700800.htm.

17   Human Rights Watch, Human Rights Views, Sri Lanka, "Child Tsunami Victims Recruited by Tamil Tigers" (January 14, 2005), http://www.reliefweb.int/rw/RWB.NSF/db900SID/SODA-68N6CF?OpenDocument.

18   Philip Gourevitch, "Killing Kadirgamar," *New Yorker* Online Only (August 25, 2005), http://www.newyorker.com/online/content/articles/050822on_onlineonly01.

19   "EU Gets Tough on Tigers," BBCSinhala.com (September 27, 2005), http://www.bbc.co.uk/sinhala/news/story/2005/09/050927_eultte.shtml.

20   UK Presidency of the EU 2005, "European Union Declaration Condemning Terrorism in Sri Lanka" (September 26, 2005), http://www.britainusa.com/sections/articles_show_nt1.asp?a=39913&i=60058&L1=41012&L2=60058&d=-1.

21   Flash News, "US Backs Strong Action Against Sri Lanka's Tamil Tigers" (September 30, 2005), EPDP News, http://www.epdpnews.com/Archive/2005/2005-September-English/news-english-2005-09-30.html.

22   Thalif Deen, "Rights Groups Hail EU Travel Ban on LTTE," Inter-Press Service (October 4, 2005), http://www.jrseurope.org/news_releases/Rights%20groups%20hail%20EU%20travel%20ban%20on%20LTTE.htm.

23   Ibid.

24   V. S. Sambandan, Interview with Chandrika Bandaranaike Kumaratunga, *Frontline*, vol. 22, Issue 24 (November 5–18, 2005), http://www.flonnet.com/fl2224/stories/20051202001104900.htm.

25   Krishan Francis, "EU Poll Monitors Condemn Tamil Tigers for Preventing Tamils from Voting in Sri Lanka," AP (November 19, 2005), http://aolsvc.news.aol.com/news/article.adp?id=20051119073009990001.

26   Peter Apps, "Sri Lanka's New President Sworn In," Reuters (November 19, 2005), http://today.reuters.com/news/newsArticle.aspx?type=tsunamiNews&storyID=2005-11-19T091918Z_01_YUE536085_RTRUKOC_0_UK-SRILANKA-ELECTION.xml.

27   D. B. S. Jeyaraj, "Why Is the LTTE Disappointed with Ranil Wickremesinghe?" *Tamiliana* (November 13, 2005), http://tamiliana.blogspot.com/2005/11/why-is-ltte-dissappointed-with-ranil.html.

28   "Australia Target in Human Smuggling Scam," *The Age* (November 19, 2005), http://www.theage.com.au/news/world/australia-target-in-human-smuggling-scam/2005/11/19/1132017016948.html.

29   "LTTE Begins Aggressive Fund Raising in Europe. Demands Large Sums for the Final War?," Lanka Newspapers.com (November 1, 2005), www.lankanewspapers.com/news/2005/11/4245.html.

GLOSSARY

AA	German Foreign Office
Abu Nidal	"Father of the Struggle"
AD	*Action Directe* (Direct Action)
ADB	Asian Development Bank
AEACT	Anti-Terrorism and Effective Death Penalty Act
AFP	Australian Federal Police
al Qaeda	"The Base" (Network established by Osama bid Laden)
ALF	Animal Liberation Front
AN	*Avanguardia Nazionale* (National Vanguard)
ANO	Abu Nidal Organization
APC	All Party Conference
ASALA	Armenian Secret Army for the Liberation of Armenia
ASP	*Associazione Solidarietá Proletaria* (Proletarian Solidarity Association)
BAC	*Brigade Anti-Criminaliste*
Basic Law	German constitution
BDA	Federation of German Employers' Associations
BfV	*Bundesamt für den Verfassungsschutz* (Federal Office for the Protection of the Constitution)
BGS	*Bundesgrenzschutz* (Federal Border Guard)
BKA	*Bundeskriminalamt* (Federal Criminal Police Office)
BMVg	Ministry of Defense
BMZ	Ministry for Economic Cooperation and Development
BND	*Bundesnachrichtendienst* (Federal Intelligence Service)
BR	*Brigate Rosso* (Red Brigades)
Bundesamt für Bevölkerungsschuz und Katastrophenhilfe	Federal Office for Protecting the Population and Assisting in Case of Catastrophes
Bundesamt für den Zivilschutz	Federal Office for Civilian Protection (Former)
Bundestag	German Parliament
Bundeswehr	German army
Carabinieri	Italian Armed Forces territorial police
CARC	*Comitati di Appoggio alla Resistenza per il Comunismo* (Support Committees to the Communist Fight)
CDU	Christian Democratic Union of Germany
CESIS	Executive Committee of the Intelligence and Security Services

CIA	Central Intelligence Agency
CILAT	Interministerial Committee for Antiterrorist Coordination
Corte d'appello	Italian judicial authority (court of appeals)
CPPT	Convention for the Prevention and Punishment of Terrorism
CSF	*Comitato di Sicurezza Finanziaria* (Committee for Financial Security)
CSPPA	Council for Solidarity of Arab and Near Eastern Political Prisoners
CSU	Christian Social Union of Bavaria
CTC	Counter-terrorism Committee
DA	*Deutsche Aktionsgruppe* (German Action Group)
DCPJ	Central Directorate of the Judicial Police
DCRG	*Direction Centrale des Renseignements Généraux*
DeNIS	*Deutsches Notfallvorsorge-Informationssystem* (Emergency Information System)
DGPN	General Directorate of the National Police
DGSE	*Direction Générale de la Sécurité Extérieure* (France)
DHKP-C	Revolutionary People's Liberation Party-Front
DIA	*Direzione Investigativa Antimafia* (Anti-Mafia Investigative Agency)
DNAT	National Antiterrorist Directorate
DPSD	*Direction de la Protection et de la Securite de la Defense*
DRM	*Direction du Renseignement Militaire*
DST	*Direction de la Surveillance de la Territoire*
EC	European Commission
ECHR	European Convention on Human Rights
EIJ	Egpytian Islamic Jihad (also Gihad)
EMETIC	Evan Mecham Eco-Terrorist International Conspiracy
EO	Executive Order
EOTF	Executive Order on Terrorist Financing
EPRLF	Eelam People's Revolutionary Liberation Front
ETA	Euzkadi Ta Azkatasuna
EU	European Union
Eurojust	European Union Judicial Cooperation Unit
Europol	European Police Office
FAA	Federal Aviation Administration
FATF	Financial Action Task Force
FBI	Federal Bureau of Investigation
FDP	Liberal Democratic Party
FEMA	Federal Emergency Management Agency
FINTER	Finter Bank Zürich
FIU	Financial Intelligence Unit (within BKA)
FLB	*Front de Libération de la Bretagne* (Liberation Front of Brittany)
FLNC	*Fronte di Liberazione Naziunale di a Corsica*
FTO	Foreign Terrorist Organization
G7	Group of Seven—Group of seven countries that participate in annual summits regarding economic affairs (France, Germany, Italy, Japan, United Kingdom, United States, and Canada; Russia is not included due to its relative economic instability)
G8	Group of Eight—Group of eight politically dominant countries who participate in annual summits regarding international affairs (France, Germany, Italy, Japan, United Kingdom, United States, Canada, and Russia)

GAP	*Gruppi di Azione Partigiana* (Partisan Action Groups)
GIA	*Groupe Islamique Armé* (Armed Islamic Group of Algeria)
GIGN	*Groupe d'Intervention de la Gendarmerie Nationale*
GMLZ	*Gemeinsames Melde- und Lagezentrum* (Federal & *Länder* Joint Communication and Situation Center)
GOSL	Government of Sri Lanka
GSG9	*Grenzschutzgruppe 9* (Anti-terror police commando unit)
GSPC	*Groupe Salafiste pour la Prédication et le Combat*
Guardia di Finanza	
	Customs and Excise Police

Hizb-ut-Tahrir	"Party of Liberation"
Hizbollah	"Party of God"
HSC	Homeland Security Council

IBT	Internet Black Tigers
IIF	International Islamic Front
IMF	International Monetary Fund
INS	Immigration and Naturalization Service
Interpol	International Criminal Police Organization
IPKF	Indian Peace Keeping Forces
IPS	Inter Press Service
ISGA	Interim Self-Governing Authority
IRA	Irish Republican Army
ISAF	International Security Assistance Force

JDL	Jewish Defense League
JRA	Japanese Red Army
JVP	*Janatha Vimukhi Peramuna*

Kalifatstaat	Turkish Islamic Group-Caliphate State
KGB	*Komitet Gosudarstvennoy Bezopasnosti* (State Security Committee)
KKK	Ku Klux Klan
Kontaktsperregesetz	
	"Contact ban law"

LAS	League of Arab States
LET	Lashkar-e-Toiba
LfV	*Länder* office
LTTE	Liberation Tigers of Tamil Eelam

MAD	*Militärischer Abschirmdienst* (Military Counterintelligence Service)
MAS	Sardinian Autonomy Movement
MEK	Iranian Mujahedin-e-Khalq
MHP	Grey Wolfs

NAP	*Nuclei Armati Proletari* (Armed Proletarian Groups)
NATO	North Atlantic Treaty Organization
NCC	*Nuclei Comunisti Combattenti* (Fighting Communist Groups)
NCCTS	Non-Cooperative Countries and Territories
NGO	non-governmental organization
NPM	Political Military Unit
NTA	*Nuclei Territoriali Antiimperialisti* (Terrirotial Anti-Imperialist Groups)

OA	*Organisation de l'armée secrète*
OECD	Organization of Economic Cooperation and Development
OIC	Organization of Islamic Conference
ON	*Ordine Nuovo* (New Order)
OSCE	Organization for Security and Co-operation in Europe
PCC	Partito Comunista Combattente (Fighting Communist Party)
PDD	Presidential Decision Directive
PFLP	Popular Front for the Liberation of Palestine
PFLP-GC	Popular Front for the Liberation of Palestine-General Command
PICAR	Program on International Conflict Analysis and Resolution
PIRA	Provisional Irish Republican Army
PJPP	Criminal Brigade in Paris
PKK	Kurdistan Workers' Party
PL	*Prima Linea* (First Front)
PLO	Palestine Liberation Organization
PLOTE	People's Liberation Organization of Tamil Eelam
PTOMS	Post-Tsunami Operational Management Structure
PRTs	Provisional Reconstruction Teams
RAF	*Rote Armee Fracktion* (Red Army Faction)
RAID	Recherche Assistance Intervention Dissuasion
Rasterfahndung	"Grid Search"
RAW	Research and Analysis Wing
Religionsprivileg	"Religious privilege"
RG	*Renseignement Generaux*
RZ	Revolutionary Cells
SAT	Antiterrorist section
SatWas	*Satellitengestütztes Warnsystem* (Satellite-based warning system)
Schleppnetzfahndung	
	"Trawl Net Search"
SCLAT	Central Antiterrorist Service
SDN	Sub-Committee on De-escalation and Normalization
SLFP	Sri Lanka Freedom Party
SLMM	Sri Lankan Monitoring Mission
SPD	Social Democratic Party
SRPJ	Regional Judicial Police Services
TELO	Tamil Eelam Liberation Organization
TMVP	Tamileela Peoples Liberation Tigers
TNA	Tamil National Alliance
TNT	Tamil New Tigers
TRO	Tamil Rehabilitation Organization
TULF	Tamil United Liberation Front
UCLAT	The Group for the Coordination of Antiterrorist Action
UN	United Nations
UNESCO	United Nations Educational, Scientific, and Cultural Organization
UNICEF	United Nations Children's Fund
VAT	Violence-Attack-Terrorism
VOCA	Victims of Crime Act

WMD   Weapons of Mass Destruction

Wehrhafte Demokratie
           "Democracy capable of defending itself"

WSG   *Wehrsportgruppe Hoffmann* (Military Sports Group Hoffmann)

ZKA   *Zollkriminalamt* (Customs Criminal Office)

ZKI   Customs Criminal Institute

ZFD   *Zollfahndungsdienst* (Customs Investigation Service)

SELECTED BIBLIOGRAPHY

Acharya, Amitav. *Age of Fear: Power Versus Principle in the War on Terror.* Singapore: Marshall Cavendish Academic, 2004.

Adams, Simon. *All The Troubles: Terrorism, War and the World After 9-11.* Fremantle, Australia: Fremantle Arts Center Press, 2004.

Alexander, Dean C. *Business Confronts Terrorism: Risks and Responses.* Madison: University of Wisconsin Press, 2004.

Alexander, Yonah, ed. *Palestinian Secular Terrorism: Profiles of Fatah, Popular Front for the Liberation of Palestine, and Democratic Front for the Liberation of Palestine.* Ardsley, NY: Transnational Publications, 2003.

———. *Combating Terrorism: Strategies of Ten Countries.* Ann Arbor: University of Michigan Press, 2002.

———. *Palestinian Religious Terrorism: A Profile of Hamas and Islamic Jihad.* Ardsley, NY: Transnational Publications, 2002.

———. *Middle East Terrorism: Current Threats and Future Prospects.* New York: G.K. Hall, 1994.

Alexander, Yonah, and Edgar H. Brenner, eds. *The United Kingdom's Legal Responses to Terrorism.* Ardsley, NY: Transnational Publications, 2003.

———. *Terrorism and the Law.* Ardsley, NY: Transnational Publications, 2001.

———. *Legal Aspects of Terrorism in the United States: 4 Vols.* Dobbs Ferry, NY: Oceana Publications, 2000.

Alexander, Yonah, and Richard Latter, eds. *In the Camera's Eye: New Coverage of Terrorist Events.* Washington, DC: Brassey's, 1991.

Alexander, Yonah, Herbert M. Levine, and Michael S. Swetnam. *ETA: Profile of a Terrorist Group.* Arsley: Transnational Publications, 2001.

Alexander, Yonah, and Donald Musch, eds. *Terrorism: Documents of Local and International Control—U.S. Perspectives, Vol. 35.* Dobbs Ferry, NY: Oceana Publications, 2002.

244

Alexander, Yonah, and Dennis A. Pluchinsky, eds. *Europe's Red Terrorists: The Fighting Communist Organizations*. London: Frank Cass, 1992.

———. *European Terrorism: Today and Tomorrow*. Washington, DC: Brassey's, 1992.

Alexander, Yonah, and Michael S. Swetnam, eds. *Cyber Terrorism and Information Warfare: Threats and Responses*. Ardsley, NY: Transnational Publications, 2001.

———. *Usama bin Laden's al-Qaida: Profile of a Terrorist Network*. Ardsley, NY: Transnational Publications, 2001.

———. *Information Warfare and Cyber Terrorism: Threats and Responses, 4 Vols*. Dobbs Ferry, NY: Oceana Publications, 1999.

Allison, Graham. *Nuclear Terrorism: The Ultimate Preventable Catastrophe*. New York: Times Books, 2004.

Archick, Kristin, and Paul Gallis. *Europe and Counterterrorism*. New York: Nova Science Publishers, 2003.

Arnold, Roberta. *The ICC as a New Instrument for Repressing Terrorism*. Ardsley, NY: Transnational Publishers, 2004.

Aust, Stefan. *The Baader-Meinhof Group*. London: The Bodley Head, 1987.

Balis, Christina V., and Simon Serfaty, eds. *Visions of America and Europe: September 11, Iraq, and Transatlantic Relations*. Washington, DC: Center for Strategic and International Studies Press, 2004.

Barnaby, Frank. *Nuclear Terrorism in Britain: Risks and Realities*. Oxford: Oxford Research Group, 2003.

Benjamin, Daniel, ed. *America and the World in the Age of Terror: A New Landscape in International Relations*. Washington, DC: Center for Strategic and International Studies Press, 2005.

Berkowitz, Peter. *Terrorism, the Laws of War, and the Constitution: Debating the Enemy Combatant Cases*. Stanford, CA: Hoover Institution Press, 2005.

Berman, Paul. *Terrorism and Liberalism*. New York: W.W. Norton, 2004.

Bloom, Mia. *Dying to Kill: The Allure of Suicide Terror*. New York: Columbia University Press, 2005.

Bohn, Michael K. *The Achille Lauro Hijacking: Lessons in the Politics and Prejudice of Terrorism*. Washington, DC: Brassey's, 2004.

Boyle, Francis Anthony. *Destroying World Order: U.S. Imperialism in the Middle East before and after September 11*. Atlanta, GA: Clarity Press, 2004.

Brisard, Jean-Charles, with Damien Martinez. *Zarqawi: The New Face of Al-Qaeda*. New York: Other Press, 2005.

Brookes, Peter. *A Devil's Triangle: Terrorism, Weapons of Mass Destruction, and Rogue States*. Lanham, MD: Rowman & Littlefield, 2005.

Brunn, Stanley D., ed. *11 September and Its Aftermath: Geopolitics of Terror*. Portland, OR: Frank Cass, 2004.

Buckley, Mary, ed., *Global Responses to Terrorism: 9/11, Afghanistan and Beyond*. London: Routledge, 2003.

Carpenter, William M., and David G. Wiencek, eds. *Asian Security Handbook: Terrorism and the New Security Environment*. Armonk, NY: M. E. Sharpe, 2005.

Céu Pinto, Maria do. *Islamist and Middle Eastern Terrorism: A Threat to Europe?* Soveria Mannelli (Catanzaro): Rubbettino, 2004.

Cheltenham, Jan Oskar Engene. *Terrorism in Western Europe: Explaining the Trends since 1950*. Northhampton, MA: Edward Elgar Publishing, 2004.

Clarke, David, ed. *Technology and Terrorism*. New Brunswick, NJ: Transaction Publishers, 2004.

Clarke, Richard A. *Against All Enemies: Inside America's War on Terror*. New York: Free Press, 2004.

Clutterbuck, Richard. *Terrorism, Drugs and Crime in Europe after 1992*. London: Routledge, 1990.

Cohen, David B., and John W. Wells, eds. *American National Security and Civil Liberties in an Era of Terrorism*. New York: Palgrave Macmillan, 2004.

Cooper, Barry. *New Political Religions, or an Analysis of Modern Terrorism*. Columbia: University of Missouri Press, 2004.

Council of Europe. *The Fight against Terrorism: Council of Europe Standards*. 3rd ed. Strasbourg: Council of Europe Publishing, 2005.

Cronin, Audrey Kurth, and James M. Ludes, eds. *Attacking Terrorism: Elements of a Grand Strategy*. Washington, DC: Georgetown University Press, 2004.

Crotty, William, ed. *The Politics of Terror: The U.S. Response to 9/11*. Boston: Northeastern University Press, 2004.

Cushman, Thomas, ed. *A Matter of Principle: Humanitarian Arguments for War in Iraq*. Berkeley: University of California Press, 2005.

Cwiek, Mark A., James A. Johnson, and Gerald R. Ledlow, eds. *Community Preparedness and Response to Terrorism*. Westport, CT: Praeger, 2004.

Dahlby, Tracy. *Allah's Torch: A Report from Behind the Scenes in Asia's War on Terror*. New York: William Morrow, 2005.

Davis, John, ed. *The Global War on Terrorism: Assessing the American Response*. New York: Nova Science Publishers, 2004.

———. *The Global War on Terrorism: Assessing the American Response*. New York: Nova Science Publishers, 2005.

de Silva, K. M. *Reaping the Whirlwind: Ethnic Conflict, Ethnic Politics in Sri Lanka*. India: Penguin Books, 1998.

Duyne, Petrus C. van, ed. *Threats and Phantoms of Organized Crime, Corruption and Terrorism: Critical European Perspectives*. Nijmegen: Wolf Legal Publishers, 2004.

Egendorf, Laura. *Terrorism: Opposing Viewpoints*. San Diego: Greenhaven Press, 2004.

Ehrenfeld, Rachel. *Funding Evil: How Terrorism Is Financed — And How to Stop It*. Chicago: Bonus Books, 2005.

Engene, Jan Oskar. *Terrorism in Western Europe: Explaining the Trends since 1950*. Cheltenham, UK: Edward Elgar Publishing, 2004.

Ferguson, Charles D. *Four Faces of Nuclear Terrorism*. New York: Routledge/Taylor & Francis, 2005.

Fijnaut, Cyrille, Jan Wouters, and Frederik Naert. *Legal Instruments in the Fight against International Terrorism; A Transatlantic Dialogue*. Leiden, Holland: M. Nijhoff, 2004.

Flynn, Stephen. *America the Vulnerable: How Our Government Is Failing to Protect Us from Terrorism*. New York: HarperCollins, 2004.

Franke, Volker, ed. *Terrorism and Peacekeeping: New Security Challenges*. Westport, CT: Praeger, 2005.

Frey, Bruno, S. *Dealing with Terrorism: Stick or Carrot?* Cheltenham, UK: Edward Elgar Publishing, 2004.

Friedman, George. *America's Secret War: Inside the Hidden Worldwide Struggle between America and Its Enemies*. New York: Doubleday Books, 2004.

Gaertner, Heinz, and Ian M. Cuthbertson. *European Security and Transatlantic Relations after 9/11 and the Iraq War*. New York: Palgrave Macmillan, 2005.

Galtung, Johan. *Pax Pacifica: Terrorism, the Pacific Hemisphere, Globalisation and Peace Studies*. Boulder, CO: Paradigm Publishers, 2005.

Ganor, Boaz. *The Counter-Terrorism Puzzle: A Guide for Decision Makers*. New Brunswick, NJ: Transaction Publishers, 2005.

Ganser, Daniele. *NATO's Secret Armies: Operation GLADIO and Terrorism in Western Europe*. London: Frank Cass, 2005.

Gareau, Frederick. *State Terrorism and the United States: From Counterinsurgency to the War on Terrorism*. Atlanta: Clarity Press, 2004.

Gerges, Fawaz A. *The Far Enemy: Why Jihad Went Global*. New York: Cambridge University Press, 2005.

Germani, L. Sergio, and D. R. Kaarthikeyan, *Pathways Out of Terrorism and Insurgency: The Dynamics of Terrorist Violence and Peace Processes*. Elgin, IL: New Dawn Press, 2005.

Gertz, Bill. *Treachery: How America's Friends and Foes Are Secretly Arming Our Enemies*. New York: Crown Forum, 2004.

Gilmore, William C. *Dirty Money: The Evolution of International Measures to Counter Money Laundering and the Financing of Terrorism*. Strasbourg: Council of Europe Publishing, 2004.

Goody, Jack. *Islam in Europe*. Cambridge: Polity Press, 2004.

Gottren, Frank, and Dana Shea. *Small-Scale Terrorist Attacks Using Chemical and Biological Agents*. New York: Nova Science Publishers, 2004.

Graham, Bob, and Jeff Nussbaum. *Intelligence Matters: The CIA, the FBI, Saudi Arabia, and the Failure of America's War on Terror*. New York: Random House, 2004.

Guelke, Adrian. *The Age of Terrorism and the International Political System*. London: I. B. Tauris, 1995.

Gunaratna, Rohan, ed. *The Changing Face of Terrorism*. Singapore: Eastern University Press, 2004.

Hannity, Sean. *Deliver Us from Evil: Defeating Terrorism, Despotism, and Liberalism*. New York: Regan Books, 2004.

Harari, Haim. *A View from the Eye of the Storm: Terror and Reason in the Middle East*. New York: HarperCollins, 2005.

Harik, Judith Palmer. *Hezbollah: The Changing Face of Terrorism*. London: I. B. Tauris, 2004.

Harris, Sam. *The End of Faith: Religion, Terror, and the Future of Reason*. New York: W.W. Norton, 2004.

Harvey, Frank. *Smoke and Mirrors: Globalized Terrorism and the Illusion of Multilateral Security*. Toronto: University of Toronto Press, 2004.

Harwood, Mark: *The EU's Fight against Terrorism: Disappointment Thus Far? Prospects for the Future?* Malta: University of Malta, 2004.

Hassan, Hamdi A. *Al-Qaeda: The Background of the Pursuit for Global Jihad*. Stockholm: Almqvist & Wiksell International, 2004.

Hastings, Tom. *Nonviolent Response to Terrorism*. Jefferson, NC: McFarland, 2004.

Hayes, Stephen F. *The Connection: How Al Qaeda's Collaboration with Saddam Hussein Has Endangered America*. New York: HarperCollins, 2004.

Selected Bibliography 249

Heinz, Wolfgang S., and Jan M. Arend. *The International Fight Against Terrorism and the Protection of Human Rights: With Recommendations to the German Government and Parliament*. Berlin: Deutsches Institut fur Menschenrechte, 2005.

Henderson, Harry. *Global Terrorism*. New York: Facts on File, 2004.

Hersh, Seymour M. *Chain of Command: The Road from 9/11 to Abu Ghraib*. New York: HarperCollins, 2004.

Hippel, Karin von, ed. *Europe Confronts Terrorism*. Basingstoke: Palgrave Macmillan, 2005.

Hollingsworth, Mark, and Nick Fielding, *Defending the Realm: Inside MI5 and the War on Terrorism*. London: André Deutsch, 2003.

Howard, Russell D., and Reid L. Sawyer. *Defeating Terrorism: Shaping the New Security Environment*. Guilford, CT: McGraw-Hill, 2004.

————, eds. *Terrorism and Counterterrorism: Understanding the New Security Environment: Readings and Interpretations*. Guilford, CT: McGraw-Hill/Dushkin, 2004.

Ignatieff, Michael. *The Lesser Evil: Political Ethics in an Age of Terror*. Princeton, NJ: Princeton University Press, 2004.

Jacobsen, Annie. *Terror in the Skies: Why 9/11 Could Happen Again*. Dallas, TX: Spence Publishing, 2005.

Johnson, Haynes. *The Age of Anxiety: McCarthyism to Terrorism*. New York: Harcourt Books, 2005.

Junaid, Shahwar. *Terrorism and Global Power Systems*. Oxford: Oxford University Press, 2005.

Kalansooriya, Ranga. *LTTE and IRA: Combating Terrorism and Discussing Peace*. Colombo: Sanhinda Printers and Publishers, 2001.

Katz, Samuel M. *Global Counterstrike: International Counterterrorism*. Minneapolis, MN: Lerner Publications, 2005.

Keeley, Jennifer. *Deterring and Investigating Attack: The Role of the FBI and CIA*. San Diego, CA: Lucent Books, 2004.

Kessler, Ronald. *The CIA at War: Inside the Secret Campaign against Terror*. New York: St. Martin's Griffin, 2004.

Kettl, Donald F., ed. *The Department of Homeland Security's First Year: A Report Card*. New York: Century Foundation Press, 2004.

Khalsa, Sundri. *Forecasting Terrorism: Indicators and Proven Analytic Techniques*. Lanham, MD: Scarecrow Press, 2004.

250   *Counterterrorism Strategies*

King, Gilbert. *Dirty Bomb: Weapon of Mass Disruption*. New York: Chamberlain Brothers, 2004.

Knop, Katharina von, Heinrich Neisser, and Martin van Creveld. *Countering Modern Terrorism*. Bielefeld: Bertelsmann, 2005.

Kohlmann, Evan. *Al-Qaida's Jihad in Europe: The Afghan-Bosnian Network*. Oxford: Berg Publishers, 2004.

Krieken, Peter J. van, ed. *Terrorism and the International Legal Order: With Special Reference to the UN, the EU and Cross-Border Aspects*. The Hague: TMC Asser, 2002.

Kronenwetter, Michael. *Terrorism: A Guide to Events and Documents*. Westport, CT: Greenwood Press, 2004.

Kunath, Jana. *RAF: die Reaktion des Staates auf den Terrorismus der Roten Armee Fraktion*. Marburg: Tectum, 2004.

Lance, Peter. *Cover Up: What the Government Is Still Hiding about the War on Terror*. New York: Regan Books, 2004.

Leeuwen, Marianne van, ed. *Confronting Terrorism: European Experiences, Threat Perceptions, and Policies*. The Hague: Kluwer Law International, 2003.

LeVine, Mark. *Why They Don't Hate Us: Lifting the Veil on the Axis of Evil*. Oxford: Oneworld Publications, 2005.

Lewis, Bernard. *The Crisis of Islam: Holy War and Unholy Terror*. New York: Random House, 2004.

Linden, Edward. *Foreign Terrorist Organizations: History, Tactics and Connections*. New York: Nova Science Publishers, 2004.

Lutz, James M., and Brenda J. Lutz. *Terrorism: Origins and Evolution*. New York: Palgrave Macmillan, 2005.

Mamdani, Mahmood. *Good Muslim, Bad Muslim: America, the Cold War, and the Roots of Terror*. New York: Three Leaves Press, 2005.

Martin, Gus. *The New Era of Terrorism: Selected Readings*. Thousand Oaks, CA: Sage Publications, 2004.

Maxwell, Bruce, ed. *Homeland Security: A Documentary History*. Washington, DC: CQ Press, 2004.

McDermott, Roger N. *Countering Global Terrorism: Developing the Antiterrorist Capabilities of the Central Asian Militaries*. Carlisle Barracks, PA: Strategic Studies Institute, U.S. Army War College, 2004.

McInerney, Thomas, and Paul Vallely. *Endgame: The Blueprint for Victory in the War on Terror*. Washington, DC: Regnery Publishing, 2004.

Mead, Walter Russell. *Power, Terror, Peace, and War: America's Grand Strategy in a World at Risk*. New York: Knopf Publishing Group, 2004.

Naftali, Timothy. *Blind Spot: The Secret History of American Counterterrorism*. New York: Basic Books, 2005.

Nassar, Jamal R. *Globalization and Terrorism: The Migration of Dreams and Nightmares*. Lanham, MD: Rowman & Littlefield, 2005.

The 9/11 Commission Report: Final Report of the Commission on Terrorist Attacks upon the United States. New York: Norton, 2004.

Noone, Michael F., and Yonah Alexander, eds. *Cases and Materials on Terrorism: Three Nations' Response*. The Hague: Kluwer Law International, 1997.

O'Day, Alan, ed. *War on Terrorism*. Aldershot, UK: Ashgate Publishing, 2004.

O'Neill, Bard E. *Insurgency and Terrorism: From Revolution to Apocalypse*. Dulles, VA: Potomac Books, 2005.

Orahovec, Zvonko, and Peter Stopa, eds. *Technology for Combating WMD Terrorism*. Budapest: Kluwer Academic Publishers, 2004.

Palmer, Monte, and Princess Palmer. *At the Heart of Terror: Islam, Jihadists, and America's War on Terrorism*. Lanham, MD: Rowman & Littlefield, 2004.

Pape, Robert. *Dying to Win: The Strategic Logic of Suicide Terrorism*. New York: Random House, 2005.

Peters, Butz. *RAF: Terrorismus in Deutschland*. Stuttgart: Deutsche Verlags-Astalt, 1991.

Peters, Michael A. *Education, Globalization, and the State in the Age of Terrorism*. Boulder, CO: Paradigm, 2005.

Primoratzm Igor. *Terrorism: The Philosophical Issues*. New York: Palgrave Macmillan, 2004.

Randal, Jonathan. *Osama: The Making of a Terrorist*. New York: Knopf Publishing Group, 2004.

Reinares, Fernando. *European Democracies against Terrorism: Governmental Politics and Intergovernmental Cooperation*. Aldershot, UK: Ashgate, 2000.

Richardson, John. *Paradise Poisoned: Learning about Conflict, Terrorism and Development from Sri Lanka's Civil Wars*. Kandy, Sri Lanka: International Center for Ethnic Studies, 2005.

Rotfeld, Adam, Roman Kuzniar, Zdzisaw Lachowski, and Hans-Joachim Giessmann, eds. *International Security in a Time of Change: Threats, Concepts, Institutions*. Baden-Baden: Nomos-Verlagsgesellschaft, 2004.

Sageman, Marc. *Understanding Terror Networks*. Philadelphia: University of Pennsylvania Press, 2004.

Satloff, Robert B. *The Battle of Ideas in the War on Terror: Essays on U.S. Public Diplomacy in the Middle East.* Washington, DC: Washington Institute for Near East Policy, 2004.

Schanzer, Jonathan. *Al-Qaeda's Armies: Middle East Affiliate Groups and the Next Generation of Terror.* Washington, DC: Washington Institute for Near East Policy, 2005.

Schmid, Alex Peter, and Albert J Jongman. *Political Terrorism: A New Guide to Actors, Authors, Concepts, Data Bases, Theories, and Literature.* New Brunswick, NJ: Transaction Publishers, 2005.

Sciascia, Leonardo. *The Moro Affair and the Mystery of Majorana.* Translated by Sacha Rabinovitch. New York: New York Review Books, 2004.

Shearman, Peter, and Matthew Sussex, eds. *European Security After 9/11.* Aldershot, UK: Ashgate, 2004.

Siegel, Marc. *False Alarm: The Truth about the Epidemic of Fear.* Indianapolis, IN: Wiley and Sons, 2005.

Sifaoui, Mohamed. *Inside Al Qaeda: How I Infiltrated the World's Deadliest Terrorist Organization.* Translated by George Miller. New York: Thunder's Mouth Press, 2004.

Sloan, Stephen. *Beating International Terrorism: An Action Strategy for Preemption and Punishment.* Revised edition. Maxwell Air Force Base, AL: Air University Press, 2004.

Smucker, Philip. *Al Qaeda's Great Escape: The Military and the Media on Terror's Trail.* Washington, DC: Brassey's, 2004.

Stout, Chris. *Psychology of Terrorism: Coping with the Continued Threat.* Westport, CT: Praeger, 2004.

Tal, Nahman. *Radical Islam in Egypt and Jordan.* Brighton, UK: Sussex Academic Press/Jaffee Center for Strategic Studies, 2005.

Thackrah, John Richard. *Dictionary of Terrorism.* Second Edition. London: Routledge, 2004.

Ullman, Harlan. *Finishing Business: Ten Steps to Defeat Global Terror.* Annapolis, MD: Naval Institute Press, 2004.

Vermaat, Emerson. *Bin Laden's Terror Networks in Europe.* Toronto, ON: Mackenzie Institute, 2002.

Walker, Clive. *Blackstone's Guide to the Anti-Terrorism Legislation.* Oxford: Oxford University Press 2002.

Walter, Christian. *Terrorism as a Challenge for National and International Law: Security Versus Liberty?* Berlin: Springer, 2004.

Walthelm, Britta. *Immigration and Asylum Policies in Great Britain and Germany after September 11: An Assessment of Policy Change in the Course of Anti-Terrorism Legislation.* Manchester: University of Manchester, 2004.

White, Jonathan R. *Terrorism and Homeland Security.* 5th ed. Belmont, CA: Wadsworth Publishing, 2005.

Whittaker, David. *Terrorists and Terrorism in the Contemporary World.* London: Routledge, 2004.

Wieviorka, Michel. *The Making of Terrorism.* Translated by David White. Chicago: University of Chicago Press, 2004.

Wiktorowicz, Quintan. *Radical Islam Rising: Muslim Extremism in the West.* Lanham, MD: Rowman & Littlefield, 2005.

Willan, Philip. *Puppetmasters: The Political Use of Terrorism in Italy.* San Jose, CA: Authors Choice Press, 2002.

Williams, Paul. *Osama's Revenge: The Next 9-11: What the Media and the Government Haven't Told You.* Amherst, NY: Prometheus Books, 2004.

Williams, Paul L. *The Al Qaeda Connection: International Terrorism, Organized Crime, and the Coming Apocalypse.* Amherst, NY: Prometheus Books, 2005.

Winn, Neil, ed. *Neo-Medievalism and Civil Wars.* Portland, OR: Frank Cass, 2004.

Woodworth, Paddy. *Dirty War, Clean Hands: ETA, the Gal and Spanish Democracy.* Crosses Green Cork, Ireland: Cork University Press, 2001.

Youngs, Tim, Paul Bowers, and Mark Oakes, *The Campaign against International Terrorism: Prospects after the Fall of the Taliban.* London: Parliament. House of Commons Library, 2001.

Zuhur, Sherifa. *Saudi Arabia: Islamic Threat, Political Reform, and the Global War on Terror.* Carlisle Barracks, PA: Strategic Studies Institute, U.S. Army War College, 2005.

CONTRIBUTORS

Yonah Alexander is currently director of the Inter-University Center of Terrorism Studies; senior fellow and director of the International Center for Terrorism Studies at the Potomac Institute of Policy Studies in Arlington, Virginia; senior fellow at the Homeland Security Policy Institute at the George Washington University; and co-director of the Inter-University Center for Legal Studies, International Law Institute, Washington, D.C. Formerly professor and director of terrorism studies at the State University of New York and the George Washington University, he founded and edited three international journals on terrorism, political communication and persuasion, and minority and group rights. He also has published over ninety books in international affairs, mostly on different aspects of terrorism.

Guillaume Parmentier is the founder and director of the French Center on the United States (CFE) at the Institut Francais des Relations Internationales. He is also a non-resident professor at the University of Paris-II. He initiated the creation of a center on the United States and France at the Brookings Institution in Washington, D.C. Educated at Cambridge, the Sorbonne, and the Institut d'Etudes Politiques of Paris, he has taught at several universities in Europe and the United States. Professor Parmentier has also served in several capacities at the North Atlantic Assembly at NATO headquarters, the French Ministry of Defense, and the French Foundation for Defense Studies. He has published extensively on European and transatlantic issues.

Ulrich Schneckener is a senior researcher of the Global Issues Unit at the German Institute for International and Security Affairs (Stiftung Wissenschaft and Politik) in Berlin. From 1996 to 2002, he was a researcher at the Institute for Intercultural and International Studies at

254

the University of Bremen. His areas of expertise include terrorism and counterterrorism, international conflict management, fragile states, and regional conflicts. His dissertation on ethnic conflict regulation (Auswege aus dem Bürgerkrieg, Suhrkamp, 2002) received various academic awards. His latest book deals with transnational terrorism and its consequences for counterterrorism (*Transnationaler Terrorismus*, Suhrkamp, 2006).

Germana Tappero Merlo teaches peacekeeping management at the University of Turin. She holds a PhD in American military history and currently researches international relations and security in the Mediterranean area. She has collaborated with the Institute for International Legal Studies of the National Research Council in researching counterterrorism strategies in the twenty-first century. She is also the author of a book on peacekeeping operations in the Middle East.

Sergio Marchisio is a professor of law and international organizations at the University "La Sapienza" of Rome. He is also director of the Institute for International Legal Studies of the National Research Council and chair of the Legal Subcommittee of the United Nations Committee on the Peaceful Uses of Outer Space. Professor Marchisio has served in various capacities in Italian and European official bodies and participated as a member of Italian delegations to numerous international conferences. He is the author of many academic publications and the editor of eight volumes of the third series of the Italian practice of international law.

Ahmed Abou-el-Wafa is a professor of international law, head of the international law department, and vice dean of the law faculty at the University of Cairo. A member of the editorial review of the *International Review of the Red Cross*, he has published several books on public international law, human rights, international humanitarian law, and the international criminal court. His latest book is *The General Theory of International Humanitarian Law*. His articles have been published in Arabic, English, and French.

Vernon L. B. Mendis is currently director-general of the International Diplomatic Training Institute in Colombo. He is one of the first diplomats from Sri Lanka, serving in many distinguished capacities at the Ministry of Foreign Affairs and abroad. Among his appointments are ambassador, chief of protocol, and deputy high commissioner. His posts included service in the United Kingdom, Canada, Cuba, the United Nations, the World Bank, and the International Monetary Fund. Dr. Mendis also was a peace fellow at the United States Institute of Peace.

INDEX